The Vanished Emperor

Percy Andreae

The Vanished Emperor

Copyright © 2012 by Indo-European Publishing

Contact:
IndoEuropeanPublishing@gmail.com

The present edition is a reproduction of 1896 publication of this work, produced in the current edition with completely new, easy to read format by Indo-European Publishing.

For an authentic reading experience, the Spelling, punctuation, and capitalization have been retained from the original text.

Cover Design by Indo-European Design Team

ISBN: 978-1-60444-616-6

IndoEuropean
Publishing.com
Los Angeles, CA, USA

BOOK I
THE MYSTIFICATION

CHAPTER I
A Missing Emperor

Those whose memories carry them back a few years will not have forgotten the sensation produced throughout Europe when, in spite of the most stupendous efforts to keep the facts from becoming public, the news suddenly leaked out that the young Arminian Emperor, Willibald II., had mysteriously disappeared.

The first intimation of this extraordinary event was conveyed to the people of Great Britain, and indeed to the world in general, by a short paragraph which appeared, printed in bold type, in a well known London morning paper, to the following effect:—

"Just before going to press, intelligence of a most unprecedented kind reaches us from Berolingen. His Majesty the Emperor Willibald is reported to be missing. The greatest consternation prevails at the Arminian Court and in official circles generally. Stringent measures have been adopted to prevent the news from spreading in the country. Last evening's edition of the 'Berolingen Gazette,' in which the first reference was made to the astounding rumour, has been confiscated, and the editor has been placed under arrest."

It is almost needless to say that the most credulous among a sensation-loving public at first received this astonishing paragraph with a smile of utter incredulity. Anything in the world would have been more readily believed of the young Emperor, upon whom since his accession to power, the eyes of all Europe had been fixed, than the fact of his having thus vanished from men's view. No other potentate was more constantly in evidence, none more deeply convinced of the paramount importance to mankind of his presence on earth. To think of him being calmly reported as missing, for all the world like the ordinary young person we occasionally read of in the police court news, who 'left her home on the afternoon of such and such a date, and has not returned since. When last seen was wearing—&c.,' seemed ludicrous beyond the power of words to express.

For weeks one of the chief topics of the European Press had been the contemplated voyage of his Arminian Majesty to the East,

1

the preparations for which had been carried out on that scale of magnificence which the public had come to regard as inseparable from the undertakings of this travel-loving young monarch. The date fixed for the imperial departure had been unexpectedly postponed on the very eve of the date itself; but the reasons given for this postponement were so plausible that no one thought of connecting it with the extraordinary news contained in the newspaper paragraph referred to.

All incredulity vanished, however, when four-and-twenty hours later every journal of importance in the United Kingdom not only confirmed the report with various additional particulars supplied by special correspondents on the spot, but devoted columns upon columns to the discussion of the possible political consequences of the event.

"There are many extraordinary features about the occurrence which has thrown so deep a gloom over Europe," wrote the correspondent of the 'Times' in Berolingen, a few days after the Emperor's disappearance. "From information which I have been able to gather from a reliable source, it would seem that the first to discover the unaccountable absence of his Majesty was his personal valet, Herr Schulzendorf. The Emperor's sleeping apartment adjoins his private cabinet on the first floor of the Royal Castle. On entering the room as usual on the morning of the discovery, and finding it unoccupied, Herr Schulzendorf's first impression appears to have been that his Majesty had absented himself on one of those secret expeditions which he has of late been in the habit of undertaking in company with his private secretary, Doctor Hofer. It was his Majesty's custom on these occasions to avail himself of a small staircase leading direct from his bedroom to a private exit in the left wing of the castle. Herr Schulzendorf's suspicion received apparent confirmation from the circumstance that Doctor Hofer's bedroom, which is situated on the same floor as that of the Emperor, was likewise empty; though the fact that the doctor's bed showed signs of having been occupied during the night should have aroused his doubts. When, however, an hour or so later, Doctor Hofer reappeared in the castle, accompanied by an officer of the Imperial guard, and it was rumoured that he had been placed under quasi-arrest at the instance of the military authorities, Herr Schulzendorf's fears were awakened, and he at once communicated the discovery of the Emperor's absence to the master of the household. The alarm soon spread throughout the palace, and by noon the news had been communicated by telegraph to the Sovereigns of the various States composing the Empire. A council of the Ministry was hastily summoned to consider the situation, but as to the outcome of its deliberations nothing has been allowed to transpire. The most astonishing part of the affair is that no one appears to possess the slightest clue to the mystery. Doctor Hofer, the imperial secretary, I am informed, has been subjected to a rigorous examination, but without any result. The doctor declares himself totally unable to throw any light upon the matter. The reason for his arrest is wrapped in complete obscurity. He is, however, a Noverian by birth, his father having been chaplain-in-ordinary to the late King of Noveria, and he is believed, in spite of the position he has occupied at the imperial court for the last twelve months, to be a strong upholder of the claim of the Duke of Cumbermere to the kingdom annexed by Brandenburg after her successful war with Austria in 1866. It is even whispered that evidence has come into the hands of the Arminian Government implicating the imperial secretary in the recent rebellious manifestations of the Guelph party in the Noverian province, which appears now to have been of a far more serious character than the world has been led to suppose. Whatever truth there may be in this rumour, it is certain that the doctor's arrest cannot have been a direct consequence of the Emperor's disappearance, since it occurred some hours before his Majesty's absence was brought to the knowledge of the military authorities. The consternation of the latter is overwhelming, and in spite of the official silence maintained by the Government, it is of course impossible to conceal the fact of the Emperor's absence from the public at large. It is new nearly a week since his Majesty was last seen by his subjects, and the most sensational reports are already flying about the city with regard to his fate.

"It is rumoured to-day that Prince Henry of Brandenburg, the Emperor's brother and heir presumptive, has been urged by the Imperial Chancellor and a few of the Southern Arminian sovereigns to assume the Regency of the Empire pending his Majesty's return. But his Imperial Highness is said to have categorically refused to accede to the request, as he declares that during the lifetime of the Sovereign, or in the absence of proof of his demise, no one but the Emperor can confer governing powers either upon him or anyone else. It is thought that, should Prince Henry persist in maintaining this attitude, serious constitutional difficulties may arise in the event of the Emperor's prolonged absence from the helm of affairs."

It was in vain that the fact of the Emperor's disappearance was now vehemently denied by the semi-official organs of the Arminian Government. When concealment, at least to the outer

3

world, was no longer possible, other means of allaying the growing sense of uneasiness in the political world were resorted to, and it was stated that his Majesty, with the knowledge of his Ministers, had gone on a political mission of great delicacy, which, while it necessitated his own personal supervision, required at the same time that he should preserve the very strictest incognito.

It was hinted that the much-vexed question of the Emperor's marriage was at the bottom of the mission, and as there was no matter the solution of which had been more eagerly and anxiously watched for ever since the young monarch ascended the throne three years before, the report, on the face of it, seemed not altogether devoid of probability. But, coming immediately after the most explicit of official assurances that his Majesty was safe and sound in his capital, the thinness of this attempt to hoodwink the public was too apparent, and beyond perhaps a few loyal souls in Arminia itself no one was deceived by it. As day after day passed, and the alarming rumours regarding the fate of the Emperor grew more and more persistent, the excitement in Europe became positively dangerous, and the Governments showed, by the extraordinary measures they adopted to calm the public feeling, that they had arrived at that stage of perplexity which, in common parlance, is defined as being at one's wits' end.

Perhaps the following few gleanings from the telegraphic intelligence of the newspaper Press of those days may serve better than anything else to recall to the reader's mind the grave state of confusion into which Europe had suddenly been thrown.

The fifteenth edition of the 'Daily Telegraph' of the 12th June—ten days after the first rumour of the Arminian mystery burst upon the world—contained the following telegraphic despatches:—

"Berolingen, June 12 (noon).

"The serious disturbances which have been taking place in all parts of Noveria during the last few weeks have now culminated in a general rising, which threatens to assume the dimensions of a revolution. The disappearance of the Arminian Emperor is believed to be connected with these troubles, and serious fears are entertained that his Majesty, who, with his usual determination, is believed to have gone incognito to Noveria to inquire personally into the position of affairs in that province, has fallen into the hands of the rebel party. These fears are strengthened by the extraordinary attitude of the Arminian Government, whose laxness in dealing with the turbulent province is now attributed to the unfortunate position of the young monarch. Should the rumours regarding his Majesty's capture prove true, there is little doubt that the outcome will be a

4

recognition on the part of Arminia of the claim of the Duke of Cumbermere to the throne of his late father, the deposed King of Noveria."

"Berolingen (later).

"There can now no longer be any doubt that the report alluded to in one of my previous despatches, according to which the private secretary of the Emperor, Doctor Georg Hofer, had been placed under arrest a few hours after his Majesty's disappearance, is substantially correct. The mystery attaching to this incident is enhanced by the fact, which now appears to be established beyond a doubt, that the order for this official's imprisonment was actually written and signed by the Emperor's own hand, and that the document was probably the last executed by the monarch before he vanished. The most startling conjectures are current regarding the connection existing between the two events. Doctor Hofer, who has enjoyed the Emperor's confidence in a remarkable degree, is said to have been a persona gratissima at Court, and his arrest at this juncture of affairs has revived certain strange stories which were afloat in society circles here a few months ago, concerning a romantic attachment supposed to been formed by his Majesty's youngest and favourite sister for a prominent official of the Emperor's household.

"These rumours were believed by many to be the mere outcome of idle Court gossip. But recent events have lent them a colour of plausibility, and it is now generally asserted that the temporary retirement of the young Princess Margaret from the Court of Berolingen at the beginning of the year, which was attributed at the time to the state of her Imperial Highness's health, was in reality due to the peremptory action of his Majesty himself, whose displeasure the young Princess had incurred by her persistent refusal to contract a marriage suitable to her illustrious birth. It is difficult, however, to reconcile this story with the circumstance that her Imperial Highness returned to Court two months ago, and has since quite regained her old position in the favour of her brother. Nor does the arrest of Dr. Hofer, whose name is now whispered in conjunction with that of the Princess, throw any light whatsoever upon the Emperor's disappearance. If true, it serves to complicate the mystery, that is all."

The fourteenth edition of the 'Evening Standard' the following day was issued with the subjoined principal headings:—
"RUMOURED KIDNAPPING OF THE ARMINIAN EMPEROR.
"THREATENED OUTBREAK OF WAR WITH FRANCONIA.
"Patropolis, June 13.

5

"The reported capture of the Arminian Emperor by the supporters of the old Noverian dynasty is generally credited here, and has caused the greatest excitement throughout Franconia. It will be remembered that, upon the demise of the late Duke of Brunsbuttel, the succession to the throne of that State devolved upon his Royal Highness the Duke of Cumbermere, the Noverian Pretender. The refusal of the Arminian Emperor to recognise the latter's claim to the Duchy, except on condition that he formally relinquished all pretensions to the crown of Noveria, produced a feeling of deep resentment among the still numerous adherents of the Duke in the Kingdom annexed by Brandenburg after the Austro-Arminian war of 1866, and the present daring coup is said to be the result. Whether true or not, it is certain that telegrams from Berolingen report the rumoured discovery of a conspiracy there, in which the most trusted confidant of the young Emperor is said to be implicated."

"Patropolis, Midnight.

"The excitement in Franconia continues alarmingly on the increase. Four Arminian subjects, one of them a distinguished member of the diplomatic service, were surrounded and set upon by a crowd of Patropolitans in one of the principal thoroughfares of the city towards six o'clock this afternoon. The interference of the police was tardy and half-hearted, and the unfortunate Arminians were not extricated from their perilous position until they had suffered considerable ill-usage at the hands of their assailants. A mob of several hundred people, among whom were a number of well-dressed citizens, afterwards proceeded to the Arminian Embassy, in front of which they made a hostile demonstration.

"This is, unfortunately, not the first outburst of popular feeling since the Arminian complication, and it is but a feeble indication of the general tendency of the hour. The Press is undoubtedly to blame for stimulating the public excitement. The trumpet call sounded a week ago by the extremist organs, has in the last three or four days been taken up by the more moderate portion of the Press, and an article entitled 'The Revenge in Sight,' which appeared this morning in the semi-official 'Patropolis Gazette,' and which is generally believed to have been directly inspired by the Government, is probably primarily responsible for the lamentable occurrence of this afternoon. The development of affairs in Arminia is being watched here on all hands with indescribable eagerness, and the sudden activity which is being displayed in naval and military departments can be taken as an indication of what may be expected. In spite of all endeavours to maintain secrecy in the matter, it is known that within the last week large bodies of troops have been amassed on this side of the Arminian frontier, and representations are said to have been made on the subject by the Arminian Government.

"Two further important items of news are being eagerly discussed to-night in the clubs and places of public resort, and, if true, will tend to render the situation more critical than ever. It is reported on the one hand that differences of a serious nature have arisen between the foremost members of the Arminian Empire, and on the other hand that grave disturbances have broken out on the Russo-Arminian frontier. The fact that these disturbances are said to have been deliberately provoked by Russia adds to the gravity of the rumour."

"New York, June 13.

"The extraordinary disappearance of the Emperor Willibald still continues to absorb public attention here. The 'New York Herald' states that the Duke of Cumbermere, the Noverian Pretender, sailed for Europe ten days ago."

"St. Petersburg, June 13.

"The sudden arrival of his Majesty the Czar in the capital yesterday afternoon from Gatschina is currently reported to have been caused by a fresh development of the Arminian mystery. A council of Ministers was held at the Winter Palace late last night under the presidency of the Czar, and it is stated to-day that a high official from the immediate entourage of his Majesty started at an early hour this morning on a secret mission to Patropolis. A Franco-Russian alliance directed against Arminia is believed to be the immediate object of this mission."

"Berolingen, June 13.

"Considerable differences of opinion are reported to exist between the heads of the various States which constitute the Arminian Empire as to the course to be pursued in view of the uncertain fate of the Emperor Willibald. The Prince Regent of Wittelsbach, it is whispered, has already taken steps to summon an immediate meeting of the confederate sovereigns, in order to consult as to the next future. The belief is that, failing the consent of Prince Henry of Brandenburg, the missing Emperor's brother and heir presumptive, to assume the temporary leadership of the Empire, the Wittelsbach monarch will move that a vice-Emperor be elected from among the sovereign rulers of Arminia. No mention of this rumour has been allowed to appear in the native Press, which, as you know, have been enjoined under threat of severe pains and penalties from referring to the subject of the Emperor's disappearance under whatsoever guise or pretence. But it is nevertheless already the common topic of conversion in the capital, where it has caused the greatest possible consternation. In fact, the feeling among the populace here is one of growing suspicion, and the situation is regarded by many as extremely ominous."

"Berolingen, June 14.

"I have ascertained on unquestionable authority that negotiations have been in progress between the courts of Wittelsbach and Wettinia respecting the proceedings at the contemplated meeting of the Arminian sovereigns. The Regent of Wittelsbach makes his appearance at the meeting conditional upon his election to the Imperial dignity. The King of Wettinia claims that dignity for himself. The prospect of any compromise being arrived at is almost hopeless."

I could supplement the above extracts by scores of others of an equally startling and alarming character. But I purposely refrain from repeating the mere sensational paragraphs with which the smaller fry of newspapers regaled their readers, under such heads as:—'Reported Death of the Emperor Willibald. Finding of the Body.' 'Berolingen in Flames. Rumoured Massacre of the Arminian Ministers. Return of Prince Ottomarck to the Head of Affairs,' and others of a similarly extravagant character. They increased, so far as it was possible to increase, the excitement of the public; but inasmuch, as they throw no light upon the real course of events, I may pass them over in silence.

Indeed, it would scarcely be possible to exaggerate the gravity of the situation. The total absence of any clue whatsoever to the Emperor's whereabouts seemed to render the prospect of a peaceable solution almost hopeless. Had he really been kidnapped or spirited away, as some asserted, with the connivance of certain exalted personages whose aim was to effect a transfer of the Imperial supremacy in Arminia to another State? Had he been made the Victim of foul play? Or was his disappearance Voluntary, and his absence really connected with some deep political design, the execution of which the youthful monarch, whose spirit of independence and arbitrary nature had become proverbial since his accession to the throne, would intrust to no one else?

The Emperor's well-known disregard of the irksome restrictions which tradition has imposed upon royalty, and the energy with which he was known to occupy himself personally with apparently paltry matters of administration that are usually left to the management of subordinate government officials, had caused him to be looked upon as self-willed and eccentric. Self-willed he undoubtedly was. Eccentric he was only in so far as he declined to be bound by what he considered obsolete customs and useless forms, and claimed the right to exercise his own unfettered judgment like every ordinary human being, and see with his own eyes and hear with his own ears that which rulers had hitherto been accustomed to see and hear with the eyes and ears of their servitors. The world shrugged its shoulders and giggled at the spectacle of a monarch who considered himself, not only in posse but in esse, the acting head and administrator of every department of his Government, and who, on the principle that every single appointment in the State, from the Prime Minister or Chancellor down to the poorest village pastor, is held by virtue of the power of representation vested in the holder of the office, by the monarch to whom theoretically it belongs, felt himself called upon, whenever the necessity arose, or the humour seized him, to temporarily take the place of the substitute and administrate the office in person.

The world merely saw the novelty of the proceeding, and called it barock and eccentric. A monarch occupying himself with the minute details of administration was something quite out of the common; hence the world's inclination was to laugh. The Emperor Willibald had been known to preach occasionally in the place of his chaplain, to pose as a teacher in the school-room, and to deliver judgment on the bench. These and other eccentricities had been made the subject of endless satires in the newspaper Press of Europe. Perhaps not unjustly. But those who knew the young monarch were aware that they were the mere extravagances of a mind which Nature had endowed with quite exceptional gifts, and with a firmness of purpose which, to use a colloquial phrase, stuck at nothing.

Personalities like that of the Emperor Willibald, which attract the public attention in an inordinate degree, are always liable to be misinterpreted or represented from a one-sided view, and there is no doubt that the young Emperor suffered in this respect what all in his position of life are more or less made to suffer. Certain traits of harshness and want of consideration towards those who had just claim's upon his respect and gratitude had in the first year of his reign prejudiced public opinion, especially in England, against him. He had entered upon a splendid inheritance with nothing to recommend him except the fact that he was the grandson of a man to whom all Europe had looked up with feelings of veneration. Young and untried as he was, he took the position of his great ancestor with an air that seemed to argue a conviction on his part that, with the Empire that had descended to him, he had also inherited the personal greatness of the man to whom it's foundation was owing. There was an absence of modesty and diffidence in his attitude which at first shocked the world. What had been natural and becoming in the grandsire seemed arrogant and unbecoming in the grandson. The one had claimed pre-eminence by virtue of mighty deeds and a life full of grand and exceptional achievements. The other asserted the same claim; but he did so as one who has yet to show himself possessed of those qualities which alone render the claim justifiable. The young Emperor was conscious that he possessed those qualities. The world had to learn that he was not mistaken. When it did so its opinion changed slowly but steadily, and in time the disapprobation with which it had at first regarded the self-reliance and assurance of the youthful ruler made way for a feeling of surprised interest, which deepened quickly into a respect as sincere, if not as profound, as that which had been felt for his illustrious grandfather.

Thus, in small things as well as in great, success is, and always will be, the criterion of merit. Whether it be a just criterion or not, the fact remains, and is incontrovertible, that he who succeeds deserves success, and he who fails apparently does not.

If I have dwelt at this length upon facts which may be assumed to be known to everyone who is not totally ignorant of contemporary history, the reader must not imagine that I therefore presume to class him among the historically ignorant. The recapitulation of these details was necessary to the full comprehension of events which are no less historical, though now for the first time to be chronicled; events which it has been my privilege to learn of from one who may claim to possess a more intimate knowledge of the subject than any other man living, not excepting even his Majesty the Emperor Willibald of Arminia himself.

CHAPTER II
Partly Diplomatic

I am alluding, of course, to Sir John Templeton.

That the famous old diplomatist should have been one of the first persons whose opinion on the extraordinary mystery that was agitating the world was consulted by those most concerned in it, will scarcely surprise anyone who is familiar with the history of the more prominent European courts during the last few decades. There are those, however, who to this day assert that Sir John Templeton at the outset grievously misjudged the case, and miscalculated its political effects. Perhaps he did. But, then, what mortal possesses the gift of looking into the future? There is little doubt that, in its earlier stages, Sir John was inclined to treat the Arminian mystery with a certain amount of indifference. He ridiculed the notion, which gradually became universal, that the Emperor's disappearance was the result of an intrigue of a phenomenal kind, the like of which history had never seen. But, whatever his views on the cause of that singular event were, its consequences could not fail to impress him in the same way as they did every one else.

Indeed, within a very short time people had ceased to marvel at the strangeness of the thing, or to seek for its explanation. The question now brought home to every mind was no longer the fate of an Emperor, but of an Empire: for Arminia was leaderless, and, worse still, was torn by inner dissensions, for which there seemed no hope of a solution, and which, coupled with the threatening attitude of the excitable Franconians, rendered the situation daily more and more critical. Since her successful great war with her hereditary foe in the west, Arminia stood, after Great Britain, at the head of the European Great Powers, and upon the maintenance of this powerful position depended in a large measure the peace of the world. Practically a confederation of a number of States under one supreme head, the Arminian Empire formed so tremendous a factor in the equipoise of Europe, that the merest suspicion touching her stability was to make every statesman on our side of the globe tremble. And it was this inner stability which was now threatened.

Unfortunately, it was not until matters political had reached their climax of confusion that official steps were reluctantly taken by the Government of Arminia to enlist the services of Sir John Templeton in unravelling the mystery that underlay it all. The reason for this reluctance is not far to seek. Sir John had on more than one occasion passed some rather severe strictures upon the Arminian authorities, whose action in silencing the Press on the subject that was exciting all Europe he pronounced a grievous blunder. His words had not, unnaturally given considerable umbrage in Berolingen; nor, if report may be believed, were his Arminian Majesty's advisers over well pleased at the fact that one of the first to consult the old diplomatist and invite him to Berolingen was the Dowager Empress of Arminia, the august relative of our own gracious Sovereign, through whom her Majesty had conveyed her desire that Sir John Templeton should place his services at the disposal of the Arminian Government.

Nevertheless, it is not a little significant of the weight that was attached to Sir John's opinions that Count Jadgberg, the Arminian Ambassador at the Court of Vienna, should have deemed it expedient to seek an interview with him in order to vindicate the course taken by his Government.

The account of this interview, which I have obtained from Count Jadgberg himself, is of sufficient interest, in view of subsequent developments, to be briefly recorded here.

"I explained at some length to Sir John Templeton," his Excellency says, in the memoir he has been good enough to draw up for me, "that in acting as they did, the Imperial Government were prompted by certain reasons, the cogency of which it was impossible to assail. The Emperor had undoubtedly on several recent occasions expressed his intention of proceeding in person to Noveria, and investigating matters in the turbulent province with his own eyes. Assuming, therefore, not unreasonably, as the authorities did, that his Majesty, in defiance of all prudence, and in spite of the urgent representations of his advisers, had ventured incognito and unattended into the very camp of the rebel party, it of course became their first care to prevent any knowledge of this dangerous proceeding from reaching the public. Indeed, the mere fact of the Emperor's disappearance, had it come to the ears of the Noverian leaders, would in itself have sufficed to put them on their guard, and open their eyes to the tremendous possibilities involved."

All these arguments, however, failed to convince Sir John.

"I have followed the career of your illustrious Sovereign with the profoundest interest, ever since his accession to the throne of Arminia," he said, "and the estimate I have formed of his character is so utterly irreconcilable with the foolhardy act which is now attributed to him, that nothing of ocular proof will convince me of it. The Emperor may be headstrong, and venturesome even to the verge of eccentricity. But, coupled with his resoluteness and self-reliance, he possesses two other sterling qualities, whose influence so far has been discernible in all his actions. Those qualities are a deep earnestness of purpose and a grasp of mind such as is rarely met with in so young a man, and more rarely still in one of his Majesty's impulsive temperament. Moreover, if the report of those may be trusted who are both competent and impartial judges, he has already given proof of considerable military genius. Compare these facts, then, with the extraordinary story we are now called upon to believe: that of a monarch staking, not only his liberty and

12

his life, but the fortune, ay, the very existence, of a mighty Empire, upon an adventure as foolish and useless in its conception as perilous in its execution. Either the facts I have mentioned are true, or the story is true; but not both.'

"Have you formed any definite theory of your own?" I asked.

Sir John shook his head.

"There is nothing I avoid more carefully than the danger of forming theories," he said. "But in this instance the conclusion to be formed from the facts is so obvious that it would be idle for me to pretend to shut my eyes to it."

"To what facts do you allude?" I inquired.

"To the facts relating to the Emperor's private secretary, Doctor Hofer," Sir John replied. "This man, it is admitted, the last person who conversed with his Majesty before he retired to rest on the night of his disappearance. He possessed the Emperor's confidence in a remarkable degree, I believe; was, in fact, more of a friend than a servant to his Imperial master."

"Doctor Hofer," I said, "if I may say so, did at one time exercise a certain influence over his Majesty. But, it is certain that this influence had not been maintained during the last two or three months."

"Which means that of late it had been observed that a certain coldness had sprung up between the Emperor and his friend."

"It is believed," I rejoined, "that Doctor Hofer had for some reason incurred his Majesty's displeasure."

"But in spite of this he was never removed from his post?"

"No."

"Nor did he cease to enjoy its exceptional privileges, such as the right of entering his Majesty's presence unannounced and at all hours?"

"I believe not."

"Yet the very last act of the Emperor," Sir John remarked, "was to issue an order which virtually deprived Doctor Hofer of his liberty."

"His Majesty's commands were that Doctor Hofer should be strictly watched, and not permitted to leave the capital under whatsoever pretence."

"And to whom was this order addressed?"

"To the general in command of the garrison of Berolingen."

"And it was to Doctor Hofer himself to whom his Majesty intrusted its safe delivery?"

"I gave a silent affirmative."

"So that," Sir John continued, "on the eve of the Emperor's

13

disappearance Doctor Hofer actually received a sealed document from his Majesty's hands containing an order for his own arrest; and being ignorant of its purport, delivered it to the general commanding the garrison, to whom it was addressed?"

Again I bowed a silent affirmative.

"There was, I understand, no reason given for the adoption of this extraordinary measure?" Sir John asked.

"None," I replied.

"It may be inferred, then, that it is in some way connected with the cause of his Majesty's absence."

"The inference is perhaps natural."

"The inference is the only possible one," Sir John said.

"Pardon my curiosity," I now observed. "But if you utterly scout the notion that the Emperor's disappearance is connected with the dynastic movements in Noveria, which are, after all, important to engage his Majesty's serious attention, to what still more important motive is it possible to assign a step which has jeopardised not only the stability of our Empire, but the peace of Europe itself?"

"Your question," Sir John answered, "is based on three grave misapprehensions. Firstly, I have not said that his Majesty's absence is unconnected with the troubles in Noveria; on the contrary, I incline to the belief that such a connection is highly probable, only I think not in the manner supposed by your Government. Secondly, you will remember that I have emphatically expressed it as my opinion that the European complications which have followed the Emperor's action are not due to that action itself, but to the arbitrary construction placed upon it by his Majesty's own advisers. Thirdly, you start from the assumption that the motive of his Majesty's step must necessarily be one of vast political importance. It may or it may not be so. To argue that it needs must be so is to fatally prejudge the case. Having said this, I can only answer your question itself by saying that I am for the present as ignorant of the real solution of the mystery as your Excellency is."

"Then how, in the name of common sense," I exclaimed, "would you propose to set to work to discover it?"

"By making myself acquainted with the only man who is apparently able to tell me what I want to know," Sir John answered.

"You allude to this Doctor Hofer," I said. "But do you imagine, that he would be complaisant enough to gratify your curiosity? You do not know the man, Sir John. Doctor Hofer is in many respects an exceptional character, and certainly not one who would be likely to tell you any more than suits him."

"What you say is deeply interesting," Sir John replied. "It is not, however, what a man tells me, but what he does not tell me, that is the most instructive information he conveys, and in this respect, it seems, I might rely upon finding this Doctor Hofer unusually communicative."

From the tenor of this conversation it is hardly to be doubted that Count Jadgberg, either on his own account, or upon instructions from Berolingen, had used this of sounding Sir John Templeton's views as to the best method of solving the difficulty in which the Government of Arminia were placed. It required, however, the pressure of personal influence, as well as that of circumstances, to induce the Arminian Government actually to invite the cooperation of the astute old diplomat in grappling with that difficulty. That such personal influence was brought to bear upon the Arminian Ministers from many illustrious quarters has already been intimated. What may have proved, however, of greater weight with them than the advice of foreign potentates, was the personal intervention of the great ex-Chancellor of the Empire, Prince Ottomarck, whose dismissal from office twelve months previously by the spirited young Emperor, though a foregone conclusion to those who were acquainted with the characters both of the master and the servant, had caused so immense a sensation in Europe.

Through King Albert of Wettinia, the truest champion of Arminian unity, and the staunch admirer of the great statesman who was its political founder, the Prince had used his utmost endeavours to prevail upon his successor in office to secure the services of Sir John Templeton.

"There are circumstances," he wrote to King Albert, "which all the resources of ordinary statecraft are inadequate to cope with, and it is time that the Imperial Government should recognise the fact that such a moment has arrived in the affairs of our common fatherland. It is my firm conviction that, until the fate of his Majesty the Emperor has been ascertained, nothing on earth can avert the disastrous consequences of the present deplorable deadlock; and I know of no man better fitted to undertake this difficult task, and possibly rectify the serious blunders which have already been committed, than Sir John Templeton, who, I am aware, needs no words of mine to recommend him to your Majesty."

What influence the opinion of Prince Ottomarck may have had upon Count Capricius, the Arminian Imperial Chancellor, I am, of course, not in a position to say. What I do know is that this letter, which was promptly forwarded to the Government in Berolingen by

15

the Wettinian monarch, bore the date of 12th June, and that on 15th June Sir John Templeton left Vienna for Berolingen.

There is nothing I regret more deeply than that just during these exciting days I happened to be absent from my post in Vienna, and thus missed the opportunity of following events, as I was so fond of doing, through the medium, as it were, of old Sir John's mind. That it would have been of more than usual interest to me to learn his views on the situation just then the reader will readily gather from the fact that I was at that very moment myself on the way to the Arminian capital for purposes of which, personal though they be, I am compelled to make brief mention here.

The fact is that the great English daily journal for which I had for many years acted as occasional correspondent, had offered me the post of its permanent correspondent in Berolingen, and it was with the object of discussing this for me momentous offer that I had obtained three months' leave of absence from my diplomatic post in Vienna and repaired to London. The result of my visit was that I agreed to act as temporary representative of the journal in Berolingen during the term of my official furlough, leaving the question of my permanent engagement to be settled at a later date.

Before I left London I had an opportunity of discussing the situation in general, and my immediate destination in particular, with our late correspondent in Berolingen, whose retirement at this particular juncture had been brought about by his contravention of the new Arminian Press laws, which made the despatch of news to foreign countries subject to the sanction of the censor.

The information I gathered from him, though full of interest from my point of view as a journalist, was surprisingly meagre in those details respecting the actual question at issue, which alone can claim the attention of the reader of this history. Indeed, beyond the facts already plainly indicated in the telegraphic despatches which I have cited, all I learned in this latter regard was that the rumour of the Emperor Willibald's capture by the so-called Guelph party in Noveria, though by no means supported by anything resembling positive proof, had a strong basis of probability. That his Majesty's love of adventure, and perhaps his tendency to trust no eye and no judgment but his own, had led him in this instance to play the part of his own detective, and thus place himself in a position of great peril, appeared in my humble opinion to be certain. It was the only plausible explanation of his strange disappearance, and, according as it did with that which was known of his independence of character and indomitable spirit, there is little wonder that a certain amount of credence should have been attached to it.

What, however, appeared to me too extravagant to believe was the alleged complicity of the Duke of Cumbermere in this daring attempt to restore by force of arms the kingdom his late father had forfeited twenty years previously, when he blindly cast in his lot with Austria in that country's unfortunate war with Brandenburg. On this point indeed, our late correspondent would express no decided opinion.

"The question is a difficult one to answer," he said. "The Duke is certainly reported upon pretty good authority to have sailed for Europe a fortnight ago, and his destination under present circumstances can scarcely be doubtful. If, therefore, the Emperor has placed himself in the power of the Noverian rebels, his Royal Highness practically holds the key of the entire position, and can dictate almost any terms he likes. On the other hand, however, there is every reason to believe that his Majesty has for some time been favourably inclined towards an amicable settlement of the Noverian question, and there are indications which tend to show that he has been conducting personal negotiations to this end with the Duke of Cumbermere. That a certain influence has been at work for several years to bring about this desired result is beyond all question. It is within your own knowledge, no doubt, that his Majesty's private secretary and, until very recently at least, his trusted confidante, is a Noverian and a stanch adherent of the late Royal house."

"You allude, of course, to the famous Doctor Hofer."

"Precisely."

"But was not this very man arrested by order of the Emperor himself at the moment of his Majesty's disappearance?"

"So it is reported. The terms of this arrest, however, are, to say the least, somewhat extraordinary, since they merely restrict the Doctor's liberty to move about at will, excepting within the precincts of the Imperial palace. But let us leave the fact of this arrest, which no one pretends to understand, out of account for the present. What we are discussing is the influence which this man has undoubtedly exercised over the mind and the views of his Imperial master. As an example of the tendency of this influence I need only adduce one incident, which, though it caused at the time considerable astonishment in Arminian political circles, naturally attracted little attention abroad. Three months ago the Emperor suddenly declared his intention of reinstating the son of the former Prime Minister of the late King of Noveria, Baron von Arnold, a young man of pronounced Noverian sympathies, and believed to be one of the most active agents in the employ of the Duke of Cumbermere, in the possessions which his father had forfeited to the crown of Brandenburg. In spite of the urgent remonstrances of the Government, who foresaw the imprudence of such a step, his Majesty persisted in carrying out this spontaneous act of grace, and Baron von Arnold returned to Arminia shortly afterwards, and quietly re-entered into possession of his family estates."

"And is it believed that this generous act on his Majesty's part was due to the influence of Doctor Hofer?"

"The conclusion is inevitable. What increases the strangeness of the incident, however, is the fact that, with the return of young Von Arnold from exile, the influence of Dr. Hofer at the Arminian court commenced to wane, and there is little doubt that, within a very short time, an estrangement ensued between the Emperor and his confidant, which, if we may credit the official version, culminated on the day of his Majesty's disappearance, in the complete disgrace and the arrest of the latter."

"But would not this tend to prove," I remarked, "that the Emperor had discovered the existence of some plot in which this man Hofer was concerned?"

"Very true. On the face of it that appears to me the most plausible explanation. Court gossip, however, throws a very different light upon the history of Doctor Hofer's disgrace. There are two versions current, either of which, if correct, would reduce the whole affair to the level of a mere court intrigue. According to the first of these two versions it would seem that Doctor Hofer had prevailed upon the Emperor to grant an amnesty to Baron von Arnold for selfish reasons, inasmuch, namely, as the young Baron, it appears, was the affianced husband of Hofer's sister, a young girl said to be possessed of very great beauty. Those who know the Emperor are aware that he never forgives an act of deception, and the discovery that he had been thus practised upon by one whom he had honoured with his confidence and friendship would indeed more than sufficiently account for what has happened. Unfortunately for the probability of this story, however, there is every reason to believe that, if Doctor Hofer had been inclined to use his position at court for the purpose of self-advancement, the extraordinary favour with which the Emperor has always treated him would have enabled him to gratify his ambition long ago, and in a manner very different from that which is now attributed to him. But his bitterest enemies cannot accuse him of pursuing selfish ends. Far from seeking advancement, he has, on the contrary, always studiously avoided it, contenting himself with a position

18

which, if influential has certainly not been productive of any undue benefit to himself."

"That disposes, then, of the first version," I said. "And the second?"

"Unfortunately it is scarcely more satisfactory than the first. You have heard, no doubt, like the rest of the world, of the strained relations which existed some months ago between the Emperor and his second youngest sister, the Princess Margaret. The cause was no secret. The Emperor wished to bestow his sister's hand upon the heir to one of the most powerful thrones in Europe, and met with a refusal on the part of the Princess which was as determined as it was unexpected. His Majesty, as you are aware, is not accustomed to brook opposition, even from those for whom he has a tenderness, and the firm stand made by her Imperial Highness, who was his Majesty's especial favourite, is said to have led to a complete rupture between the brother and sister, culminating at last in the banishment of the latter from court. The Princess is reported at the time to have declared her intention never to marry at all. Whether true or not, rumour at once busied itself with the reason for such a determination in one whose attractions are universally acknowledged to be of a very superior kind. It was whispered that an unfortunate attachment for a certain person of quite inferior rank, who held a confidential position at the Imperial court, was the real cause of the Princess's wish to remain single, and among those pointed out as the probable object of this attachment was his Majesty's private secretary, Doctor Hofer. The gossip subsided after a while, as gossip usually does, but it has been revived within the last fortnight, and the quarrel between the Emperor and His favourite sister is now asserted by some to have a distinct bearing upon the subsequent disgrace of his Majesty's secretary. Unfortunately, again, for the upholders of this version, there is the fact that, only a few weeks prior to the disappearance of the Emperor and the mysterious arrest of Doctor Hofer, the banishment of the princess was revoked, and a reconciliation between the illustrious parties to the quarrel took place, which circumstances, as you will readily admit, is scarcely compatible with the theory advanced by the court wiseacres in explanation of her Imperial Highness's enforced retirement from the capital."

All this was of course deeply interesting to me, but at the same time extremely puzzling.

"It is strange," I said, "that, in whatever direction one looks in this mysterious business, the only result one obtains is a negative one. It is like wandering in a maze of blind alleys. There seems to be no single affirmative fact, if I may so call it, to start from in investigating the matter."

"Just so," my companion rejoined. "It is that which emphasises the seriousness of the situation, and you may believe me, in spite of all outward appearances, affairs look nowhere more serious than in the Arminian capital itself. There is a savour of revolution in the very atmosphere one breathes there."

"But surely," I said, "it is not by means of a revolution that the people of Berolingen can hope to rescue their Emperor from the hands of the Noverians."

My informant shrugged his shoulders.

"A populace does not reason," he said. "The people's confidence in their Government has entirely vanished. The attempts of the authorities to conceal what everyone knows to be the truth, coupled with his rumoured meeting of the Arminian princes in the capital to deliberate on the situation, have caused the most extravagant suspicions. What their outcome will be I will not venture to foreshadow. But you will have an opportunity of seeing and judging for yourself."

And so indeed I had.

As I lay in bed that night, previous to my departure for the Arminian capital, ruminating on the amazing change which had taken place in the aspect of political affairs throughout the entire civilised world within a short fortnight, in consequence of the disappearance of one solitary mortal from the scene of action, I could not help dwelling upon the extraordinary instability of our human affairs generally.

Let the reader recapitulate for himself the stupendous mass of events which had crowded into that comparatively brief span of time.

It was on the 31st of May that the first rumour of the Arminian Emperor's disappearance reached the public through the medium of a London morning paper. Within a few hours the report confirmed on indubitable evidence by every newspaper of note in Europe, and its truth maintained in spite of the most strenuous denials issued by the Arminian Government. A wave of the greatest conceivable excitement instantly passed over the world. The Cabinets of every State in Europe were hastily summoned to deliberate on the situation and its possible consequences. Alas, to how little purpose! Within ten days, Franconia had practically mobilised her army, frontier troubles of the gravest kind had arisen between Arminia and her colossal neighbour in the East, apprehension had seized the mind, and was guiding the actions of every statesman in Europe; in short, complications of the most alarming nature had set in on all sides. Troops were being mustered, armies strengthened, and other military measures adopted by every power who had any interests to protect—and what power has not? In Arminia itself differences and dissensions were reported to have broken out between the component sovereign members of the huge Empire, a rebellion had suddenly taken place in Noveria, and Berolingen, with its population of over a million souls, was on the eve of a terrible revolution.

Viewed calmly and dispassionately, even at the distance of time which has since elapsed, this rapid metamorphosis seems to us now almost incredible. Yet, when I say that the picture is not overdrawn nor exaggerated in one single particular, I do so knowing that the testimony of every contemporary observer will bear out the truth of the assertion.

Doubtless, history records more than one instance of international complications as intricate and menacing as those we are now dealing with, but assuredly none in which the source, the primary cause, of the complications was of so strangely simplex a nature. The conflicting political interests of the great powers of the earth, to reconcile and adjust which the combined intelligence of the most eminent statesman and diplomatists frequently spends itself in vain, have before now set the world ablaze, and brought untold misery and disaster upon suffering humanity. But here was a case of a different, a totally unprecedented kind. Not the aims and ends of scheming statecraft, not the clash and the entanglement of irreconcilable interests of State and State, nor the colliding angry passions of rival races, were the primary elements of the gathering storm. Its origin was assignable to one single fact, one solitary event, upon the elucidation of which it depended whether war or peace, hope or despair, calm or tempest, was in store for mankind. In a word, the fate of the whole civilised world hung upon the answer to the one problem, the terribly simple problem: What had become of the Arminian Emperor?

BOOK II
COMPLICATION

CHAPTER III
Imperial Berolingen

If it merely required a relation of my own personal experiences to place the reader in possession of the remarkable facts of the present story, my task would be light and easy indeed. The circumstance, however, that I happened at this juncture to be sent to Berolingen as special correspondent of one of the most distinguished English newspapers, and that I thus had the good fortune to live, so to speak, in the thick of subsequent events, is a coincidence which, though it enables me to supply from my own stock of knowledge a good many details bearing upon the subject matter of these pages, does not place me in a position to deal as an historian with that subject matter itself.

I wish the reader, before I proceed, clearly to grasp this fact. The collection of those more or less disjointed records which form the really historical part of my story has been a labour of some years, to which I have devoted no little energy and persistency, and for which I may justly claim some recognition. Without my experiences, gathered both in London and in Berolingen, I should perhaps not have been able so to piece these records together, supplementing, where needful, those general details which they lack, as to produce a perfectly complete and consecutive narrative. On the other hand, were it not for the main facts, for which I am indebted to other sources, the account of my own experiences, pure and simple, would possess no more interest, and certainly no more value, than the reminiscences of any fairly able journalist whom chance has placed as an eye-witness in the midst of events of an unusually stirring character. It is the combination of these two distinct sources of information which qualifies me to write this history, and it is this combination, then, with all its necessary drawbacks, which I must ask the reader to bear with patiently.

Having thus, as I venture to think, satisfactorily explained my position, I will now proceed to lay before the reader that part of my material, the true source of which he must use his own skill and ingenuity to discover.

Those who can claim even the slightest acquaintance with Berolingen are aware that what is known there as the Royal Castle, a huge pile remarkable rather for its squareness than its beauty, marks, as it were, the boundary between the older portion of the city, which extends hence towards the north and the east, and comprises a considerable number of industrial suburbs, with their legion of factories and storehouses, in its wide area, and the more modern extension of the town, which covers a still larger area in the west and south. In the immediate vicinity of the Castle stands the great dome, and at a somewhat greater distance, arrayed, seemingly, without any regard for symmetrical order, upon a comparatively small space, there are the museums and picture galleries, the Hall of Glory, with its piled-up mass of trophies, and the University buildings. Opposite the latter, to the left, stands the Grand Opera House, flanked by two royal palaces. One of these, once known as the palace of the Crown Prince, is now the Berolingen residence of her Majesty the Empress Mother; whilst the other, once the regular abode of his late Majesty the Emperor Willibald the Victorious, and facetiously termed 'the chest of drawers' by the Berolingen wits, on account of its resemblance in shape to that useful article of furniture, has since the decease of that glorious monarch been left untouched by his successor for reasons of historic piety.

From here the world-famed Grand Avenue of Limes stretches for considerably over half-a-mile towards the historical Arch of Victory, forming as fine a boulevard as any capital in Europe, not excepting Patropolis itself, can boast of. Beyond lies the aristocratic, or at least wealthier, western quarter of Berolingen, with its unique forest park, its shady avenues, canal-walks, and villa residences. But it is within the immediate precincts of the great alleys of limes that royal and official Berolingen lives and breathes. Here is the centre of the great metropolis, where the world of fashion congregates. Here the people from every quarter, north, south, east, and west, assemble in their hundreds of thousands when court pageants or military displays are expected, for the numerous palaces of the different members of the Royal and Imperial house are all situated within a ten minutes' radius of this centre, and whether court processions or military reviews, royal receptions or departures, or any other State functions, form the programme of the day's performance, both start and finish can only be witnessed on this spot, and nowhere else.

At the time we are speaking of, that is to say, two days after the conversation recorded in the preceding chapter, there was little in the aspect of this portion of the city to denote the existence of any unusual popular excitement. In the great Square in front of the principal entrance to the Royal Castle the crowd of gazers who always idle about here in anticipation of catching a glimpse of its illustrious occupant was perhaps a little larger than usual, and the mounted police stationed at all points and corners were obliged to display somewhat more than their ordinary energy in enforcing the regulation which prohibited the gathering of groups in the public thoroughfares. But the demeanour of the people was on the whole extremely orderly, and beyond a certain look of anxiety on some faces, and an air of vacant curiosity, mingled, however, with a peculiar expression of distrust on others, the keenest observer could have detected no sign of that spirit of dissatisfaction and resentment which, according to those accustomed to gauge the state of the public pulse, pervaded the town.

In the Castle itself, into which it will now become my privilege to introduce the reader, everything wore its usual tranquil appearance. In the various departments of the Imperial household work was proceeding with its wonted clockwork regularity. In the immense vestibule leading from the inner courtyard to the Imperial State apartments on the ground floor of the central building, a host of lacqueys in their gorgeous liveries were to be seen solemnly pacing up and down between the statues and vases with which the place abounded, or standing at attention near the grand entrance itself, as if expecting every moment to hear the cry of the sentry in the courtyard without heralding the approach of the Imperial carriage, and to see the guard stationed in the gateway opposite turn out and present arms as his Majesty drove up and alighted at the entrance.

No one could have guessed from the empty expression on their stolid countenances that they had been waiting in this vain expectation for over a fortnight. Carriages, it is true, had driven up in considerable numbers during that period, but their occupants, princely or otherwise, had rarely alighted, and the duties of the be-liveried gentlemen in the vestibule had consisted all this time in the mere reiteration to these would-be visitors, of the now well-worn phrase, specially constructed and issued from the office of the Imperial Chief Court Marshal, "that his Majesty would receive no one."

24

The words were harmless, and deceived nobody. They simply meant that the situation, which was no longer a secret to anyone, remained unaltered; and so they were received, with a sigh by some, with resignation by others, and deferentially yet sadly by one and all.

The grand staircase which mounts from the entrance hall to the first floor of the main body of the Castle leads to the principal staterooms, amongst which the two most important are the great banqueting hall, in which several hundred guests can be seated with ease, and the throne room, a chamber of colossal dimensions, used only on extraordinary occasions when State ceremonies of a specially formal character are enacted. Immediately at the top of the staircase a spacious corridor branches off to the left wing of the Castle, where the Emperor's private apartments are situated. These, although most sumptuously furnished, are comparatively few in number, consisting, indeed, merely of three large rooms, the middle one of which, approached through an ante-room, is his Majesty's private audience chamber, and the two others respectively the Emperor's study and his sleeping apartment, the latter immediately adjoining the study.

Besides these three rooms, however, which are exclusively reserved for the Emperor's own use there is a large library, separated only by a small closet from the Imperial study, and leading on the other side to a further set of two rooms, which constitute—or rather constituted at the period in question—the official abode of the Imperial secretary, Doctor Georg Hofer.

Even in this portion of the Castle, the description of which must suffice the reader for the present, there was nothing in the general appearance of things to indicate the occurrence of that extraordinary event which was engrossing the minds of the outer world. The Emperor's apartments were empty, it is true; but for all the evidence to the contrary his Majesty might have been out riding or driving, or holding a review of his troops, or surprising the garrison of the capital—a pastime much affected by his Majesty—or, in short, engaged on any other business necessitating a temporary absence from home. The approach to the Imperial apartments was as carefully guarded as ever. The ante-chamber was occupied by the Imperial aide-de-camp on duty, as if at any moment the call-bell from the inner apartment might sound and summon him to the presence of his illustrious master; whilst outside, the usual array of orderlies stood about, ready to hasten off with commands or despatches at the shortest notice. Chamberlains and other household dignities were continually passing to and fro between the ante-room and the various official departments of the Castle; stalwart lacqueys stood stiff and erect at their posts before the door to the Imperial chambers and along the passage leading to it. In a word, the scene generally presented as animated an appearance as it had ever done at the best of times.

In one of the rooms adjoining the library, the situation of which I have described above, sat, at this moment, two men engaged in earnest conversation. One of these, a tall, wiry figure, slightly bent with age, yet in every limb still expressive of a vitality that would have arrested attention even in a younger man, was Sir John Templeton himself. The other, a man of commanding presence, with a handsome, though somewhat stern cast of features, who was seated at a large writing-table strewn with a mass of books, papers, and official documents, was no other than the famous Imperial private secretary, Doctor Georg Hofer.

The gossip concerning this man and his relations to the missing Emperor will have awakened sufficient curiosity in the mind of the reader to justify a somewhat more detailed description of this interesting personage than that already given.

As regards his age, he might have been anything between 25 and 35. His head was rather round than oval in shape, but his face had a marked individuality of its own in all its parts. Each feature was sharply defined and well-proportioned, the nose tending somewhat to the aquiline, the forehead high and arched, the eyebrows finely curved, and the lips strong and determined. His hair was of a dark brown colour, matching with that of the beard, which he wore slightly pointed. By his dress one could not fail to recognise in him a man accustomed to move in circles where fashion is a power, if not a deity. His attire was faultless, yet quiet, and in the latter respect accorded with his general demeanour, which was grave and reserved, almost excessively so in one of his years.

This picture, however, so far as it goes, conveys but a slight idea of the real character of the man. This was not stamped on any feature; it revealed itself in the eyes alone. No one could have met the firm, dignified expression in these eyes without being instantly struck with the sense of power which spoke in them; ay, and something even beyond that—a certain subtle influence difficult to define, but which few can resist, the influence of a mind concentrated in itself, like that of the magnetiser, who by the sheer force of his will can direct the thoughts and guide the actions of his less gifted fellow-mortals.

This, then, was the man who, if report could be believed, had succeeded in accomplishing what the greatest statesman of the century, if not of all times, had failed to accomplish; that is to say, to gain an ascendency over the strong-willed young monarch who sat on the throne of Arminia. True, to all outward appearance this success had not been lasting. Even now, he who had once been the powerful favourite, sought after by many, envied by all, was to all intents and purposes a prisoner; confined in a palace, indeed, yet none the less a captive; treated with consideration and respect, yet not free to move at will, to come and go when and where he liked. And more strange than all this, the Emperor, whose friendship he had succeeded in gaining—he alone of the hundreds who had striven for it, and intrigued for it, and fought for it—the master to whom he apparently had known how to make himself indispensable, had vanished completely from view, as if suddenly removed from the face of the earth.

Here was a curious reversal of fortunes. Those who had but yesterday sued for his favour, the very Ministers and generals who had eyed him with that keen distrust which is born of fear and jealousy, and which no smiles can effectually conceal, were now his gaolers, responsible for his safe-keeping, but responsible also for his safety and wellbeing. They knew, or they fancied they knew, that he alone had enjoyed the confidence of their Sovereign; a misplaced confidence, of course, they thought, as, indeed, what monarch's confidence is not misplaced in the opinion of those upon whom it has not been bestowed? Perhaps even, in spite of the suspicions of the Berolingen populace, they were inwardly convinced that the key to the mystery which baffled them and threatened to spread disaster throughout the length and breadth of the world was in this very man's possession. And yet they felt their hands tied, their actions fettered, by the sovereign commands of the Emperor himself, whom to disobey, even with the most loyal intentions, meant to offend and displease for ever. What if it all were but a feint to try that spirit of blind obedience which the young autocrat demanded from all who served him? The favourite had fallen, but might he not rise again? He had lost the influence that had once been his, but might he not regain it? After all, he was perhaps only checked, not overthrown, rebuffed, but not discarded. In short, the position was altogether anomalous. The history of royal favourites afforded no parallel instance from which some conclusion as to the true meaning of the riddle might have been drawn.

The man who now sat opposite the object of all these doubts and fears seemed as unconscious of them as he was unmoved by the evident air of haughty reserve with which his companion treated him. Different as they were in external appearance, these two men were strangely well-matched in respect of those finer qualities of the mind in which man's real strength lies; and they felt it, too, the one proudly, suspiciously, the other with undisguised satisfaction, and with an interest as keen as that of the champion who for once meets a foeman of his own peculiar stamp.

Sir John Templeton, true to the principle from which he rarely deviated, that, although facts concerning the action of men may be conveniently learned at second hand, no reliable opinion as to the motives underlying them can be formed from such intermediary courses, had lost no time, after his arrival in Berolingen, in seeking out the one man whom he believed to be possessed of the key to the mystery he had undertaken to solve. It was characteristic, too, of his method of procedure that he should have declined to hold speech on the subject of his mission with anyone, whether a member of the Government or not, until he had been brought face to face with the man of whose character and individuality he desired above all things to form a free and independent judgment.

This decision considerably surprised the ministerial councillor who had been his travelling companion from the frontier, and with whom, at such times when he was not occupied in studying the official report which, at Sir John's own request, that gentleman had been charged to convey to him, he discoursed pleasantly on every possible topic except the all-important one on which it might have been supposed that his whole interest was concentrated. The astonishment of the Arminian official, however, was greater still when they arrived in Berolingen, and Sir John Templeton, on being received at the station by the Imperial Chancellor's private secretary, who was in waiting to conduct him forthwith to the Chancellor himself, courteously but firmly declined that honour as if this was a mere trifle. He would wait upon his Excellency later in the day, Sir John said. For the present he merely requested that instructions should be given at the Royal Castle which would insure his admittance to the presence of his Majesty's private secretary, whose personal acquaintance he was anxious to make.

Thereupon he had taken a courteous leave of his travelling companion, and driven straight to the British Embassy, a handsome palace forming the corner of the famous Willabald-street and the Avenue of Limes in the centre of the town, where he was to stay as the guest of Sir Edward Hammer, her Majesty's representative at the Arminian court. Two hours later he was closeted with Doctor

Georg Hofer, the Emperor's much-talked-of private secretary, in his apartments in the Royal Castle.

It is marvellous how quick kindred minds are to recognise each other. These two men had been together but a short quarter of an hour, and they had never met before that day. Yet each had already gauged the other's power, and was prepared to put his own against it.

With what result the reader will now learn.

CHAPTER IV
An Interview with the Imperial Secretary

Sir John Templeton was not the man to clothe his intentions in ambiguous language, or to beat about the bush when his purpose was to effect a definite understanding. He had come to offer a compact, and after the first formal interchanges of courtesies between him and the Imperial secretary, he had frankly stated the object of his visit, and explained the nature of the mission which had brought him to Berolingen.

Doctor Hofer's countenance, while listening to the brief exposition of the circumstances which had preceded his visitor's arrival in the Arminian capital, was inscrutable. Had the speaker been expatiating upon the most commonplace of occurrences, the effect of what he said upon his listener could scarcely have been less stirring. Once or twice, when Sir John made passing mention of the grave political crisis in Europe, to which the Emperor's disappearance had given birth, he raised his eyebrows ever so slightly, showing thereby that the facts alluded to were new to him. But, with these few exceptions, he merely sat listening with polite attention, his eyes fixed the while upon his visitor with a quiet, studious gaze.

"You do me a signal honour by this visit, Sir John Templeton," he said, with a faint touch of irony, when the old diplomat had concluded, "and it is one that I can appreciate the more, as I have of late not been over-burdened with such distinctions. But, since it is apparently based upon the assumption that I possess intelligence bearing upon the matter you have at heart, I fear I cannot claim to merit it. I possess no such intelligence, and can therefore be of little service to you."

There was a ring of determination in these words, which might have escaped a less practised ear than that of the man to whom they were addressed.

"Were it merely a question of rendering me a service," Sir John said, "I should not have ventured to trouble you, Doctor Hofer. Let me assure you, to begin with, that I have sought you less as being the person chiefly concerned in the mysterious disappearance of his Majesty the Emperor than as the individual most deeply interested in his safe return."

"In other words," the Doctor replied, "you have come to render me a service?"

"Possibly," Sir John rejoined.

"And in what may that service consist?"

"For the present merely in soliciting your assistance in the task that lies before me."

"My assistance?" the other said, with a bitter smile. "That sounds more like a pleasantry. You see me here virtually a prisoner within these four walls, cut off from all communication with the outer world, and consequently more ignorant of the event's that are moving it than any living creature in this city."

"True," Sir John Templeton said, gravely. "And you might add, consequently, the less able to gauge the extent of the danger that threatens you."

"Me?"

"You."

"From what quarter?"

"From those who may hold you responsible for the Emperor's fate—whatever that fate may be."

"And upon what grounds would they be justified in thus holding me responsible for that of which I know as little as they themselves?"

"The grounds are numerous. But one will be sufficient. You were the last person who saw his Majesty alive."

"Possibly. What does that prove?"

"In itself little. But in conjunction with the fact that his Majesty's last act was to issue an order depriving you of your freedom, it might lead to an ominous conclusion."

"I fail to see the logic of such conclusion."

"The logic is simple. His Majesty is not accustomed to act without a purpose, and the interpretation that will be placed upon his intentions in this particular instance, in the event of his absence continuing indefinitely, is not likely to be favourable to yourself."

"Well?"

"That is your danger. It might occur—nay, it probably has occurred—to those to whose safe-keeping you have been consigned that, in solving the mystery attaching to the arrest of the Emperor's private secretary and confidant on the eve of his Majesty's strange disappearance, the explanation of that disappearance itself may be found."

An expression of genuine surprise came into the doctor's eyes.

"What you say there," he observed, after a moment's reflection, "is more interesting to me than you perhaps imagine. Indeed, he who enlightens me as to the reason for the extraordinary treatment to which his Majesty has thought fit to subject me will confer an inestimable boon upon me."

"You yourself, then, can assign no reason for it?"

"It is a mystery more profound to me than that of his Majesty's disappearance itself."

"And yet, if I am correctly informed," Sir John said, "there had been signs that his Majesty had ceased to regard you with the same favour as of old."

"Even so, the fact enhances rather than lessens the mystery. You are not the first, Sir John Templeton," Doctor Hofer went on, falling once more into his former tone of curt and frigid hauteur, "who has thus plied me with questions since his Majesty's disappearance. It is a pity that those who have sent you to me did not spare you the trouble of repeating a process the results of which can only be a negative one. I have, as I have already said, nothing to divulge. I am detained here," he exclaimed, growing warmer as he proceeded, "a captive, humiliated and disgraced without cause or reason, an object of distrust and suspicion to those who watch and guard me, and yet ignorant of the very nature of the crime they apparently impute to me. The Emperor, whom it seems I have offended, though by what action of mine I know not, has mysteriously left his palace and his capital, and because I, forsooth, was the last person with whom he is supposed to have conversed, it appears that I am to be held answerable for his non-return. It is but one instance more of the famous spirit of Brandenburgian justice. Had I not the misfortune to be a Noverian—but enough, why dwell upon it? I know only too well towards what this all tends."

His speech had grown quick and animated, and he pulled himself up towards the close, as if regretting that he had allowed himself to be entertained upon debatable ground.

31

"The misfortune," Sir John remarked, "is not alone that you happen to be a Noverian, Doctor Hofer, but that the Emperor is believed by some to be at this moment, detained a prisoner by the party who have recklessly raised the standard of rebellion in the kingdom to which his Royal Highness the Duke of Cumbermere lays claim."

"I have heard that extraordinary story," Doctor Hofer, said coldly. "Do you believe it?"

"I believe exactly so much of it as you do yourself," Sir John Templeton replied, somewhat ambiguously.

"And assuming it were true," Doctor Hofer went on apparently ignoring the reply, "by what stretch of fancy could I be supposed to be implicated?"

"You are an avowed friend of the Duke of Cumbermere," Sir John said, "and are known to have maintained a secret correspondence with him up to the very date of his Majesty's disappearance."

"Well?"

"Is it necessary for me to point out the possible construction that may be placed upon this circumstance? His Majesty the Emperor—"

"Has been perfectly cognisant of the fact of this correspondence, sir," Dr. Hofer broke in haughtily.

"Precisely," Sir John rejoined; "for the correspondence has passed through his Majesty's own hands."

Doctor Hofer gave a slight start.

"That is indeed new to me," he said slowly. "But since his Majesty has always been aware of my sentiments, even this alleged violation of privacy of my letters can have resulted in nothing more than a confirmation of that which he already knew!"

"Possibly that may be so," Sir John answered. "Only the question is not what his Majesty knows, but what interpretation his Government may place upon it."

"Am I to understand, then, that my correspondence with the Duke of Cumbermere is in the possession of the Arminian Government?" Doctor Hofer asked, with the shade of a frown upon his face.

"The Government possesses copies of all letters that have passed between you and his Royal Highness the Duke of Cumbermere since the beginning of this year," Sir John replied.

"You are therefore doubtless acquainted with their contents?"

"I am."

"You have certainly the merit of being strangely frank, sir," Doctor Hofer said, after a pause, during which he eyed his visitor with an undisguised expression of interest.

"I know of no better weapon against deception," Sir John answered, simply. "My object is to undo, not to add to, the mischief which has been caused by the blindness and duplicity of those upon whose discretion and wisdom I believed the Emperor has relied. Even you must be to some extent aware of the terrible consequences with which their foolish policy of secrecy and concealment has already been fraught. Arminia is on the verge of total disruption. Franconia threatens her in the west, and Russia is encroaching upon her in the east. Meanwhile her own fears paralyse her actions, and render her even incapable of coping with the most ordinary of her inner difficulties. In another week, Doctor Georg Hofer," he concluded, impressively, "unless the Emperor returns to his capital, or something definite is ascertained regarding his fate, a European war will have broken out; with what result to Arminia I may leave you to conceive."

Doctor Hofer was silent for a moment.

"The picture you draw is a desperate one indeed," he said, at last. "But let us trust that it is somewhat exaggerated. Even supposing all this were to come about as you predict, are not the Arminian sovereigns able to hold their own? If their Emperor has forsaken them, there are others among the monarchs of Arminia who will be capable of replacing him."

"And, peradventure, as anxious to do so as they are capable," Sir John remarked, drily. "It is just here where Arminia's chief and most immediate danger lies; and if it is to be averted, no time must be lost. Even while we are speaking, the Sovereigns of the Arminian States are hurrying from all sides to the Imperial capital, and will assemble here in full conclave to deliberate on the very measure you have mentioned."

"Well? And do you think—"

"I think, sir," Sir John said, "that such a meeting of the Arminian Sovereigns at this particular juncture will produce a revolution, but not an Emperor."

"A revolution? What, in Berolingen?"

"Not only in Berolingen, but throughout the entire Kingdom of Brandenburg, without whose support and cooperation an Arminian Empire would be a body without a backbone, mere flesh without muscle. Believe me, sir, Franconia could wish for no better opportunity of reclaiming what it has lost than the moment when

33

the Sovereigns of Arminia assemble in the Imperial capital to adjust that which is not adjustable."

"Yet surely," the other exclaimed, impressed in spite of himself by what he had heard, "it is imperative that something must be done to meet this unheard-of position. Where, then, in the name of all reason is the Emperor, whose unaccountable absence is the cause of all this confusion?"

"That," Sir John replied, "is the question I have set myself to solve."

"And do you think you will succeed?"

"With your aid—yes. Without it, only if time and events do not forestall me."

"With my aid?" Doctor Hofer said. "I do not follow your meaning. In what respect, pray, can my humble aid serve you?"

"In so far that you can save me the trouble of finding out for myself, as I undoubtedly shall, for what purpose you have entered the service and gained the confidence of the Arminian Emperor. Nay, why start up and frown? We are two men, Dr. Georg Hofer, well, if not equally, matched. Why should we fear to speak our thoughts to each other? It requires but little wisdom to tell me that you had a purpose in availing yourself of the useful friendship of a monarch, the cause of whose enemies you confessedly uphold. It is no less obvious to me that that purpose has been discovered by his Majesty, and that to know it means to know the solution of the mystery which is now convulsing Europe."

Doctor Hofer had risen, and now regarded his companion with a penetrating look. Gradually a lofty smile crept into his face, and he said calmly:

"I have heard something of your powers of perception, Sir John Templeton. In this instance, however, you will forgive me if I fail to appreciate them. I am a Noverian by birth and by sympathy. The Emperor knows it, and has always known it, for I have never endeavoured to conceal the fact. I have been credited, I know, with an influence on his Majesty which I have never possessed. By heaven," he exclaimed, with an angry outburst, "has it not even been asserted that it was I who induced the Emperor to grant an amnesty to this double-faced scoundrel Von Arnold, and restore to him the estate which his father forfeited when he loyally threw in his lot with his ill-fated King? That act of restitution, for which I never pleaded, was his Majesty's own spontaneous inspiration; for what cause I know not, unless it be that he hoped thereby to deprive the cause of the Noverian dynasty of its most influential supporter; in which

34

case," he added, bitterly, "it would seem that he has only too well succeeded."

"You are of opinion, then," Sir John broke in, "that Baron von Arnold has suddenly become a traitor to the cause for which he has hitherto sacrificed so much?"

"And if I were of that opinion, sir?"

"The opinion seems somewhat strange in the face of the fact that the Baron has just espoused the sister of the very man who holds it."

"His Majesty is aware that this marriage never had my approval; indeed, that I opposed it to the very utmost limit of my power and means."

"Why?"

The directness of the question seemed momentarily to disconcert the Doctor.

"The reason is self-evident, I think," he said, evasively. "But we are wandering from the subject. My private affairs can scarcely be suspected to have a bearing upon the important matter which is at present engaging your attention. Pshaw," he went on, more calmly, "loyal Noverian though I am, I am well aware that if the rights of the Duke of Cumbermere are to meet with just recognition, it is not by dint of arms, nor by puny attempts at rebellion made by a band of well-meaning and fanatic devotees, that such recognition is to be obtained. If his Majesty has really been deceived by this rising it is not the fault of the Duke of Cumbermere, without whose privacy, you may rest assured, it has taken place. As for the purpose you are good enough to credit me with, I have certainly availed myself of the friendship extended to me by this Majesty, in order to open his eyes to the just claims of the Prince whose heritage he withholds from him. If this fact can be construed as the result of premeditated purpose, you are welcome to the interpretation. I shall be the last person to deny it."

The tone of these words was unmistakable. It meant that, so far as the speaker was concerned, the matter ended there.

Sir John Templeton rose quietly.

"I must of course accept your answer, Dr. Hofer," he said. "Unfortunately, however, for your opinion as to the Duke of Cumbermere's privity to the incidents in Noveria, there is a circumstance which places this matter in a somewhat different light. It will possibly be news to you to learn that the Duke of Cumbermere sailed for Europe more that a fortnight ago, that he landed on the Belgian coast the day before yesterday, and is at this moment presumably well on his way to join his faithful followers in the realm which his late father forfeited."

As he spoke he drew a copy of an English newspaper from his pocket, and handed it gravely to the Imperial secretary.

Dr. Hofer had grown strangely pale, and his hand trembled perceptibly as he took and glanced at the paper. But he seemed conscious that his companion's eyes were riveted upon his countenance, and he regained his composure almost instantly.

"Pooh!" he said, crushing the paper in his hands and throwing it down with an air of disdain. "The thing is a fable, must be a fable, or—"

"Or you have been grossly deceived," Sir John Templeton said, quietly. "That is what you would say. And, indeed, is it not more than probable that you have been deceived, Doctor Georg Hofer, and in a quarter from which you least expected it?"

"It is impossible, totally impossible, I say!" Doctor Hofer exclaimed, pacing the room in great agitation.

"Impossible that you, the Duke of Cumbermere's trusted friend and correspondent, who has been in constant communication with his Royal Highness, could have been left in ignorance of that which so deeply concerns, not only his Highness's plans, but your own safety?"

"It is impossible," the other repeated once more.

"May I ask," Sir John said, "when you last received a communication from the Duke?"

The question seemed to surprise the Doctor. But he made no reply.

"But I can save you the trouble of answering the question," Sir John continued. "The Duke's last letter reached you three weeks ago, a day before his Majesty's disappearance. From the copy," he added, tranquilly, "of that letter, which I have been permitted to inspect—"

Doctor Hofer bit his lip fiercely. But Sir John went on apparently without noticing it.

"From this copy it is clear that the writer either had no intention of starting for Europe at the date of the writing, or that it did not suit with his plans to acquaint his correspondent at the court of Arminia with the fact that he harboured such intention. Your own letters unfortunately throw no light upon the matter, so that the Arminian Government are left to choose between the two alternative assumptions. It is not difficult to guess upon which one their choice will fall."

36

"And that is?"

"I will explain it briefly. They think the Emperor has fallen into a trap set him by the Duke of Cumbermere, perhaps with the aid and connivance of certain exalted personages whose names I refrain from mentioning, and that the principal instrument in luring his Majesty to his fate is the man whom the Emperor, conscious no doubt of the risk he was incurring, has left in the safe custody of his advisers—in other words, yourself."

"And by what means is it supposed that I have succeeded in thus deluding his Majesty?"

"It would take too long to enumerate the many theories propounded in this regard," Sir John replied. "But what combinations are possible hardly requires much thought to conceive. Recall the facts for yourself, Doctor Hofer. On the 15th January the Emperor, disregarding the advise of his responsible Ministers, and, as it is supposed, at the instance of his Noverian secretary, grants a free pardon to Baron Frederick von Arnold, the son of the late King of Noveria's Prime Minister, and one of the confidential group of friends surrounding the Noverian Pretender, the Duke of Cumbermere, in his American retreat. Four weeks later Herr von Arnold returns to Arminia and re-enters into possession of his family estates, selecting as his residence, not his possessions in the Noverian province, but the property of Arnoldshausen in Brandenburg, not thirty miles from Berolingen. Coincident with the young Baron's return are two events, the connection between which would appear to be obvious. I mean the sudden activity of the Noverian party in the annexed province, and the estrangement between his Majesty the Emperor and the man upon whom he had until that moment bestowed his confidence and friendship, and for whose sake his act of clemency towards Herr von Arnold is believed to have been accomplished. Of Herr von Arnold's movements, after his return to his own, little is ascertained. He lives almost as a recluse upon the smallest of his vast estates, which he never leaves, apparently visiting no one and visited by none. Meanwhile the disturbances in Noveria increase, and the Emperor treats them with inexplicable leniency, until they reach a pitch which can no longer be disregarded. Then the extraordinary event happens upon which the whole mystery turns. The Emperor vanishes on the very eve of a long premeditated voyage to the East, and simultaneous with his strange disappearance comes the news of the Duke of Cumbermere's departure from America and return to Europe. These facts, Doctor Georg Hofer, combined with the apparently trivial incident of the order for the practical arrest of the man whose sister

37

has so recently become the wife of Baron von Arnold, suggest, as you will admit, the not unnatural conclusion—"

"That Doctor Hofer and Herr von Arnold, acting as the agents of the Duke of Cumbermere, have conspired to lead the Arminian Emperor into the power of the Noverian rebel party; a truly wild conclusion, in all faith. And do you share it?"

"If I shared it, sir," Sir John said, "I should not be standing here now."

"You have formed some definite opinion, then, as to his Majesty's purposes in thus vanishing from his capital?"

"I have formed certain conclusions as to what were not his purposes, sir, and they are so comprehensive that few possible ones remain for closer investigation."

"And when do you suppose you will have succeeded in solving the problem?"

"When I have succeeded in solving the simpler one which I have already mentioned; the cause of your presence at the Imperial Court of Arminia, Doctor Hofer."

The Doctor made an impatient gesture.

"You still adhere, then, to the belief that I am concerned in this unfortunate mystery?"

"Our conversation has rendered the belief a conviction."

"In short, that I have sacrificed the liberty, and perhaps the life, of his Majesty the Emperor Willibald of Arminia for some alleged hidden purpose of my own?"

"On the contrary," Sir John answered with a smile, "that his Majesty the Arminian Emperor has thwarted this alleged purpose of your own, as you please to term it, by acting as he has done."

The Doctor looked at him in silence.

"Were any other man but Sir John Templeton to tell me this," he said at last, "I should conclude him—"

"To be a fool, Doctor Hofer. Possibly. You scout my conclusion. Yet you yourself have just now propounded a theory scarcely less astonishing than mine."

"What theory, sir?"

"The theory that Baron Frederick von Arnold, the husband of a lady who, if report is true, excels even her brother in her loyalty to the house of Noveria, has traitorously forsaken that cause in order to regain possession of the estates which his father sacrificed for it."

The other shrugged his shoulders contemptuously.

"Unfortunately," he said, "history records many parallel instances of such treachery."

"But surely none," Sir John observed, "where the traitor signalises his treachery by espousing a passionate adherent of the very cause he has betrayed."

"You are singularly well acquainted with the sentiments of the lady you speak of," said the Doctor, eyeing him suspiciously. "Am I to infer from this circumstance that not even the correspondence between my sister and myself has escaped the prying attention of his Majesty's advisers?"

Sir John bowed an assent.

"I have had the privilege of reading some of Demoiselle Hofer's letters to her brother," he said, "from which I have gathered that hatred of the house of Brandenburg is the first and most important article of the creed she has been reared in from her earliest infancy."

The Doctor turned away with a shrug, and made no reply.

"Does it not strike you as at least worthy of consideration," Sir John continued, without heeding the gesture, "that his Majesty's Government should have taken so entirely different a view of the relationship existing between the Emperor and this latest Noverian protege of his?"

"If you mean by that, sir," Doctor Hofer rejoined sharply, "that his Majesty's Government distrust this man, I see practically little difference between our respective views, for so do I."

"True; but the suspicion the Arminian Government entertain against him—"

"Is preposterous, sir," the other exclaimed, with some petulance. "Have not you yourself admitted it?"

"With a certain reservation, yes," Sir John Templeton replied. "I am, as I have already said, convinced, Doctor Hofer, that you possess no knowledge of the Emperor's whereabouts."

The Doctor inclined his head with an ironical smile.

"But I am equally convinced," Sir John went on, quietly, "that Baron Frederick von Arnold does."

"Then, in heaven's name!" the Doctor exclaimed, with a passionateness which was startlingly sudden, "if such be the views of his Majesty's Government, why do they not lay hands on this man? They have him in their power, and if he alone on God's earth knows what fate has befallen the Emperor—"

"Would his mere seizure suffice to secure the principal object the Government seek to attain; that is to say, to bring his Majesty safely back to his capital? You forget, Doctor Hofer, that the Emperor's absence is not believed to be voluntary, and, moreover, that it is supposed to be connected with the rebellious manifestations in Noveria. Under these circumstances his Majesty's Government have been content for the present merely to watch Herr von Arnold's movements with the view of intercepting any communication that may pass between him and the rebel leaders."

"A wise proceeding, forsooth," the Doctor said, contemptuously. "And, pray, with what success has it been attended?"

"Hitherto with none," Sir John replied. "It has, on the contrary, been established, I think beyond a doubt, that Baron von Arnold holds no communication whatever with the outer world, but is living tranquilly on his estate at Arnoldshausen, enjoying the first sweets of his married life."

Doctor Hofer strode impulsively to the window and gazed out. Presently he returned, and faced his companion with a searching look.

"Why do you tell me all this?" he said, in a short, almost fierce tone.

"As I have already explained," Sir John Templeton, answered calmly, "to warn you of the danger to which you are exposed—not only from the Arminian government, to whose vigilant care the Emperor, for reasons known to himself alone, has confided you, but from a far more formidable quarter. Events, if I mistake not, are rapidly striding towards a crisis unprecedented even in Arminia's chequered history, and though the Sovereign's commands may protect you from the wrath of those to whose custody he has consigned you, not many days may elapse before even they will require to seek protection from the senseless fury of the people whom they have foolishly sought to delude."

Hofer paced the room gravely, a stern expression upon his handsome features.

"You believe, in short, that the people of Berolingen will rise and overthrow the government."

"Berolingen is at this very moment in the throes of a revolution."

"Caused by the absence of the Emperor?"

"Caused by the folly of those who have converted his absence into a national calamity, sir."

"And this assemblage of the Arminian princes, you think, will be the match that ignites the revolutionary flame?"

"A populace whose suspicions are once aroused is quick at forming conclusions. That the imperious nature and independent character of the young Emperor have caused many heartburnings among the confederate sovereigns who acknowledge his supreme leadership is a matter of common history. The indecent haste shown to replace him by another of their own choice has not unnaturally given rise to the wildest conjectures among a populace already highly excited. The fire is smouldering; it requires but a breath to fan it into flame."

"And this breath—" Doctor Hofer said reflectively.

But at that moment a rattling of carriage wheels, and a succession of shouts, accompanied by the clatter of feet and the beating of drums, as the guard turned out to render a royal salute, sounded in the castle courtyard without, and interrupted the speaker's sentence. Stepping quickly to the window, Sir John Templeton looked out.

"There," he said gravely, pointing to the occupant of the Imperial equipage which had just driven up to the grand entrance, "is the first of symptom of the coming storm."

Doctor Hofer, who had followed him to the window, gazed with some surprise at the royal visitor, who now alighted.

"The Prince Regent of Wittelsbach," he murmured.

"The first of the Arminian Sovereigns to arrive in Berolingen," Sir John said. "The rest will follow. Is not the fact suggestive? Twenty years ago, Doctor Georg Hofer, the then ruler of Wittelsbach, Brandenburg's most jealous rival in the Arminian confederacy, was the first to acclaim the venerable King Willibald of Brandenburg as Arminian Emperor. That was on the soil of conquered Franconia. You know, as well as I do, what it cost to induce proud Wittelsbach to submit to the political leadership of the great rival State. The wound to its pride was never healed. Powerful as Brandenburg is, and paramount among the Sovereignties of Arminia, let Noveria, that trophy of Brandenburg's victorious war with Austria and the Southern Arminian States, be once more wrenched from her and restored as an independent Arminian kingdom, and the preponderance of Brandenburg's power is no longer such as to outweigh the ambition of its proud Southern rival; more especially," he added, fixing his companion with a meaning look, "if, with the return of the Duke of Cumbermere, Wittelsbach should gain a grateful ally where Brandenburg loses a great territory."

Doctor Hofer fell back with an air of bewildered surprise.

"Do you mean," he said, "that the Regent of Wittelsbach has taken advantage of the Emperor's disappearance to league himself with the adherents of the Noverian dynasty, and by restoring the kingdom to its rightful owner, the Duke of Cumbermere, to gain the latter's support in the Imperial Council? By the powers, the idea is so well conceived that I could almost wish it were true."

"If it should prove true, sir," Sir John Templeton said solemnly, "rest assured that you will not live to see it accomplished. For the present the idea is merely the outcome of popular fancy and suspicion run wild. Yet, such as it is, it bodes little good to one in your position."

He paused for an instant; then he resumed in his ordinary tone—

"I have done what in me lay to open your eyes to the grave peril in which you stand, and I have no more to say. If I must work without your aid there is no help for it. Perhaps," he added with a peculiar look, "we separate, both of us, wiser men than we met. Before I go, one more word of warning, Doctor Hofer, if you value the life of him to whose cause you have devoted so much, take no step without consulting me. The advice is that of a friend. Follow it."

Before Doctor Hofer could answer he had left the room and was gone.

For the space of a full hour the Imperial secretary paced his room like a caged lion, stern and wrathful. Outside, the unusual stir and bustle caused by the advent of the royal visitor continued. There was much rushing to and fro, and clangour of swords and other military display. A constant stream of equipages was flowing into the great castle-yard, and their occupants alighted and passed into the building—some with slow, phlegmatic movement, some briskly, and with an eager, expectant mien. Princes of the Royal house of Brandenburg, Ministers, generals, and court and State dignitaries of every kind and description were among these prompt visitors, all apparently hastening to pay their respects to the illustrious guest whose arrival was looked upon as an omen of the gravest significance. This change in the aspect of the Castle surroundings was a strangely striking one; and, indeed, had it been caused by the long-hoped-for return of its Imperial lord himself, it could scarcely have been greater.

Doctor Georg Hofer took no note of all this, but pursued his restless promenade, wrapped in thoughts which to all appearances were totally unconnected with the events that were passing around him. They were stormy thoughts, too, as was evidenced by the passionate way in which he would ever and anon stop short and clench his hands, like a man reduced to the extremity of despair. Could Sir John Templeton have taken a glimpse now of the calm and haughty personage with whom he had just held an apparently fruitless converse, he might well have stood amazed at the metamorphosis he had meanwhile undergone.

Whether the spectacle would have enlightened him on the one point on which he was avowedly seeking enlightenment it is, however, difficult to say.

CHAPTER V
The Dowager Empress Fritz

Sir John Templeton was right. Within forty-eight hours of the interview, recorded in the last Chapter, the Prince Regent of Wittelsbach's arrival had been followed by that of nearly every reigning sovereign in Arminia.

It would be impossible to conceive a more extraordinary contrast than that afforded at this period between the life at the Imperial Court of Berolingen and the demeanour of those classes of society of which nine-tenths of the population of the metropolis was composed. In keeping with the sorry farce enacted by the Arminian Government to blind the country, and indeed the world generally, to the palpable fact that a crisis of the most momentous nature was pending, the Imperial Court had not only maintained its ordinary appearance, as if nothing had occurred to affect it, but had developed an even greater activity than was customary at this time of the year.

The Emperor's absence, in this sphere of society, was never alluded to in words. It was tacitly accepted as a matter of course. At the Royal Castle, the abode of the Sovereign, there was under the circumstances naturally no sign of that gay and festive life which, to the outer world, is the gilt that hides the rough substance of care, and toil, and worry, and anxiety, which constitutes the reality of royal existence. But in other directions the usual parade of gaiety went on uninterrupted. During these last three weeks function had succeeded function, festivity followed upon festivity, until the people, who were usually only too ready to feast their eyes from the distance upon these brilliant shows, grew sated with the incessant display, and witnessed each fresh pageant with an increasing sense of sullen bewilderment. They read with amazement of these Court balls and State concerts, receptions, and ceremonies, which followed one another in such rapid succession; and they went, as they always did, in their tens and tens of thousands curiously to witness the grand military reviews held "by command of the Emperor," as the 'Gazette' gravely put it, on the parade ground outside the north-western quarter of the city. But they felt the imposition notwithstanding, and regarded these persistent attacks on their credulity with growing resentment.

The fiction, they saw, was to be kept a outrance, and the only thought it roused in them was as to when and how it would all end. One thing they felt sure of, that if the members of their Royal House affected this show of indifference and unconcern in the face of a calamity which threatened the very foundation of the Empire, they did so, not of their own free will, but under compulsion, though under what sort of compulsion they would have been at a loss to determine.

In spite of the smiling countenance of the Empress-Mother and her daughters, the sisters of the reigning Emperor, wherever they appeared in public, the Berolingers were quick to perceive the lines of anxiety and care with which the suspense of these last weeks had furrowed their brows. Rumours, too of all kinds, were in circulation respecting the attitude assumed by the Imperial family, and more especially by Prince Henry, the Emperor's only brother, towards those who advocated the summoning of the Arminian Sovereigns to Berolingen, ostensibly to devise measures for the government of the Empire during the Emperor's absence.

The Prince, a sailor, with something of a sailor's bluffness, was credited with having categorically refused to lend his countenance to proceedings which the Emperor's death alone could justify. Report even declared that a correspondence of a very heated character had passed on the subject between him and the Regent of Wittelsbach, as the spokesman of the Arminian princes, in which he had announced his intention of signifying his disapproval of the contemplated action of the Arminian rulers in a marked and unmistakable manner.

Whether this report was correct or not, it is certain that an hour before the arrival in Berolingen of the Regent of Wittelsbach, Prince Henry had left the city and taken up his quarters in Carolinenburg, the well-known Royal summer resort situated not three miles from the capital itself. It was scarcely possible to misinterpret the meaning of this movement. Though the Prince could not prevent the assembly of the monarchs in the Arminian metropolis, he was at least determined to take no part in their reception.

The people had noted this significant circumstance, and they were not slow to approve and applaud it. The arrival of the Regent of Wittelsbach had taken them quite unawares; for the fact of the Royal journey to Berolingen had been kept a profound secret. But when, late that same evening, the news spread through the city that the arrival of the Wittelsbach Sovereign had been followed within a few hours by that of the Kings of Suabia and Neckarstadt, the sense of surprise gave away to one of stern displeasure, and the railway termini of the capital were beleaguered during the next two days by a multitude which defied all the endeavours of the police, assisted by soldiery, to repress and disperse it.

Monarch now followed upon monarch, and what with the incessant receptions, and the driving to and fro of innumerable State coaches with court and military dignitaries in gala attire between the various Royal palaces and the railway stations, the occasion might have passed for one of some rare festivity, such as a Royal jubilee or coronation.

What the people commented upon, however, was not so much the inappropriateness of all this outward display of pomp and splendour, as the extraordinary precautions for the maintenance of order and decorum in the streets with which it was accompanied. The three first arrivals had been accomplished with a singular absence of ostentation and show. But at the first sign of the awakening of the popular curiosity all this simplicity vanished, and the reception of the Royal visitors assumed quite a different character. Troops now surrounded the stations and lined the routes to and from them and the centre of the town. Military escorts accompanied even the petty Princes and Sovereign Dukes who constituted, what may not inaptly be termed the smaller fry of the Confederate Monarchs, and the police swarmed everywhere in such numbers that one might have supposed they had been called out to quell a disturbance rather than to effect the comparatively simple manoeuvre of keeping the roads clear for the passage of a few Royal visitors.

Strangely enough, as it chanced, the streets of Berolingen had never before been filled with more orderly crowds than they were during these two days. No attempt was made in any single quarter to give open vent to the feelings of exasperation which pervaded all classes of the community; although, as will be seen presently, the occasion did not pass without a startlingly significant demonstration of quite an opposite description. The masses surged in the streets from morning till night, surrounding the stations and thronging the open spaces in front of the Royal palaces, apparently intent upon nothing else but to catch glimpses of the illustrious personages who passed in review, as it were, before them. To all appearances, it was only the ordinary curiosity of a spectacle-loving populace that had enticed them from their every-day occupations, and brought them out to gape and gaze.

One thing alone distinguished them from an ordinary assembly of curious sightseers. This was the almost total silence maintained by these vast crowds from one end of the city to the other. Not a cheer was raised, not a cap lifted, as the princely visitors swept past in their gorgeous coaches. And yet, once—and for one instant only—did this air of apparent apathy and indifference which characterised the loitering crowds during those two memorable days vanish completely, as if dispelled by some hidden magic, making way for an outburst of such demonstrative enthusiasm that none who witnessed it can have failed to be deeply impressed by it.

This incident was brought about by the chance appearance of her Majesty the Dowager Empress in the streets of Berolingen. Returning from Carolinenburg, whither she had gone to visit her son, Prince Henry, her Majesty, accompanied by her daughter, the Princess Margaret, happened to enter the Avenue of Limes on her drive back to her palace just at the hour when, in consequence of the expected arrival of the King of Wettinia and the Grand Duke of Zahringen, both of whom were to take up their quarters in the Royal Castle, that great thoroughfare had become densely packed from end to end with a surging mass of spectators.

At the first glimpse of the imperial carriage and its occupants, as they emerged unexpectedly through the colossal Arch of Victory at the further end of the boulevard, a sudden shout of delight went up from the throng collected there, and rolled in an ever-increasing roar along the whole route, being taken up by the countless thousands who filled it for considerably over a mile.

A strangely impressive spectacle now followed. Those who had hitherto stood for hours and hours silent and impassive behind the troops that lined the route in single file on both sides, now pressed forward with so sudden an onrush that the lines were instantly broken through in all directions. Caps were thrown up, handkerchiefs waved, and such a deafening noise of cheers and acclamations rent the air, that the words of command issued to the astonished soldiers by their irate officers were completely drowned by it. The demonstration was so sudden and unexpected that it was

46

impossible to cope with it, and for the time the military, the police, and the public, were all mingled in one entangled, struggling mass, which closed round the Imperial carriage, and followed it as it proceeded on its way down the grand Avenue toward her Majesty's palace at the other end. All that the troops could do was to avoid being carried away altogether by the overwhelming stream of excited peopled. To oppose it, or attempt to stem the impetuous tide and restore order, was out of the question. Indeed, many of the soldiers, in spite of their being mounted, were unable to extricate themselves from the rushing crowd until they had been swept along for a considerable distance, and the police, the greater number of whom were on foot, proved, or course, totally powerless to help them.

The wonder was that the progress of the Imperial carriage itself was not impeded by the frantic mob that surrounded it. But the pace at which it proceeded scarcely slackened perceptibly for one moment, and not a muscle in the familiar face of the Empress betrayed the faintest apprehension at the stirring scene about her, as she sat bowing right and left in proud acknowledgment of the wild and frenzied greeting that was offered to her. She understood, and appreciated its meaning only too well.

Ten minutes later, when the troops had barely recovered their order and had formed once more in an unbroken line along the route which had just been the scene of this extraordinary demonstration, a detachment of Imperial Guards, heralding the approach of the two Royal visitors whose arrival had been the cause of the vast congregation of spectators in the Avenue, issued forth from under the Arch of Victory, followed by two four-horsed equipages with outriders, containing the august guests and their suites, while another detachment of the same troop formed the escort in the rear.

In the opposite direction, the sounds of cheering and shouting could still be faintly heard from the distance, as they were carried across by the breeze which blew over the city from the north. But they died away almost immediately.

And now what a contrast, as the brilliant procession drove slowly along the same route that had just before been traversed by that one solitary carriage amid a scene such as Imperial Berolingen had rarely witnessed! The moment it came into view a hush fell upon the multitude, and in like manner as but a few minutes ago a wave of the wildest enthusiasm had swept over it, carrying all and everything before it, so now a wave of cold, stern silence passed over the same crowds. It preceded the Royal cortege along the whole way; nor was the strange, ominous, stillness broken until long after it had vanished from sight.

The Berolingers had given vent to their sentiments, plainly, unmistakably, and this one spontaneous outburst apparently contented them for the moment. Was it a warning of that spirit of determination which, according to those best informed, was seething beneath their outer surface of gloomy calm? And if so, would they to whom it was addressed take timely heed of it?

Doubtless the Government of his vanished Majesty were only too sensible of the tremendous responsibility that was crushing upon them. One and twenty sovereign Kings and Princes of Arminia were already within the walls of Berolingen, and four more would arrive in the course of the next four-and-twenty hours, thus completing the full number of those whose territories were comprised in the vast Empire they had come to safeguard. The fate of Imperial Arminia was to be decided by these five-and-twenty monarchs. Did it occur to any one of them that they were perchance blindly placing their own fate in the hands of the people in whose midst they had elected to assemble?

There was at least one person in Berolingen who was painfully alive to this possibility. That person was no one less than the Imperial lady whose appearance that day had been the signal for so remarkable a demonstration on the part of the populace of Berolingen.

The duties of the chosen ones of the earth necessitate the abnegation of self, with its predilections and interests, in a higher degree than those of an ordinary mortal, however onerous his position may be. Had her Majesty the Dowager Empress, or the Empress Fritz, as she was more commonly styled in commemoration of her late lamented husband, been an ordinary mortal, she would perhaps have heartily applauded the spirit displayed that day by her son's subjects. She would certainly have regarded it with greater equanimity than, under the circumstances, she was able to. But, alas! the very suspicion of turbulence on the part of the people, even if it be prompted by excess of loyalty, is alarming to the occupants of thrones, and the Empress had seen enough that day to fill her with sombre misgivings on this score in regard to the near future. Her own inclination would have led her to withdraw from the city, like her son Prince Henry, or at least to shut herself up in the seclusion of her palace and plead her sorrow and anxiety, or what not, as an excuse for declining to receive the illustrious Sovereigns whose presence in the Imperial capital was a deep chagrin and a source of distrust and anger to her. But, though she disapproved of the policy that had brought them there, and, indeed, looked upon it with alarm and suspicion, etiquette demanded that she should conceal her real feelings and extend a Royal welcome to these self-invited guests. Nay, not only the exigencies of Royal custom rendered this necessary; the very demeanour of the people, which was a secret source of pride to her Majesty, made it imperative that she should not appear to resent the intrusion of the unwelcome visitors, and thus encourage the churlish spirit in which they had been received.

Towards evening on the day which had witnessed the end, or nearly the end, of the influx of Arminian princes into the capital of the Empire, her Majesty sat in her private apartment in the north wing of her palace, engaged, as was her wont when the duties of State permitted, in the pursuit of the art in which she found her most cherished recreation.

The room, which was situated on the upper floor of the palace, for the sake of the better light afforded there, resembled a painter's studio more than the boudoir of a Royal lady. Several easels with half-finished paintings stood about; lay figures, some draped with costly materials, others without the accompaniment of cloth or drapery and posed in various attitudes, were arranged in more or less conspicuous positions in front of them, and groups of statuary, busts, canvasses, framed and unframed, gems, models, and curios—in short, works of art of every class and description—were distributed here and there in picturesque disorder, giving the whole place an aspect of luxurious, but somewhat Bohemian, splendour.

Before one of the easels near the great bow window in the centre of the apartment sat the Empress herself, ostensibly occupied with brush and palette in putting the finishing touches to the huge canvass which towered before her. I say ostensibly, for her Majesty's attention was manifestly divided between the great clock over the chimneypiece opposite and the door of the room on her left, rather than directed upon the work before her.

Presently one of her gentlemen entered, received a sign from her, bowed, and withdrew. A few moments afterwards Sir John Templeton was ushered in.

The Empress had risen, and now advanced to meet her visitor with an eager, questioning look.

"You bring good tidings, I trust, Sir John Templeton," she said, in a tone in which hope and doubt were equally mingled.

The old diplomat bowed low over the hand she extended to him.

"I fear I am destined to disappoint your Majesty," he said.

49

"Ah," she exclaimed, "do not tell me that you already despair of accomplishing your task."

"I despair by no means, Madam," he replied. "Only it requires time; and whether I shall accomplish it before it is too late to avert the disaster it is designed to avert, that is a question which fills me with grave anxiety. Certain events are fast approaching that may be fraught with consequences which not even the safe return of his Majesty the Emperor will be able to undo."

The Empress sighed deeply.

"Yet you still believe in my son's ultimate safe return?" she asked anxiously.

"Implicitly."

"You have progressed, then? Tell me what you have learned. What may we hope?"

"I must pray of your Majesty to be content for the present with the knowledge that I am progressing," Sir John answered. "Had I the cordial support of those who have summoned me to their aid, I could promise to accomplish in hours what may now occupy days. And every moment is precious. Unfortunately I am hampered where I should be assisted, and thwarted where I should be encouraged. My advice is disregarded—indeed, I fear it is even received with suspicion; and unless your Majesty condescends to become my ally—"

"Does it need my assurance to convince you that you may count upon me?" the Empress said. "I have neither power nor influence over my son's Ministers. But such assistance as I may be able to afford you is yours. What can I do?"

"Two things, Madam. Firstly, to use such influence as your Majesty possesses to prevail upon the Arminian princes to defer this projected meeting in full conclave for another few days at least."

"I will use every endeavour," the Empress said. "But I fear it will be difficult."

"Doubly difficult, doubtless, as matters now stand."

"Have fresh troubles, then, arisen?"

"No fresh troubles, Madam. But those we already have to cope with have assumed more definite proportions. The Franconian question has to-day entered into an acute stage. The demand for the withdrawal of the troops with which the garrisons in the annexed Franconian provinces were recently reinforced by command of the Emperor has been pressed with an imperativeness that borders on positive insolence. The latest communication received from his

50

Excellency the Franconian Ambassador is, I understand, virtually an ultimatum."

"You have seen the Chancellor?"

"I have this moment left his Excellency in conference with their Majesties the Kings of Suabia and Wettinia and the Prince Regent of Wittelsbach."

"And the proposed meeting of the Sovereigns—"

"Will take place at noon the day after to-morrow, unless your Majesty can prevent it."

"War threatening us from without, and revolution from within. What will be the fate of Arminia?" the Empress murmured.

"Arminia's more immediate fate, Madam, rest assured, depends upon one thing only—the return of his Majesty the Emperor before this meeting of Sovereigns takes place."

"And If he returns too late to prevent it?"

"Then, Madam, I fear he will return to find himself the only monarch left in Arminia."

"What?" the Empress said. "Do you imagine the people would dare to lay violent hands on their princes? Ah, you forget. We have the army. Berolingen is garrisoned by fifty thousand of our finest troops."

"The majority of whom are children of Berolingen, Madam, the sons of the very people they will be called upon to oppose."

"True, true," the Empress murmured. "Yet they are loyal to their Emperor. Have I not seen the proofs with my own eyes?"

Sir John Templeton made no response. Perhaps he felt no call to point out that a revolution prompted by loyalty may end by destroying the very idol it had started to set up. If he had, history would no doubt have afforded him more than one parallel instance in illustration of the fact.

The Empress remained silent for a while, plunged in her own thoughts. Presently she turned to him again, and said—

"You spoke of a second matter in which my assistance would be of avail. What is it?"

"It is this," he answered. "To-morrow night your Majesty gives a State ball in honour of these princely visitors. I have come to ask your Majesty to command the addition of one more name to the list of the guests."

"That is a simple matter," the Empress replied. "Who is it?"

There was a slight pause before Sir John answered.

"It is his Majesty's private secretary, Doctor Georg Hofer," he said.

The Empress drew back with a look of displeasure.

"You cannot be serious," she said, coldly.

"Your Majesty is mistaken. The occasion would indeed be a sorry one for a jest."

"You forget that Doctor Hofer has incurred the Emperor's grave displeasure."

"Can your Majesty tell me through what serious offence of his Doctor Hofer has had the misfortune to displease the Emperor?" Sir John asked, quickly.

"I have not made it my business to inquire into the private affairs of my son's household," the Empress replied, in a tone which was half-haughty, half-evasive. "But the character of his offence matters little. Such a mark of favour, as you suggest is, under the circumstances, impossible."

"As a mark of your Majesty's favour—perhaps. Yet, if I am correctly informed, there was a time when Doctor Hofer would not have required my humble intermediation to obtain so slight a favour at your Majesty's hands."

"You show a strange interest in this man, Sir John Templeton," the Empress said, giving him a look which indicated plainly that this manifestation of interest on his part was distasteful to her.

"I do not deny it, Madam," he rejoined. "It is through him alone that I can hope to solve the one problem upon which this whole mystery turns."

"And that is?"

"Why his Majesty the Emperor has left his capital."

"You suspect Doctor Hofer of being privy, then—"

"I think not," Sir John answered.

"Then I do not understand you. You are propounding a riddle which appears to admit of no answer."

"It is precisely a riddle we are dealing with, Madam," he said, "and a riddle to which I maintain Dr. Georg Hofer alone possesses the key."

"And yet he refrains from using it?"

"If he knew how to use it, or were even at liberty to do so, his Majesty the Emperor would be now safe in his palace at Berolingen."

"Then Doctor Hofer's captivity, in other words, is not the effect, but the cause of the Emperor's absence?"

"I believe it to be both, Madam."

"But if it were indeed the cause," the Empress exclaimed, "the simplest means of securing his Majesty's return would be—"

"To set Doctor Hofer at liberty, precisely. It is this advice which I have just ventured to tender to his Majesty's Government."

"And they have rejected it?"

"Indignantly."

The Empress gazed at him for a moment in silence.

"I do not profess to understand the reasons that prompted you in offering such advice," she said at length. "But since Doctor Hofer, as you know, is strongly suspected of having instigated the rebellion in Noveria—"

"Your Majesty cannot but applaud the decision of the Government," Sir John said. "May I ask, Madam, if you share these suspicions against Doctor Hofer?"

The Empress made a little movement of impatience.

"I know no longer what suspicions I share, and what I do not share," she replied, almost desperately. "It is all dark and entangled. If his Majesty were at liberty to return, what greater inducement could he possess for doing so than the knowledge of the terrible position in which the Empire is now placed?"

"It is indeed impossible to conceive of any stronger inducement," Sir John assented, gravely.

"Is not this a proof, then, that he is not at liberty to return?"

"Might it not also be a proof that he lacks the knowledge your Majesty has just mentioned?" Sir John asked.

"Is that likely?"

"It is more than likely; it is certain, Madam."

"Certain, you mean, always assuming that the Emperor is really free to return?"

"Not necessarily. His Majesty may be detained by those whose power to hold him will vanish with the first breath of that knowledge which he so sorely needs."

"And that breath, you think," the Empress said, after a moment's reflection, "would reach him through Doctor Hofer?"

"As surely, Madam, as I believe it would have reached him long ago through the public Press of the country, had the latter not been enjoined to maintain strict silence on the subject of his Majesty's absence."

"You persist, I see, in believing that the Emperor's absence is voluntary."

"That it was originally so—yes."

"Yet this sudden resolve to leave his capital—"

"Sudden, Madam? It was far from sudden."

"How so?" the Empress said, startled by his tone.

"I mean that it was long premeditated."

"What leads you to this conclusion?"

"The fact that his Majesty had already fixed the exact date for his departure three full months ago," Sir John said.

"Three months ago!" the Empress cried. "And you profess to know this?"

"Nay, more, Madam," Sir John said; "I think I can designate not only the day, but the very hour when his Majesty fixed that date."

The Empress regarded him with a look of incredulous surprise.

"And when was that?" she asked, slowly.

"It was the moment when his Majesty issued his commands to the naval authorities to commence preparations for the intended Imperial voyage to the East."

The Empress reflected an instant.

"It is true," she murmured; "the Emperor disappeared on the very eve of this contemplated voyage."

"When, therefore, the most elaborate measures had been devised for the carrying on of the Government during his Majesty's sojourn upon the high seas," Sir John remarked.

"Then you maintain," the Empress said, "that these extensive preparations were merely effected—"

"To enable his Majesty to leave his capital secretly without any inconvenience arising to the Empire from the prolonged absence of its sovereign head; I have no doubt about it, Madam."

The Empress was visibly impressed.

"But if this conclusion should be correct," she exclaimed, with sudden animation, "and indeed it sounds wonderfully plausible—it would surely afford proof positive that his Majesty's absence is unconnected with the rebellious uprising in Noveria."

"Your Majesty has touched the core of the matter," Sir John said. "The Emperor's plans, whatever they were, had been conceived and carefully matured long before the rebellion in Noveria was thought of. It is of this fact that I have vainly endeavoured to convince the Imperial Government."

For some moments her Majesty stood with an air of indecision, wavering apparently between two conflicting resolutions.

"Tell me," she said at last, abruptly, "for what purpose do you desire Doctor Hofer's presence at the Court ball?"

"Does your Majesty insist upon an answer to that question?"

"Not if you have reasons for with holding it. Nay, I am willing to grant this strange request, Sir John Templeton," she went on

54

more warmly, "on one condition: that you pledge me your word that this is not a stratagem to enable Doctor Hofer to escape from his custodians. The Emperor's commands are law, and I will not be a party to their contravention."

"Your Majesty," Sir John Templeton said, gravely, "will please to accept my solemn assurance that nothing is further from my thoughts than to connive at so heinous an offence. I will answer for Doctor Hofer's safety with my own person."

Twilight had set in during the progress of this conversation, and the dusk was now increasing apace, enveloping the vast chamber, with its curious assortment of statues and easels, its costly draperies and many-coloured stuffs, interspersed here and there with painting paraphernalia of every kind and description, in an indistinct haze which lent it an almost weird appearance. From outside came the distant muffled hum of the traffic in the great city, now broken for an instant by a few short, sharp cries of command and a monotonous military tramp of feet in the street immediately below the windows of the studio, where the sentinels stationed before the portals of the Imperial palace were being relieved. These sounds died away quickly, and left the stillness, or rather the semi-stillness, more impressive than before.

The Empress had quitted Sir John Templeton and approached a magnificent bureau standing in an embrasure between the two great middle bow-windows—a masterpiece of the designer's art, executed most elaborately in ebony inlaid with silver. The workmanship of this exquisite piece of furniture, which was a memento of the visit of her Majesty's late husband to the Holy Land and Persia, was the most perfect thing imaginable, and its value was priceless.

Drawing from one of its recesses a letter fringed with a thin black border and bearing on the top of its front page the familiar initials, "V.R." she stood for a moment perusing it in silence. At last she turned again to Sir John Templeton.

"The Queen is anxiously awaiting some hopeful tidings," she said. "What may I tell her, Sir John Templeton? The messenger goes back to-night. Can I give her some assurance that will confirm her confidence in your power to unravel this mystery? Stay," she added, "you shall judge for yourself of the trust she reposes in you. 'That you now have the advice of Sir John Templeton,' her Majesty writes, 'is a great solace to my heart, which bleeds sorely for you in your dire trouble and sorrow. You may trust it implicitly. I have experienced its sterling value.'"

A flush of pleasure mounted to the old diplomatist's face, and his expressive gray eyes lighted up with a quick brightness.

"I would wish her Majesty to know," he said with a profound bow, and speaking in a soft, vibrating tone, which reflected the emotion that had been stirred within him, "that I seek no higher ambition than that of justifying the trust her Majesty so graciously places in me." He paused for an instant, and then, as if inspired by a sudden impulse, he added: "Madam, will you convey to her Majesty my assurance that, if I fail in this, I shall consider it the disaster of my life; and by heaven!" he exclaimed, with unusual animation, "unless that has been done which no mortal hand can undo, I shall not fail."

The Empress replaced the letter silently in the drawer of the bureau from which she had taken it. Then she extended her hand to him with a grateful smile.

"I believe you, Sir John," she said simply. "May heaven, then, prosper your work."

CHAPTER VI
Princess Margaret of Brandenburg

On leaving the Empress's studio, Sir John Templeton was received in the ante-chamber through which he passed by her Majesty's personal attendant, a stalwart lacquey in the Imperial livery, and conducted to the head of the grand staircase, on to which this apartment gave. Here he was again met by another lacquey, who bowed automatically as he approached, and receiving him, as it were, formally from the first one's hands, preceded him silently with grave, ceremonious steps down the first flight of stairs to the floor below, where a whole array of similar automata were stationed at regular intervals, like gorgeous sign-posts in human shape, apparently to guide the hapless wanderer who chanced to go astray in the maze of corridors and passages that gaped here invitingly at him on all sides.

With a stately gesture the nearest of these statuesque beings motioned the visitor in the direction he was to take, and which, had he followed it, would have led him to the central staircase that descended from this first floor of the palace to the entrance hall below, whence, under ordinary circumstances, those who had passed through the ordeal of an Imperial reception were not a little relieved to make their speedy escape into the easier atmosphere of the everyday world without.

But Sir John Templeton seemed in nowise pressed for time, and stood at the foot of the stairs gazing furtively around, as if in search of something or some one whom he expected to meet here. Nor was he deceived in such expectation; for just as the statuesque gentleman aforementioned, who had observed his tendency to loiter in the precincts of the Imperial apartments with an air of dignified disapprobation, advanced towards him with the obvious intention of "moving him on," if so mean a term is applicable to so exalted a personage, an officer in the uniform of the Imperial Guard, emerging apparently from nowhere in particular, stepped suddenly on to the scene, and quickly approaching the old diplomatist, saluted him in stiff, military fashion.

The statuesque gentleman and his associates drew back at once, and resumed their former attitude.

"Sir John Templeton, I believe?" said the officer.

Sir John bowed acquiescently.

"You have received her Imperial Highness's commands, I presume?" the officer asked.

Sir John bowed once more, this time with the shadow of a smile.

"I have received a note from her Imperial Highness informing me of her wish to speak with me," he said.

"Then have the goodness to follow me," the officer rejoined, curtly. And raising his hand once more by way of salute, he wheeled round without anything further, and passed on in a direction leading apparently to the left wing of the palace. Sir John Templeton followed in silence.

Those who know Arminia and the military spirit which pervades all classes of its people, more especially in Brandenburg, will not, I trust, commit the fatal mistake of supposing that this Imperial guardsman intended any rudeness by his abrupt and unceremonious manner. Far from it. He was performing a duty, and the very essence of such performance, according to Arminian ideas, consists in its being unaccompanied by any unnecessary word or phrase which might indicate what I will call a sense of the personal identity of the performer. Military rank in this vast Empire, with its standing army of over half-a-million disciplined soldiers, governs society from the highest grade to the very lowest, and the degree of deference accorded by the wearer of one uniform to the wearer of another—and who does not wear uniform in Arminia?—is determined simply and solely by the number of stars on their respective epaulettes, or whatever other outward sign of their military position the wearers may possess. Sir John Templeton, being, as I need hardly say, pre-eminently of the civilian order, wore of course no uniform at all, and he was consequently as complete a nonentity from the military point of view as it is possible for a breathing human being to be. Indeed, had the most distinguished and illustrious man of the century, for whom possibly our guardsman in his un-uniformed human character would have felt the deepest personal veneration, been in the old diplomatist's place without some such distinctive badge of the only recognised rank in the country, his mode of reception would doubtless have been the same.

This, I beg the reader to believe, is no exaggeration. It is a fact that, at the recent opening of the new Houses of Parliament in Berolingen, the venerable President of the Arminian Legislative Assembly, one of the most eminent men in the country, and, for the nonce at least, one would have supposed, second in importance only to his Majesty the Emperor himself, was actually relegated at the great opening ceremony to a back seat among the crowd of beardless lieutenants and subalterns, where he languished in obscurity throughout the whole proceedings, for no other reason than because he happened in his military capacity to have attained no higher degree than they.

This curious incident was, it will be remembered, much commented upon at the time in the foreign Press; and in Arminian official circles, too, considerable indignation was called forth by the absurd fact—not, I mean, that the illustrious President of the Parliament should have been only a sub-lieutenant in the Imperial Army, but that a mere sub-lieutenant in the Imperial Army should have been elected President of the Parliament.

But I have digressed.

The particular portion of the palace to which Sir John Templeton was now conducted was situated at no great distance from the spot where his guide had met him; nor would the way thither have been difficult to find, had he been left to seek it for himself. It was, in fact, merely a long, straight passage, with no outlet on the other side, leading to a suite of apartments to which access was gained by a pair of large folding-doors at the end. Passing through these at the heels of his military conductor, Sir John Templeton found himself in a kind of inner vestibule with doors on every side. Approaching one of these doors, the officer motioned him to enter, saluted once more in the same stiff fashion as before, and retired without another word.

The apartment, an octagonal chamber of ordinary dimensions, was lighted by two shaded lamps, one a standard placed almost in the centre of the room, in close proximity to a reading-desk of carved rosewood, the design of which displayed the letter 'M' in every possible shape and form, the other an ordinary table lamp, fitted to a receptacle of chased silver, and standing upon a side table near a curtained door on the opposite side. The appointments of the room were rich and dainty, and the surroundings generally could scarcely have been more different from those Sir John Templeton had just quitted. There was no sign here of that artistic disorder which characterised the Empress's favourite haunt. This room was a lady's boudoir in the fullest and most particular sense of the term.

When Sir John Templeton entered it was empty. But he had barely had leisure to glance curiously around him, when the curtained door at the further end was opened, and a slim, girlish figure stepped into the room. She hesitated for a moment upon the threshold, and fixed a look, half proudly curious, half timidly apprehensive, upon her visitor. Then, as if suddenly shaking off her passing fit of timidity, she closed the door behind her, and advanced with a quick, resolute movement into the middle of the room.

"I have to thank you, Sir John Templeton, for complying so readily with my wish to see you," she said, speaking with a rich, musical voice, and in the purest English.

"I shall consider myself fortunate if I am able to be of service to your Imperial Highness," Sir John answered.

There was a ring of something more than pure formality in the tone of the words. And, indeed, they would have been no mere figure of speech in the mouth of any man possessed of some sense for feminine grace and beauty.

Princess Margaret of Brandenburg, the second youngest daughter of the Arminian Empress, showed her English origin, like all her sisters, in her appearance as well as in her speech. She was, in fact, the very type of that rare English beauty which perhaps none are quicker to perceive and readier to admire than foreigners. Her Guelph descent through her mother was traceable in every line of her face; yet there were certain features in it, more notably, perhaps, the slightly pursed lip and the determined curve of the chin, which stamped her just as unmistakably as of the house of Brandenburg. It was in these latter characteristics that her resemblance to her brother the Emperor was most marked. They gave her, as they did him, that air of haughtiness and stubborn resolve which is the distinctive feature of that whole illustrious race. And yet it was rather the quality of self-reliance than pride, rather, perhaps, that of wilfulness than obstinacy, which they really betokened; and in the Princess they were wonderfully softened by the feminine charm of her whole countenance, culminating, as it occasionally did, in the bewitching smile that proclaimed her, more than anything else, the true daughter of her mother.

There are some people who smile with their lips only; there are others the essence of whose smile lies in their eyes. The Princess Margaret belonged to the latter class, and though she smiled rarely—more particularly at the period we speak of—the memory of one smile from those large expressive brown eyes of hers dwelt long and sweetly enough with him upon whom it happened to be bestowed to make him forget the length of the interval that ensued between it and its successor.

"You can render me a very great service, Sir John Templeton," she said, sinking upon a large divan in the centre of the room, flanked on either side by a croup of taper-leaved palms, and inviting him with a graceful gesture to a seat near her. "Need I tell you what has caused me to ask you for this interview?"

"I think not, Princess," Sir John answered. "There is but one thought dominating every mind in the country at this moment, and I scarcely need your Imperial Highness's assurance that it is uppermost in yours; the anxiety concerning the fate of his Majesty the Emperor."

"I would give my life to bring him back," the Princess exclaimed, clasping her hands in front of her with a sudden passionate gesture. "Can nothing be done, nothing to solve this dreadful mystery? Whatever it is, if my help can avail, it is yours unasked."

There was something despairing, and yet suggestive, in her tone and in the action that accompanied it, which struck Sir John Templeton strangely.

"Princess," he said, bending slightly forward towards her, and gazing full into her eyes, as if he expected to read in them the answer to what he was about to say, "permit me to ask you one question. Did the Emperor part with you in anger?"

She returned his look with one of surprise.

"No, no," she said. "You mistake me. It is not that. He was tenderness itself towards me. Ah, only too tender."

She added the last words as if on an after-thought—fondly, regretfully.

60

"His Majesty never gave you the slightest reason for supposing," Sir John asked, "that it was his intention to absent himself from his capital, or to embark upon any undertaking involving peril to his own person?"

"None whatever," the Princess replied. "My brother's last words to me—I remember them only too well—were these: 'When we meet again, Sissy, I shall have news for you worth more than a kiss. So hold yourself prepared to pay special tribute.'"

"Your Imperial Highness, of course, knew to what his Majesty was referring," Sir John observed.

"Not surely," the Princess exclaimed, with a start, "to anything connected with his strange absence?"

Sir John Templeton did not answer at once. Apparently a train of thought had been started in him which for the moment absorbed his attention. Presently he turned to her with a quick impulse.

"Am I right, Princess," he said, with an abruptness that was softened by his tone of respectful sympathy, "in assuming that you have sent for me because you think you possess some knowledge which may throw light upon the cause of his Majesty's absence?"

"I have sent for you, Sir John Templeton," the Princess replied, studying his face with a curiously scrutinising gaze, "because I have heard you spoken of as one whose advice is to be trusted, and because I know that my mother places all her hopes in your ability to fathom this terrible mystery."

"And do you share her Majesty's confidence?" he asked.

"I hope to share it," she replied.

"Then I may speak without reserve, Princess," he continued, "without fear of giving offence, even if I should venture to trespass upon a subject which may be painful and distressing to your Imperial Highness?"

The Princess turned just a shade paler, and her slender fingers toyed nervously with the leaves of a palm that curved invitingly towards her.

"What subject could be more painful and distressing than the one we are discussing?" she said in a low voice. "You may speak freely. I desire it."

Sir John Templeton bowed greatly.

"You occupied, I believe, a place very near his Majesty's heart," he said, "and he confided in you more fully than in any other member of his family; is it not so, Princess?"

"Possibly," she replied; "I can scarcely say. My brother loved me and placed great trust in my affection. But he was never inclined to be lavish with his confidence, even towards those whom he loved."

Sir John paused for the space of an instant before he continued.

"Did he ever confide to your Highness the cause of the sudden distrust which he conceived towards his private secretary, Dr. Georg Hofer?"

The question was evidently not an unexpected one. Yet, save for an almost imperceptible tremor of the Princess's lips, which betrayed her emotion, there was nothing in her manner of receiving it to denote that it affected her more than any ordinary question would have done.

"He did not," she answered simply. "But perhaps—"

She hesitated now, and a slight flush mounted to her cheeks.

"Perhaps?"

"Perhaps it required no explanation on his part to enable me to guess the true cause," she said. "But why do you ask this?" she continued, with a sudden return to her former agitated manner. "You do not suppose that any possible connection can exist between my brother's relations with this man and his unaccountable disappearance?"

"Would it be so extraordinary," Sir John answered, "if I supposed what your Imperial Highness yourself firmly believes?"

"Ah, if I believed it," she exclaimed, half rising, and with a quick flash of anger in her eyes; "but can I, dare I believe it?"

"Princess," Sir John said, impressively, "there is indeed but one road to the knowledge we are seeking, and he who would find it must first possess himself of the secret which Doctor Georg Hofer alone holds: the cause of his quarrel with his Imperial master."

The Princess gazed at him with a steady, searching look.

"You are absolutely convinced of this?" she asked.

"Absolutely."

"Have you seen Doctor Hofer?"

"I have both seen and spoken with him."

"And you believe him capable of betraying one who trusted and confided in him?"

There was a touch almost of angry menace in the tone in which she asked this question, which perhaps escaped Stir John's notice. At any rate, he took no apparent heed of it, but unanswered unmoved—

"I am as ignorant, Princess, of the part played by Doctor Hofer at the Imperial Court, and the purpose which brought him here, as I am of the cause of the sudden difference which has arisen between him and the Emperor. One thing only I know—as certainly as I know of my own existence. It is that the discovery of the real purpose pursued by Doctor Georg Hofer at the Court of Berolingen, not only was the cause of the Emperor's altered attitude towards his private secretary, but is also the cause of his Majesty's absence."

Again the troubled look crept into the Princess's face, and she sat for a while in silence, apparently weighing what she had heard.

"Tell me, Sir John Templeton," she said, presently, in a low, anxious voice, "do you believe the Emperor's life is in danger?"

"No one can say to what danger his Majesty may be exposed," he replied.

The Princess rose once more, with the same abrupt lapse into passion as before.

"If his life should be endangered," she exclaimed, "if one hair of his head should have been injured to further the plans of any mortal man, whoever it may be, he shall know at least that a sister's curse rests upon him; ay, he shall learn that a woman may possess the courage to avenge her own blood, and will avenge it, even if—"

"Even if she should tear out her own heart in doing so, Princess," Sir John said, in an earnest tone.

"Even if she tear out her own heart in doing so," the girl echoed, returning his gaze proudly, yet speaking scarcely above a murmur. "You have said it. Now go and tell Doctor Georg Hofer what you have heard, and whose were the lips that uttered it."

Sir John's eyes rested upon her with a regard of undisguised admiration, as she stood before him, her figure proudly erect—so youthful, yet so queenly; so sternly resolute, yet so impetuous and passionate. He, too, had risen to his feet when she rose.

"Were it not better, Princess," he said, deliberately, "that Doctor Hofer should learn all this from your Imperial Highness's own lips?"

"From my lips?" she asked, with a startled expression. "What opportunity will be vouchsafed me of speaking my mind to Doctor Hofer?"

"The opportunity is near at hand," Sir John replied. "The question is whether your Imperial Highness will deign to avail yourself of it. Doctor Georg Hofer will be present at the court ball to-morrow night."

"Ah," the Princess exclaimed, with an involuntary impulse of joy, "then he is free again?"

Sir John Templeton shook his head.

"He is not free, Princess," he said. "At least, he is no more free than he has been for the last four months."

"For the last four months?" the Princess repeated in a puzzled tone. "Do you mean that he was already a prisoner before the Emperor left us?"

"To all intents and purposes, yes," Sir John replied. "Doctor Hofer has not been at liberty to quit the capital since the day on which he had the misfortune to forfeit his Majesty's confidence."

The Princess made a movement of annoyance.

"You are trifling with me, Sir John Templeton," she said, coldly. "Why this pretended ignorance of the origin of my brother's displeasure? You know it as well as I do."

"If I knew it as well as you do, Princess," Sir John rejoined, drily, "I should be ignorant indeed; for your Imperial Highness, of this I am at least sure, is gravely mistaken."

The Princess flushed and drew back.

"Yet you tell me that Doctor Hofer has been virtually a captive in my brother's palace for the last four months?" she said.

"Since his Majesty learned the nature of his secretary's correspondence with his Royal Highness the Duke of Cumbermere, yes."

"That correspondence, then, has fallen into the Emperor's hands?"

"It was first brought to his Majesty's notice by Baron von Ellermann, the Minister of Police, since when no letter has been received or despatched by Doctor Georg Hofer without his Majesty being supplied with a copy."

"You have read these letters?"

"With the greatest care."

"And their contents are of a treasonable nature?" the Princess pursued, with blanched lips.

"Their contents are such as to prove of the very deepest interest to his Majesty the Emperor," Sir John replied.

"In view of the questions pending between him and the Duke of Cumbermere?"

"In view of the questions pending between his Majesty and the Duke of Cumbermere," Sir John affirmed.

There was a short pause.

"You know more than you profess to know, Sir John Templeton," the Princess said, darting a quick look of suspicion at him.

"I know more than I dare confide even to your Imperial Highness," he answered. "But unfortunately it does not tell me where his Majesty is, nor why he has left his capital."

She turned away from him with a petulent gesture, and stood for a few instants wrapped in thought.

"I will see Doctor Hofer," she said at last, with a sudden resolution.

Sir John bowed.

"May I inform him of your Highness's intentions?" he asked.

"It is unnecessary," she replied.

"Yet," he persisted, "it might be prudent, Princess, under the circumstances—"

"It is unnecessary," she repeated, peremptorily. "I will see Doctor Hofer during the ball to-morrow night. Where and how are questions that need trouble neither you nor him."

"I am satisfied, of course, to leave the matter entirely in your Highness's hands," Sir John said. "Only I would venture to point out that there will be many eyes watching the movements of Doctor Hofer to-morrow night."

"You mean that he will be guarded?"

"Under the circumstances, no doubt, with redoubled vigilance."

"If he comes at all," the Princess said, haughtily, "I presume it will be as the Empress's guest, not as a State prisoner. In any case, provided he does come, I shall not fail to gain speech with him. With what result," she added, "you will learn in due time."

The tone of the last words meant that Sir John Templeton's audience was at an end, and bowing profoundly he withdrew.

There was that in the Princess's manner towards him that told plainly of some inner struggle which was tearing her heart; a struggle between doubt and belief, trust and mistrust, resentment and love. She had received her visitor as a friend, claiming his support and asking his advice. She dismissed him more like a foe whom she suspected than an ally in whom she confided.

Sir John Templeton felt all this, and pondered over it as he went. But the smile it evoked from him was one of intelligent sympathy rather than disappointment or perplexity.

Outside in the vestibule he was received once more by the officer who had conducted hither, and who approached him now with an expression of mingled curiosity and respect. Saluting him again in the usual stereotyped fashion, he placed two letters in his hand.

"For you," he said, in his curt, military tone, "The matters are urgent, I believe."

Sir John Templeton glanced at the letters. One was sealed with the official seal of the Chancellor of the Empire, and bore above the address the superscription; 'On Business of the State, Urgent.' The other bore the seal of the British Embassy surmounted by the Royal Arms of England. Opening the latter first, to the evident surprise of the Imperial guardsman, Sir John rapidly perused the few words it contained. They were written by her Majesty's Ambassador, Sir Edward Hammer, and ran as follows:—

"Private advice from London. The Duke of Cumbermere reached Noveria safely yesterday afternoon, and has placed himself at the head of the rebel troops. The news is official."

Sir John Templeton crushed the note in his hand with a peculiar smile, and proceeded to open the second one.

It merely contained a tersely worded request that Sir John Templeton would repair with convenient despatch to the Ministry for Foreign Affairs, where a communication of importance awaited him. The document was signed: 'Von Capricius, Chancellor of the Empire.'

Sir John read it without betraying any surprise, thanked the officer, and quickly made his way out of the palace.

It was nearly half-past 9 when he found himself once more in the street. Here a fresh change had come over the aspect of things generally; for instead of the quiet which usually reigned at this end of the great boulevard, there were now signs of some considerable commotion noticeable. Excited groups were clustered round lamp-posts and other rallying points, reading evening papers or eagerly discussing some absorbing piece of intelligence. A constant stream of foot passengers was hurrying westward towards the opposite end of the Avenue, where, in the distance, Sir John, as he stood for an instant upon the slightly elevated ground outside the Empress's palace, could distinguish at a glance that a vast concourse of people had gathered. The gestures of those in his more immediate neighbourhood indicated the existence of some strong excitement. But it was evidently a pleasant excitement.

Accosting a passer-by, Sir John asked the reason of the unusual stir. The man, whose appearance bespoke him to belong to the class of superior tradesmen, regarded his interlocutor with some surprise.

"Eh, eh," he cried, "haven't you heard the news? Prince Ottomarck has arrived in Berolingen, and has taken up his quarters at the Hotel Victoria, just off Willibald-street. I fear there is no getting near the place to catch a glimpse of him."

He saw the impression his tidings produced, and added with a gleeful laugh:

"Eh, my friend, that's a piece of news for you? We shall have a man at the helm at last."

And he hurried on to join the crowd flocking in the direction of Willibald-street.

Prince Ottomarck at Berolingen? It was news indeed. The great ex-Chancellor, who had never set foot in the Imperial capital since the famous rupture which had caused him to quit the service of his autocratic young Sovereign, was once more returned to the scene of his glorious past. The people, it was evident, greeted the event as if it signalised the end of all anxiety and suspense. To them, for the moment, such was the confidence they reposed in their great statesman, it meant that all immediate danger was over.

Sir John Templeton knew that it meant something altogether different. Indeed, had any doubt still existed in his mind as to the seriousness of the crisis in which Arminia was now involved, nothing could have more effectually dispelled it than this one unlooked for event—the return of Prince Ottomarck to Berolingen.

CHAPTER VII
A Midnight Conference

Until far past midnight the famous Willibald-street—the Downing-street, only on a somewhat larger scale, of Imperial Berolingen—was packed throughout its entire length by a jubilant multitude.

Prince Ottomarck, an hour after his arrival in the capital, had driven straight to the Ministry for Foreign Affairs, where he remained for some while in close conference with the Imperial Chancellor, the President of the Council, and several of the greater Arminian sovereigns now in Berolingen, who had hurried post haste to join in the conference upon receipt of the news of his Highness's arrival.

These latter had stayed, some a quarter of an hour, others somewhat longer, and had then driven away again—as the imaginative populace who observed them thought—with chagrin and disappointment writ large on their countenances; a circumstance which was hailed as a proof that the Iron Chancellor had promptly sent them about their business, as, figuratively speaking, he had so often done in the good old days of his greatness and glory.

But alas for the highly-strung sentiments of loyal Berolingen! Their hero was a hero indeed. But in this instance they credited him with achievements that were beyond even his powers. He had come to Berolingen at the urgent desire of the King of Wettinia, his unfailing friend and admirer, and, though cordially welcomed by the Arminian Ministers, who had joined in the invitation of the King, he was there to advise only, not to dictate. None knew this better than the great statesman himself.

Twice during the progress of the conference, the ex-Chancellor had appeared on the balcony of the room in which it was being held, in response to the vociferous call of the crowds outside. But he had merely bowed a silent acknowledgment of the homage paid to him, and withdrawn again at once. What was passing inside that room remained a secret to the expectant people without; nor, indeed, had they known it, would it have left them any wiser than they were before. All they cared to learn was what had become of their Emperor, and if the truth must be told, this was a matter which at that moment had almost ceased to occupy the minds of those in whose deliberations they were so deeply interested. The Ministers had the immediate situation to grapple with, and to do it effectually it was imperative that they should accept the fact of their Sovereign's absence as definite and unalterable. This, at least, was the view of the Imperial Chancellor, and recent events had tended to strengthen it.

Count Capricius was a military commander of some eminence. He had also given proof of considerable administrative powers. Yet, when all was said and done, he was a soldier still, not a statesman. And what chafed him most in his present difficult position was the enforced inactivity to which he saw himself condemned. Noveria was in revolt, and he dared take no measures to quell it. Franconia was advancing the most insolent demands, and he was compelled to submit patiently to their discussion until such time as he would be in a position to sternly repel them. His sovereign's absence crippled him everywhere. In whatever direction he looked, he dared take no decisive step for fear of the consequences that might ensue to the Emperor, of whose whereabouts no one knew anything.

Amid all these difficulties his one hope was concentrated upon the meeting of the Arminian princes. He had hailed the plan with eager approval, and had so far carried it through in the teeth of all opposition, even that of the Imperial family itself, confident as he was that by this means alone the Empire could be saved.

And was he now to be checked by the threats of an unreasoning Berolingen mob? Was he to delay what he believed to be of paramount urgency to suit the fads of some foreign meddler, whose ignorance of matters military—an almost convertible term in the Chancellor's opinion with 'matters Arminian'—was simply appalling? Sir John Templeton, whose services he had never desired, who had been forced down his throat, as it were, by the combined insistance of so many illustrious personages whom he could not afford to displease, treated the most burning question of the hour, the offensive attitude of Arminia's hereditary foe, Franconia, as if it were a mere trifle, to be disposed of off-hand whenever a convenient opportunity might offer. Noverian affairs scarcely awakened this man's interest—in fact, beyond making one or two absurd propositions, and raising up bugbears in which his Excellency had no belief, he had scarcely acquainted himself with any of the true difficulties of the situation, but had gone his own way, consulting no one, and keeping his ideas and plans, if indeed he had any, strictly to himself.

All this was a sore grievance with the Imperial Chancellor, and it formed the burden of his eloquence when he found himself alone with Prince Ottomarck after the departure of the Royalties who had come to assist at their conference. He had never believed in Sir John Templeton's ability to fathom a secret which had baffled the united intelligence of every official military and otherwise, in the country; and, moreover, such knowledge of his doings as he had elicited excited his disapproval, if not his grave suspicions.

He now held in his hand what he considered irrefragable proof of the incompetence of the man whose presence in the capital, modest, and unobtrusive as it appeared, had nevertheless hampered him and interfered with his policy at every step. He knew that Prince Ottomarck had been chiefly instrumental in bringing Sir John Templeton to Berolingen, and it afforded him a sort of grim satisfaction to be able to disconcert the sage old diplomat, in whom so many placed their trust, before the eyes of his most stanch admirer.

Prince Ottomarck was pacing the room in which their conversation was passing with giant strides, silent and thoughtful. From the street below there sounded every now and then a low roar, as some one started a cheer in the hope of its inducing the idol of the hour to show himself once more at the brilliantly-lighted window. But the expectation was a vain one.

69

It was now 11 o'clock, and still Sir John Templeton, whose arrival the two statesmen were awaiting, remained absent.

In outward personal appearance a certain faint resemblance might be detected between the ex-Chancellor and his successor. But it is a resemblance of form only. Count Capricius is a fine soldierly figure, with an imperious look and a dignified bearing—every inch of him a warrior. The Prince, too, as is well known, possesses all the characteristics of one born and bred, so to speak, in military surroundings. Only in him the soldier is but the one-half—and in deed the lesser half—of the man. So far, then, and no farther, the likeness goes. In every other respect a greater contrast could scarcely be conceived than that existing between the veteran statesman who built up the great Arminian Empire and the man who has taken his place at the helm of affairs.

Indeed, many a more striking figure than that of the worthy Count would dwindle into pigmy insignificance when placed side by side with the most imposing personality the century has brought forth. Only those who have been brought into actual personal contact with the great Chancellor can realise the impression of colossal power which he produces upon his fellow men. Nor is this impression due exclusively to the intellectual superiority which distinguishes him from his kind. It is the weightiness of the whole man, physical as well as moral, that creates it. The ponderous figure, towering far above the average human height, with its martial bearing and the firm, almost massive, features; the great fearless eyes, overshadowed by thick bushy eyebrows, beneath which their glance shoots out straight at the object before them, like the quick flash of a search light, sudden and disconcerting; the proud, determined lips, breathing irresistible energy and resolution—all these outward characteristics seem but the external shape and form, the corporal expression, as it were, of the commanding genius which men have learned to regard as identical with the very name of Ottomarck.

At this moment the countenance of the ex-Chancellor was slightly flushed with the excitement consequent upon the discussion in which he had just taken part. The precarious state of Imperial affairs had, of course, been generally known to him. Yet, when regarded in detail, the gravity of the situation had exceeded even his worst expectations.

Was it indeed, he reflected, no longer a question of "Where is the Emperor?" but rather of "What is to be done without him?" Again and again, whilst the Imperial Chancellor in loud strident tones was explaining such details of the position of affairs with which his companion was of necessity still unacquainted, the Prince took up and perused a much-handled document which lay in a conspicuous position, among a heap of maps, charts, and official papers of every description, upon the huge square table in the centre of the room. His mind seemed concentrated upon the contents of this one document, and it is to be feared that the Chancellor's eloquent discourse fell upon deaf or unheeding ears.

At last the door opened, and the long expected visitor was announced. A moment later Sir John Templeton entered.

As he tarried for the space of an instant upon the threshold, his keen eyes wandered with an inquiring glance from one to the other of the two statesmen. The one, he was well aware, regarded him with anything but friendly feelings. The other he knew to be his friend and well-wisher, and his instinct, or perhaps the knowledge he had gained since he quitted the palace of the Empress, told him that he might have need of his weighty support.

Prince Ottomarck greeted him with great cordiality. The Chancellor, on the other hand, received him with a stiff and somewhat haughty inclination of the head, which Sir John Templeton acknowledged with a smile and a respectful bow.

"If I have not been able to obey your Excellency's summons earlier," he said, in a tone of easy apology, "it is chiefly due to the fact that the approaches to Willibald-street are at this moment practically impassable to all but Royalty."

The Chancellor received this explanation with the shadow of a frown and a wave of the hand. It was not pleasant to him, as may be conceived, to be reminded of a fact which, among other things, emphasised rather invidiously the respective positions held by himself and his great predecessor in the estimation of the people of Berolingen.

"I have desired your attendance here, Sir John Templeton," he began with characteristic abruptness, "in order that you may have an opportunity of communicating to his Highness the results of the investigation you have been conducting at the Court of Berolingen."

Even a less quick ear than Sir John's would have caught the sarcastic intonation of the last words. He understood the challenge they conveyed, and accepted it.

"These results, as your Excellency is well aware," he replied, "are as yet scarcely of such a definite nature as to permit of my recounting them to a third person with any profit to him or myself."

"Yet, such as they, are," the Chancellor pursued, "they appear to have warranted you in arriving at certain deductions."

71

"Which are not shared by your Excellency," Sir John broke in, drily. "Precisely. Perhaps for that very reason I am acting wisely in maintaining my own counsel until such time as I may find myself in possession of facts convincing enough to prove the correctness of those deductions even to your Excellency's satisfaction."

"You still adhere, then, to these deductions?" the Chancellor asked.

"If your Excellency means whether I still adhere to my opinion that it would be expedient to release his Majesty's private secretary from his present position of semi-captivity—yes. I have seen no cause, since I last had the honour of suggesting this course, to alter a view which, as your Excellency knows, is based on the conviction that no man is less deserving of the suspicion that rests upon him than Doctor Georg Hofer."

"The friend of the Duke of Cumbermere?"

"The friend of the Duke of Cumbermere, if your Excellency so pleases."

"Ha," the Chancellor exclaimed, struck by something in Sir John's tone. "Do you now doubt this friendship?"

"By no means. I am convinced that his Royal Highness the Duke of Cumbermere possesses no stancher friend in the world than Doctor Georg Hofer."

The Chancellor cast a significant glance across at the Prince, who stood listening to this conversation with his arms crossed and a look of curious interest on his iron countenance.

"Since this is your deliberate conviction, Sir John Templeton," Count Capricius said, approaching the table and taking up the document that had so deeply engaged the Prince's attention just before the old diplomat entered, "I would commend the contents of this despatch to your earnest consideration."

And he placed the document in Sir John's hands, with the air of a man who, having carefully laid a mine and applied a match to the fuse that is to fire it, retires calmly to a distance to watch the explosion.

Sir John Templeton took the paper and read it quietly. I ran thus:

"Headquarters of the IV. Imperial Army Corps in Noveria."

"The Duke of Cumbermere has succeeded in passing through all lines and has assumed command of the rebel forces now encamped in a strong position two miles from Celle. Unless we advance promptly, the situation may become serious. Impossible to temporise any longer. The Duke's proclamation, which has been posted throughout the province, in spite of our vigilance, has excited the people to fever-heat. All the old resentment has broken out afresh. Thousands are daily flocking to the rebel standard. Disaffection is increasing by leaps and bounds, and there are indications that it is spreading to our own troops. Our inactivity is interpreted as weakness. Rumours still persistent that rebels hold important captive. Solicit immediate orders to attack.

"VON GROBEN, General in Command of the IV. Noverian Army Corps."

"A truly interesting document," Sir John said, when he had perused it. "And what, may I ask, does your Excellency propose to do?"

The quiet interrogative tone incensed the Chancellor.

"I will tell you, Sir John Templeton," he said, planting his somewhat burly form squarely before the old diplomat. "It is the opinion of the Government that the time has arrived for them to adopt stringent measures against the man whom his Majesty the Emperor has left in our custody for a very obvious reason. If we are obliged to proceed with due caution in our dealings with the rebel Prince who has dared to lay hands on the person of his Majesty the Arminian Emperor, there is at least nothing to hinder us from dealing summarily with this audacious friend of his, whose complicity in the treasonable scheme no sane man can now doubt. Do you follow me?"

"Perfectly," Sir John replied. "Your Excellency alludes to Doctor Georg Hofer. I understand, then, that it is the intention of the Imperial Government to proceed against his Majesty's secretary as a rebel and a traitor?"

"Exactly."

Sir John Templeton reflected a moment.

"This is a definite and final decision?" he asked. "I mean, the Government have already resolved irrevocably upon this course?"

"A council of Ministers is summoned for 11 o'clock to-morrow morning, when the necessary order will be issued."

"Then," said Sir John, simply, "I would beg that your Excellency at the same time to inform the council that, upon the issue of this contemplated order, I shall withdraw my services and return to Vienna."

The Chancellor bit his lip angrily, and Prince Ottomarck, who had meanwhile seated himself and remained silent during the whole conversation, rose with a gesture of concern.

"You disapprove of this course, then?" the Chancellor asked.

"Totally," Sir John answered curtly.

"Why?"

"For two reasons. Firstly, because I know it to be conceived under the fatal misapprehension that Doctor Hofer has anything to disclose worth learning by his Majesty's advisers, and secondly, because I am particularly interested in the welfare of his Majesty's private secretary. Sir," he went on impressively, "I can only repeat once more that there is no man who has less knowledge of the Emperor's fate and whereabouts than Doctor Georg Hofer."

"Very good," the Chancellor exclaimed angrily. "We shall see if he persists in this profession of ignorance when he learns what such persistence may cost him."

Sir John Templeton inclined his head gravely.

"Your Excellency," he said, "is of course the best judge of your own affairs. I have expressed my views, and have nothing more to say."

Prince Ottomarck now advanced, in order to interpose a few words. But before he could carry out his intention he was interrupted by the Chancellor's secretary, who entered the room hurriedly, and placed a letter in his Excellency's hands.

"From the Minister of Police, Baron von Ellermann," he said; "to be delivered to your Excellency without delay."

The Chancellor hastily broke the seal, and read the note. As he did so, a look of triumph lighted up his face, and, turning to Sir John Templeton, he exclaimed, almost roughly—

"Now, sir, read this, and if you should then still be desirous of discussing the question of Doctor Hofer's innocence, you will find me at your service."

Sir John took the note, which contained an enclosure, and read as follows:—

"I have to inform your Excellency that the accompanying communication addressed to Doctor Georg Hofer, his Majesty's private secretary, was delivered this evening at the Royal Castle by a man professing to be an ordinary street messenger. The individual, who declares the missive was handed to him for instant delivery by a person unknown to him, has been arrested and subjected to a rigorous examination; so far without result. He is now in the police cells awaiting your Excellency's pleasure."

The communication referred to, which Sir John Templeton merely glanced at with a curious smile, contained these few words:—

"The Duke of Cumbermere has reached Noveria and placed himself at the head of the rebel forces. Take no step to-morrow night without consulting him who sends this, or you will imperil a life more precious to you than that of Doctor Georg Hofer.

"A Friend."

"Well?" the Chancellor exclaimed, as Sir John quietly returned the documents to him.

Sir John glanced up at him with a half-amused smile.

"The police are wary, indeed," he said. "I have only to deplore the harsh fate that has befallen the unfortunate messenger; for, in truth, no man ever suffered more innocently."

"Have the goodness to explain your meaning, Sir John Templeton," the Chancellor said, with a dawning suspicion that there was a mistake somewhere.

"I mean, sir," Sir John said, "that your Excellency need not put yourself to the pains of seeking for the sender of this seemingly dangerous missive. He stands before you."

Prince Ottomarck gave vent to an audible chuckle, and resumed his seat.

"You?" the Chancellor cried, half in astonishment, half in anger. Then, flinging the letter passionately upon the table, he added, after a pause: "You knew, then, of the Duke's appearance in Noveria before you entered this room?"

"I did," Sir John replied,

"From what source?"

"From a source, sir, to which I have owed most of the information his Majesty's Government have thought fit to withhold from me? Had I known the contents of that despatch twelve hours ago, when it was already in your Excellency's hands—"

"Well, what then?" the Chancellor asked haughtily.

"I should now be twelve hours nearer the solution of the problem on which the fate of Arminia is hanging, that is all," Sir John replied.

The Chancellor was silent; perhaps because he felt at a loss what to say. He had conceived an intense dislike of old Sir John, which grew the deeper the more conscious he became of his inability to worst him. It is not pleasant to be corrected, especially if you happen to be an Imperial Chancellor: and somehow all Sir John's actions had a tendency to put the Imperial Government in the wrong, a position conceivably intolerable to so august a body.

"For what purpose," Count Capricius asked at last, "did you communicate this news to Doctor Hofer?"

"Because I believe him to be as deeply interested in it as the Government to whom it is addressed," Sir John replied.

"It appears to me," the Chancellor observed, "that you are playing a dangerous game, sir, which may involve trouble to others besides the person who plays it."

"The game I am playing, since your Excellency pleases so to term it," Sir John retorted, "is not of my seeking. It has been forced upon me by circumstances, of which no one is better aware than your Excellency. It rests, of course, with the Imperial Government to decide whether they will once more reject the advice I have tendered them. If they do so, I shall, as I have already intimated, resign my task into the hands of those who intrusted me with it."

There was no mistaking the ring of determination with which those words were delivered. Sir John Templeton was in earnest, and both Count Capricius and Prince Ottomarck recognised the fact. The latter had watched the play of the old diplomat's features throughout this somewhat heated discussion with keen attention. Turning to him now, he said:—

"One question, Sir John, which may save many others. Are you quite assured that you will succeed in accomplishing the task you speak of?"

"Quite."

"That is to say, to bring his Majesty the Emperor safely back to his capital?"

"Precisely."

"This in spite of what you have just learned here?" the Prince pursued, lifting up the despatch from the Noverian headquarters, and letting it fall back upon the table.

"In spite of it."

"You attach no importance, then, to the Duke of Cumbermere's action, which, assuming that the Emperor is really still a free agent, can only be regarded as that of a man?"

Sir John Templeton paused before he replied.

"Your Highness," he said, "touches a question of vital interest, on which I would prefer to maintain silence. The Duke of Cumbermere's arrival upon the scene of action alters the whole complexion of affairs. I had scarcely dared to expect it," he added, almost reflectively.

"Then you admit at last," the Chancellor interposed, "that this fact is at variance with the conclusions upon which you have hitherto been acting?"

"Your Excellency," Sir John said, "unfortunately credits me with that which I have never possessed. It was precisely a conclusion which I wanted. And the despatch I have just read has supplied it in the most unexpected manner."

"Ha," the Chancellor ejaculated, taken somewhat aback. "And this conclusion is?"

"This conclusion," Sir John answered, with a whimsical look at his interrogator, "is that his Majesty the Emperor Willibald, your illustrious Sovereign, is at this moment master of the political situation."

Even Prince Ottomarck could not help giving vent to an exclamation of incredulous surprise at this seemingly extraordinary statement.

"With all due respect for your opinions, Sir John," he said, in a tone of slight raillery, which was peculiar to him, "that sounds under present circumstances almost like a Franconian despatch. But, even assuming what you say is correct, the chief question, it seems to me—"

"The chief question is, and always remains: where is the Emperor?" Sir John said. "Indeed, your Highness is right. Yet even that question is now nearer solution. Were less at stake, I would venture to recommend an experiment which might end all further suspense. But in view of what may possibly be his Majesty's intentions, I dare not risk it without the certainty of success."

"Well?" the Prince asked. "And what is it?"

"The arrest of Baron von Arnold, the husband of Doctor Hofer's sister," Sir John answered.

"Ah," cried the Chancellor with some animation, "there we meet on more congenial ground, sir; though, for my part, I confess, had I the choice, I would rather arrest the wife than the husband. Commend me to a woman for downright rabid partisanship. This fair Noverian spitfire is more likely to be concerned in whatever hidden conspiracy we may be dealing with than either her brother or her husband."

"Your Excellency knows her, then?" Prince Ottomarck inquired.

"I know her from her letters," the Chancellor replied, "and they prove her to be inspired with a hatred of Brandenburg and its royal house which would do credit to the Duke of Cumbermere himself."

"Her letters?" the Prince asked, "To whom?"

"To His Majesty's secretary, Doctor Georg Hofer," the Chancellor rejoined. "We have a fair collection of these precious documents; and they afford interesting reading, as Sir John Templeton will no doubt testify."

"And was his Majesty," the Prince pursued, "aware of these sentiments of hatred which his secretary's sister harboured against the country whose sovereign he was serving?"

"Baron von Ellermann assures me," the Chancellor said, "that his Majesty has been repeatedly warned; within the last four months, both against Doctor Hofer and his sister, whose relations with this Baron von Arnold had aroused the Minister's suspicions. But—you know the Emperor. He sent his warners about their business, took the matter entirely into his own hands, ordered every letter written to or despatched by Doctor Hofer to be submitted to him, and told Baron von Ellermann in plain words that he was 'an ass,' and that before long he—his Majesty himself—would teach him a lesson in his own profession, from which he trusted that he would benefit."

"This sounds interesting," Prince Ottomarck observed. "What does Sir John Templeton say to it? You have read these letters of Demoiselle Hofer, now Baroness von Arnold?"

"I have," Sir John said, "and I can confirm his Excellency's statement that they afford most interesting and instructive reading. Only, politically speaking, I should say they have about as much value as the sentimental outpourings of any average Berolingen schoolgirl."

"Schoolgirls may prove dangerous in circumstances," the Chancellor observed. "At any rate, there can be no doubt that the sentiments entertained by Demoiselle Hofer against the illustrious sovereign whose bread her brother is eating are genuinely sentiments of the deepest and bitterest hatred."

"That is beyond question, of course," Sir John answered. "But I think his Majesty was perfectly alive to the fact that he possessed no friend in the beautiful Demoiselle Hofer. Under these circumstances, her marriage with Baron Frederick von Arnold becomes significantly suggestive."

"It is on account of this marriage, I conceive," Prince Ottomarck asked, glancing curiously at the speaker, "that you would advise the arrest of this Noverian Baron?"

"Partly," Sir John answered. Then, turning suddenly to the Chancellor, he said, with an apparently abrupt change of the topic, "the Emperor and his secretary fell out some months ago. Has your Excellency any explanation to offer for this sudden estrangement?"

The Chancellor raised his eyebrows slightly. "It has been attributed to various causes," he replied. "Possibly one of them may have been the unfortunate gossip which whispered Doctor Hofer's name in connection with that of her Imperial Highness the Princess Margaret."

"I have been too long absent from Court to be au courant of these things," said the Prince. "Pray explain. Do I understand that this bourgeois secretary, who appears to have infatuated his Majesty in an extraordinary degree, has dared to lift his eyes to the Emperor's own sister?"

"My dear Prince," the Chancellor said, "the history of this Imperial infatuation, as you rightly term it, is wrapped in a good deal of obscurity. The Emperor's acquaintance with this man Hofer, as you know, commenced at the university, when his Majesty was still simple Prince Willibald. Already there, in spite of his open espousal of the cause of the Noverian Pretender, he appears to have made a strong and abiding impression upon the Sovereign. When his Majesty came to the throne, he offered his old university comrade a position in his service, which was declined. They are known to have corresponded very frequently, but all inducements held out by his Majesty to this strange personage were unavailing. He would accept no favour at the Emperor's hands. At last, about a year ago, the Court was startled by the sudden appointment of Doctor Georg Hofer as private secretary to his Majesty. It is averred—with what truth I am unable to say—that the suggestion in this instance came from Doctor Hofer himself, who, yielding to the Emperor's repeated and pressing invitation, declared himself willing to accept a confidential position in his Majesty's immediate entourage, on the condition that by doing so he should forfeit neither his character as his Majesty's friend nor the right to hold his own independent political views. It must be acknowledged that during the period of his office he has proved himself singularly free from the usual faults of those who enjoy Imperial favour. At least, there are no indications that he has ever used his Majesty's friendship for the purposes of his own advancement. But presumably this reticence was a mere cover to hide a loftier and more daring ambition, which, when discovered by his Majesty, led to the estrangement that culminated three weeks ago in the secretary's practical arrest."

"And the Princess Margaret?" Prince Ottomarck inquired.

The Chancellor shrugged his shoulders. "The Princess, as you know, was removed from Berolingen for a time," he said. "And here is the strangest marvel of all. As suddenly as she had been banished, she was recalled to Court again, and up to the time of Doctor Hofer's arrest there was not the faintest sign to show that his Majesty suspected the fact of a tacit attachment existing between her Imperial Highness and the man in connection with whom her name had once been mentioned."

"Which would appear to negative the alleged reason for her Imperial Highness's absence from Berolingen," the Prince remarked. "But to return to this interesting lady, the present Baroness von Arnold," he went on, addressing Sir John Templeton. "Did she accompany her brother to the Court of Berolingen?"

"By no means," Sir John answered. "Demoiselle Hofer, who has been brought up in the strictest seclusion, has steadfastly refused to set foot in the Arminian capital. Although apparently full of affection and reverence for her brother, she never approved of what she termed his weakness towards the man who had deprived his lawful Sovereign of his inheritance. Consequently, when Doctor Hofer accepted the office he now holds, he was compelled to leave his sister under the care of the lady who had been intrusted with her education at Friedrichsdorf—a townlet, as your Highness possibly knows, situated not many miles from the estate of Arnoldshausen, of which Demoiselle Hofer has since become the mistress."

The Chancellor regarded the speaker with some astonishment.

"Whence do you derive this knowledge, pray?" he asked. "You speak as if you had seen and conversed with this Demoiselle Hofer."

"I have studied the correspondence between her and her brother, that is all," Sir John replied; "perhaps, however, with greater care than your Excellency and others have bestowed upon the task."

"Do you not think it possible," the Prince asked suddenly, "that his Majesty possessed some secret intelligence, known to himself alone, incriminating his secretary and proving his complicity in the treasonable occurrences in Noveria?"

"I am convinced, on the contrary, sir," said Sir John, "that Doctor Hofer is totally innocent of any participation in the rising in Noveria."

"Yet his correspondence with the Duke of Cumbermere proves—"

"It proves him in one respect at least to have been the dupe, not the deceiver," Sir John said.

"But how about his sister, the Baroness von Arnold?" the Prince asked. "Do I gather that, in spite of the violent sentiments she has given proof of, you hold her incapable of being implicated in any conspiracy against his Majesty the Emperor?"

"I believe, on the contrary," Sir John rejoined, "that she has even been the means of thwarting certain designs upon his Majesty—unwittingly, of course, but none the less surely."

"In what way?"

"By marrying Baron von Arnold."

The Chancellor, who had moved away, turned round sharply at these words, and darted a look of keen interest at the speaker. The Prince, to whom the reply came quite unexpected, remained silent.

"What you have just said," the Chancellor remarked, addressing Sir John Templeton for the first time in a tone of some consideration, "is interesting. It is a singular fact," he went on, turning to the Prince, "that his Majesty himself should apparently have held a very similar opinion on the subject of Baron von Arnold's marriage. When this man Hofer succeeded in persuading his Majesty to reinstate Baron von Arnold in his possessions—"

"Is your Excellency so sure," Sir John here broke in, "that this reinstatement was the work of Doctor Hofer?"

"Do you doubt it?"

"I do not doubt that Doctor Hofer welcomed with gratitude the clemency extended by his Majesty to so fervent a patriot and adherent of his Royal Highness the Duke of Cumbermere. But I have reason to believe that the act was entirely spontaneous on his Majesty's part."

"Well, be it so," the Chancellor conceded, with unusual graciousness. "It matters little now who was the originator of Baron von Arnold's recall. But it is a fact that his Majesty, although to all appearances exceedingly incensed with his secretary on learning that the first fruit of this act of grace was the alliance of Demoiselle Hofer with the Noverian Baron, declared to me on more than one occasion with his own lips that this contemplated marriage only confirmed him in his opinion of Von Arnold's honourable intentions towards the Arminian Government, which had reinstated him in his possessions."

"Though the lady he had married was admittedly so implacable a foe of everything and everyone Arminian that she even declined to set foot in the capital?" Prince Ottomarck asked in astonishment.

"It sounds strange, yet so it is," the Chancellor affirmed. "Indeed, but for the extremely strong views entertained by his Majesty on the subject of his newest Noverian protege, I should not have hesitated to adopt the very measure Sir John Templeton has just hinted at, and to have both Herr yon Arnold and his precious wife brought to Berolingen."

"And now," Sir John asked, "does your Excellency see any reason to waive these scruples?"

"I do not, sir," the Chancellor replied. "In recalling Baron von Arnold his Majesty can have had but one purpose, that of conciliating the still powerful faction which has hitherto steadily refused to recognise the new order of things in Noveria. To arrest Baron von Arnold would be to certainly frustrate that purpose, whilst the advantage to be gained by such arrest is at best a very problematical one."

Sir John Templeton bowed.

"And Doctor Hofer?" he continued. "Does your Excellency see fit to reconsider the contemplated proceedings against his Majesty's private secretary?"

The Chancellor was about to reply, when an interruption occurred of an unforeseen kind. While Sir John Templeton was still speaking, the clock of a neighbouring church had chimed out the hour of 1. Prince Ottomarck, who had been pacing the room in silent thought, stopped at the sound, approached the window, and, drawing back the heavy curtain that hung before it, gazed out.

A loud roar from without, continuing for fully a minute after the statesman had hastily replaced the curtain, showed that outside in the streets the multitude was still standing on guard patiently waiting to see, perhaps even to hear, some reassuring words from the man whose mere presence in the capital had momentarily at least lifted the weight of anxiety from their breasts.

Suddenly, high above the vociferous cheering and the persistent cries of "Ottomarck! Ottomarck!" a stentorian voice rang out the words, "Give us back our Emperor!" A moment's total silence ensued. Then the words were taken up, echoed and re-echoed, again and again, by thousands of throats, frantically, deliriously.

The three men listened, each with a different expression—the Chancellor with curling lip, but his countenance just a shade paler than before; Sir John Templeton grave and pensive.

The Prince stood with brows slightly contracted, grim, yet startled. The sudden demonstration outside had struck him almost like a comment upon his own thoughts, confirming and amplifying them. All he had heard that night was practically new to him, and though he was unable to piece it together, he knew him from whom he had learned it too well to doubt that, if any man were capable of doing so, he was that man.

As the din in the street slowly subsided and died away in the distance, his Highness strode gravely across the room towards the Count, and laying his hand upon his arm, said—

"If your Excellency follows my advice, you will not disregard that warning."

And he pointed with his left hand significantly towards the street.

"Your Highness thinks—"

"I think," the Prince went on, "that he who would save Arminia from the most hideous of the dangers now threatening her must bring the Emperor back to his capital. I know not if it still be possible. But, if mortal man can accomplish it, rest assured that it is he who stands before us."

The Chancellor glanced across at Sir John Templeton, hesitated, and frowned. He, too, had his pride allowed him to own it, was at heart shaken by what had passed that evening. But there was still a lingering obstinacy within him, which prevented him from yielding without some show of resistance.

"Your Highness's recommendation," he said, "is, of course, of the very gravest weight. But in consideration of the very grave evidence that has accumulated against this man Hofer."

"I would myself take the very course your Excellency has proposed," the Prince said quickly; "only not at the cost of losing services which I am convinced will prove of more advantage to Arminia than any knowledge that this man Hofer may be forced to disclose. Surely," he added, "the Imperial Government have enough to do to keep the ship of State afloat among the political breakers that are surging around it. Let them not add to their troubles by blindly rushing into new dangers."

Almost unconsciously the Prince had drifted into the emphatic, dictatory tone which years of unlimited power had rendered natural to him. Count Capricius, now his successor, had formerly been his subordinate, and had, perhaps, not forgotten the habit of bowing to the decision of one who had once been his chief—and, indeed, what a chief!

"Well," he said at last, reluctantly, "be it so, then. If Sir John Templeton is satisfied with this concession to an opinion which is, to say the least, strangely at variance with the facts, I am willing to suspend the contemplated proceedings against Doctor Georg Hofer until the Sovereigns shall have met in council. But that is all I can and will do. Grant heaven I may not have to regret it!"

Thus ended an interview, the result of which was destined to have a more important bearing upon the future of Arminian affairs than the conference of crowned heads and Ministers that had preceded it.

Five minutes later Sir John Templeton was driving with Prince Ottomarck through the still densely-packed Willibald-street, amid the wildest demonstrations of the excited crowds, towards the Victoria Hotel in the Avenue of Limes.

It was half-past 1 o'clock when they reached the hotel. When Sir John Templeton left it again, the first rays of the morning sun were already glistening through the rich foliage of the trees in the Avenue. But the city was now quiet, and its inhabitants were wrapped in peaceful slumber.

CHAPTER VIII
The Empress's State Ball

All the world knows of the famous ball which took place at Brussels on the eve of Waterloo. How many of those who danced gaily that festive night lay stiff and stark, crippled or mangled, a sight of blood and horror, within a few hours of that strange, ill-timed frolic. The mind is curiously fascinated by contrasts of this description, however dire and terrible they be, and it has clung to this one with peculiar tenacity, and will no doubt continue to cling to it and dwell upon it as long as history lasts.

If one were to seek for an event to compare with the doings of that fateful night, one might do worse than fix one's choice upon the no less historical festivity of which it is my purpose now to speak: the State ball given by her Majesty the Dowager Arminian Empress in honour of the five and twenty sovereigns who had assembled in Berolingen to discuss the fate of the much threatened Empire of her absent son.

Here, too, a contrast is afforded of a nature scarcely less striking than the one just dwelt upon; and yet how different, both in character and in circumstance. There, the contrast we now contemplate with a feeling of curious awe was that of black night following upon sunny day, of blood and battle succeeding the sweets of happy revelry. Those revellers of eighty years ago made merry with the zest of beings for whom the future is as a thing unborn— gray, indistinct, and intangible; yet they knew of that which was to come, surely, inevitably. Here, present and future mingled, were blended together, as it were, in one incongruous picture. The grim demon of war—ay, and of worse than war—stood, visible to all, threatening upon the threshold; yet none knew whether he would cross it, nor when. And the merrymaking was a feint, a sorry show of gaiety hiding hideous doubt and gnawing anxiety. Not outwardly a sorry show, indeed; for nothing could have surpassed the splendour of the function, nor the dazzling display of rank and wealth and power and beauty which graced it, making it stand forth unique even in the annals of a court renowned for such brilliant spectacles.

Two thousand four hundred guests all told thronged the halls of the Imperial Palace that night, and among them were five-and-twenty crowned heads, each with their attendant suites and noble following. Almost every species of gorgeous uniform known in the civilised world, every variety of fashion in dress and costume, was to be met with in this motley, ever-moving crowd that filled every available space in the vast palace.

To describe anyone individually and in detail would be an impossible task. Even had the eye had time to rest upon any single toilette amid this kaleidoscopic movement of colour, colour everywhere, it would have been too much dazzled by the blaze of light that was reflected back from the countless jewels glittering in the hair or shining on the dress of the fair wearers to arrive at any adequate judgment of its individual taste and beauty. Nor were matters mended in this respect by anything in the nature of quietness and simplicity in the dress of the sterner sex. The agreeable relief usually afforded by the sober, if sombre, black of the ordinary male evening dress, or even the comparatively simple court dress worn, at least by the general crowd of male guests, on similar State occasions in this country, was here sought for in vain. Indeed, in respect of colour and brilliancy of personal adornment, the men vied with the ladies, and presented an almost equally dazzling spectacle.

Ambassadors and diplomatists in their gorgeous full-dress uniforms. Ministers in their tight-fitting court attire, thickly weighted with gold braid; military attaches of foreign Powers, wearing the more or less picturesque uniforms of their respective regiments; Arminian court dignitaries and State officials, with the badges and insignia of their office; and last, not least, in number as well as in quality, military grandees of every rank and description in the Arminian Army, most of them with their breasts covered with stars and orders, plumed helmet in hand, resplendent in cuirass or double-coloured cloth, pomaded, betasselled, and ubiquitous; of such and their like was the male contingent of the brilliant assembly composed.

The general company had the freedom of every room and hall excepting one apartment reserved for the Empress and her circle; in the present instance a Royal circle in a truly multiple sense. Here her Majesty, assisted by her three daughters, several Princes and Princesses of the house of Brandenburg, and the foremost officials of her court, did the honours of the festival to her Sovereign guests, before commencing her progress at their head through the rooms thrown open to her lesser guests. From this central point—for the apartment was open on both sides, disclosing a long vista of rooms blazing with light and thronged with eager and expectant crowds— the initiated onlooker versed in the mysteries of heraldry and the Golden Book might have observed a kind of graduating decline in the social status of the multitude, these who occupied the rooms nearest the Imperial presence doing so by a kind of tacit right and privilege in virtue of their superior blood, whilst the farther one wandered from this august centre the less distinguished became the throng—to the well-instructed observer, of course, for the ordinary unaided eye would have detected but little difference.

Punctually at a quarter-past 10 her Majesty, giving her arm to the King of Wettinia, and preceded by her Chief Court Marshal, led the way to the ballroom, where the dancing was, as usual, to be formally inaugurated by the performance of a Royal polonaise. Immediately behind her Majesty followed the Prince Regent of Wittelsbach with the Emperor's eldest sister, whilst a line of more than twenty-couples, in strict order of precedence according to the sovereign rank of the guests, brought up the rear.

As the Royal procession passed through the wide lane formed by the bowing crowd in the adjoining apartments, the strains of orchestral music could be faintly heard in the distance, where the musicians stationed in the grand ballroom had now struck up the first bars of the national march. Responding graciously right and left to the respectful greeting of her guests, her Majesty proceeded slowly on the arm of her Royal partner, interrupting her conversation with him every now and again to bestow a glance of recognition or a kindly smile on this or that favoured personage whom she met and distinguished among the bowing throng on her way.

A more queenly figure than that of her Imperial Majesty of Arminia it would not be easy to find. Although in stature, like her venerable mother, rather below than above the normal height of women, she possessed that which neither height nor shape, nor, indeed, any other mere external physical attribute can bestow—a truly regal presence.

Her dress was a magnificent robe of black satin and velvet, veiled with priceless old Venetian point, which was caught up at the side with white ostrich plumes and carried down the immense black train that flowed in a graceful curve from her right shoulder. She carried a bouquet of the rarest mauve orchids in her hand, and among other costly jewels she wore in her hair a tiara of rubies set with diamonds, which flashed forth a red fire as she swept along, proud and stately, the cynosure of every eye.

There were many, more gay of attire and youthful in appearance, that followed in her wake; but they scarcely attracted more than a passing notice. The murmur of admiration which buzzed through the assembly as the procession wended its way through, lasting for some time after it had vanished from view, was unmistakably called forth by this picture of Imperial Majesty at its head.

Notwithstanding, there was one among that admiring throng on whom its effect was apparently lost; a solitary figure—distinctly solitary even in the midst of the crush that surrounded him—standing half concealed behind a gigantic marble statue of the Greek Apollo in the grand corridor leading to the State ballroom. He was one of the few whose costume was simple evening black; a circumstance which in itself would have marked him out among the rest. But there was something beyond his costume that made him conspicuous in spite of his half concealed position.

The most casual of observers would have recognised at a glance from the mien of those in his immediate neighbourhood that he was a personage whose presence was shunned. He was aware of it, too; not sensitively or resentfully. The disdainful curl of the lip, and the proud half-smile that settled on his handsome face, when this or that individual whom the pushing, hustling crowd had brought unawares into immediate contact with him shrank back again startled and concerned, proved the contrary.

As the Royal procession approached the spot where he stood, he bent forward impulsively, and his eyes rested for the fraction of a second upon the illustrious pair who headed it. Then, with a quick, almost nervous movement, they wandered anxiously along the line of those who followed behind, returning again and halting abruptly at the couple that came fourth in the order of precedence: her Imperial Highness the Princess Margaret of Brandenburg on the arm of her uncle, the Grand Duke of Zahringen.

The Princess, her head slightly inclined, and a pensive look on her countenance, was listening with apparently deep interest to her partner's earnest conversation. But there must have been something magnetic in that steady gaze which rested upon her; for of a sudden, with a scarcely perceptible start, she raised her head, and turned her eyes slowly in the direction from whence it came. A faint flush tinged her cheeks, fading away again as quickly as it came. That was all. Before even he who had thus attracted her notice was conscious that her eyes had met his, she had passed by.

A few minutes later, when the rush of the guests who immediately closed up behind the procession and followed it to the grand ballroom to witness the Royal polonaise, had subsided, leaving the corridor comparatively deserted, a distinguished-looking personage, with an unmistakably British type of countenance, detached himself from a small knot of men, comprising one or two noted diplomatists, who had not joined in the general rush, and deliberately crossing the space that separated him from the solitary figure beside the pedestal of the Greek statue, greeted him in English.

"I was told that I should meet you here to-night, Doctor Hofer," he said. "May I express the pleasure I feel in doing so?"

Doctor Hofer turned to him as he spoke, half-surprised, half-annoyed. But he took the hand extended towards him, and responded with a smile that had even something of cordiality in it.

"You are very good, Sir Edward Hammer," he said. "Your informant, I presume, was the person to whom I owe the unlooked-for privilege that has been accorded me."

The Ambassador nodded an assent.

"Shall we seek a cooler atmosphere?" he said, with a wave of his hand in the direction whence the royalties had just come. "These closed rooms are stifling at this season. The terrace is more inviting."

The Doctor cast a furtive glance towards the ballroom, where the stately opening dance was now in full progress. Then he looked inquiringly into the Ambassador's face.

"You have something to say to me?" he asked, without stirring.

"Nothing of importance," Sir Edward answered. "Shall we go?"

The invitation was too pointed to be declined without some definite reason, and Doctor Hofer was fain to accept it with a good grace.

As they walked along side by side through the various rooms which had just been traversed by their Imperial hostess and her royal guests, many a curious look was cast upon them by those whom they passed. Sir Edward noticed them and smiled. But Doctor Hofer was too much absorbed in thoughts of his own, either to heed the attention bestowed upon him, or even to reply to the light and chatty observations which his companion addressed to him on the way.

It was not until they had left the more or less crowded apartments of the inner palace and passed through the handsome winter-garden, which forms almost a separate wing of the building, covering an area of considerably over fifty square yards, and opening out about midway on to the terrace which stretches the entire length of the palace on the garden side, that the Doctor apparently awoke to the consciousness that he had a companion at his side.

"Why am I here to-night, Sir Edward Hammer?" he asked, almost brusquely, when they had stepped out into the cool and fragrant night air.

"I have not the remotest idea," Sir Edward replied.

"To be watched and spied upon, I presume," he continued, rather sternly than bitterly, and scarcely awaiting the answer to his question. "As if all their watching and spying could drag that from me which I do not possess. If it is indeed Sir John Templeton whom I have to thank for this questionable privilege—"

The Ambassador interrupted him by laying his hand lightly upon his arm.

"I think there is no doubt," he said, "that you have to thank Sir John Templeton for this privilege, Doctor Hofer. Perhaps, you have to thank him for even more. If I may so far presume upon our acquaintance as to offer you a word of friendly advice, I would urge you not to despise the friendship of a man in whose perfect sincerity you may place implicit faith."

"You would render me a still greater service, Sir Edward Hammer," Doctor Hofer rejoined, "if you would inform me to what circumstance I am indebted for this unsolicited display of interest on the part of a man whom I never saw until four days ago, and who, I understand, is serving the Government that holds me here a captive contrary to all law and justice."

"If you knew Sir John Templeton as I do, Doctor Hofer," Sir Edward replied, "you would not need to be told that whomsoever he serves he serves for the purposes of truth and right, and for none other. To what circumstance you are indebted for his friendly interest I do not know. That you possess it is proof abundant to me that you are not undeserving of it."

"Are you so sure, then, that I possess it?"

"As sure, sir, as I am of the fact that you owe to it the very air you are now breathing."

Doctor Hofer started.

"You mean that I owe my life to this man?"

"You owe it to him at least that you have not been obliged to purchase that life at a cost dearer perhaps than it is worth—to yourself."

Doctor Hofer gazed at the speaker long and searchingly.

"Has Sir John Templeton commissioned your Excellency to tell me this?"

"The question is perhaps natural, Doctor Hofer, but it is scarcely courteous," Sir Edward retorted drily.

Doctor Hofer felt the rebuke and coloured.

"Moreover," the Ambassador went on, "Sir John Templeton, I can assure you, is not the man to employ a mouthpiece—were it even a British ambassador," he added with a smile, "to proclaim that which, if he so desired, he could proclaim with his own lips. I know that but for him you would yesterday have been arraigned before an Arminian court-martial to answer a charge of conspiring with the Duke of Cumbermere against the liberty and the life of his Majesty the Arminian Emperor; with what result, in view of the fact that his Royal Highness is at present waging war against his sovereign, I need hardly stop to explain. I was of opinion that this piece of news would interest you, Doctor Hofer. If I have been mistaken I have only to regret my mistake, and apologise for troubling you with so insignificant a matter."

"You punish me somewhat severely for a hasty utterance, Sir Edward," Doctor Hofer answered, with an air of quiet dignity. "But perhaps I may not unfairly plead my exceptional position in extenuation of an offence that was certainly not intentional. I can only repeat that I find it difficult to understand this display of interest in a comparative stranger on the part of a man whose alleged purpose is to serve those who distrust and persecute him. Does it not occur to you that Sir John Templeton, in bestowing so much unmerited attention upon my humble person, is perhaps neglecting the chief duty he has taken upon himself to perform at the Court of Berolingen: that of restoring the Emperor to his loyal subjects?"

"I think not," Sir Edward answered simply. "I have never known Sir John to act without the most cogent of reasons. In this instance it happens that he believes his Majesty the Emperor is safe and that you are not."

"By heaven," Doctor Hofer exclaimed, with an earnestness that startled his companion; "I wish I could share this happy view."

"Of the Emperor's safety, or your own peril?" Sir Edward asked.

"Sir," Doctor Hofer said, almost passionately, "to be assured of his Majesty's safety I would—but pshaw, we are trifling with words. I appreciate your solicitude, Sir Edward, fully and sincerely," he went on more calmly, "but rest assured that it is not in Berolingen, nor from the quarter you imagine, that the gravest danger threatens me. Of this, pray acquaint Sir John Templeton. It may save him much fruitless trouble. Meanwhile, if he would not go hopelessly astray and jeopardise the safety of the Emperor, whom it is his desire to serve, bid him beware of Noveria. There is more villainy afoot there, Sir Edward Hammer, than either he or those whom he advises dreams of."

With which warning, solemnly uttered, he turned abruptly on his heel, and left Sir Edward standing alone on the terrace.

"Singular," the Ambassador murmured to himself, as he gazed after the Doctor's retreating figure. "A profession of ignorance and knowledge in the same breath. What if Sir John should be mistaken after all."

This reflection, as he slowly wandered back into the palace, pursued him, filling him with a sense of uneasiness which he could not shake off. He had intended to convey a well-meant warning to a man with whom, during the short time he had known him, he had always stood on friendly terms, and for whom, in spite of all appearances against him, he felt still a genuine esteem. Instead of this, he had himself received a warning, and it was one that could not shake his faith in the innocence of him who had uttered it.

When Sir Edward Hammer rejoined the crowd in the general reception rooms, the royal polonaise had concluded and dancing was in full swing in the apartments reserved for that purpose. The atmosphere was close and oppressive, in spite of open windows and other more ingenious contrivances to moderate the temperature, and the languid air and flushed countenances of those who moved in it proved that its effect was telling with unpleasant consequences. Indeed, more than one member of the fair sex had only saved herself from total collapse by a timely recourse to smelling salts and other reviving remedies, and it was even whispered—with what truth probably few knew—that one of the Imperial princesses had been suddenly overcome by the heat and been obliged to retire to her private apartments.

Sir Edward Hammer was anxious to gain a few minutes' speech with Sir John Templeton, with whom he had conversed for a short time at the beginning of the evening. But he found it impossible to accomplish his purpose. A British Ambassador at a State ball is not a free agent, and he had scarcely shown himself near the Royal circle, when he was espied by the Empress, who sent for him and engaged him for some time in conversation. Later on, when he was again at liberty to follow his own bent, he chanced at last upon the object of his search, but only to find him engaged in close conference with his Majesty the King of Wettinia.

While he was wafting at a respectful distance in the hope that their conversation would soon end, he was startled by a merry little voice close beside him, which accosted him with these words—

"Will you be my cavalier for three minutes, Sir Edward?"

The light, sparkling blue eyes that gazed, half roguishly, half deprecatingly into his face, as he turned quickly to respond, would have proved irresistible to an older and sterner man than our Sovereign's distinguished representative at the Court of Berolingen. Sir Edward Hammer was the most perfect courtier imaginable, and though he did so with an inward sigh, he acceded to the request from these fair lips without a moment's hesitation.

"Certainly, Comtesse," he said; "until you weary of me or dismiss me. Where may I conduct you?"

"I do not know," she answered demurely, placing her little hand in the arm he offered her. "Let us walk. Exercise is so refreshing."

The assertion, under the prevailing conditions, had certainly a smack of originality about it. But Sir Edward possessed far too much tact to express surprise at it. He merely sighed once more—only inwardly, of course—and obeyed.

There was not one among all the men present that night, however high his rank, who would not have envied him the unlooked-for distinction that had been conferred upon him; for the charms of the Comtesse Renee von Seckendorf, the inseparable companion of her Imperial Highness the Princess Margaret, to whom she acted as lady-in-waiting, constituted in the most literal sense of the word a power in the household of her Majesty the Empress. Comtesse Renee could dare to do what no one else at the Imperial Court could dare to do; and she did it with a grace which none could withstand. She stood in high favour with the Empress, whose wrath, much feared by those who had experienced it, was rarely proof against one of the Comtesse's penitent smiles. Indeed, so potent were these that it was even said the Emperor himself had for their sake once overlooked what he had never been known to overlook before—a breach of military discipline. In the strict sense of the term the Comtesse was not a beauty; but she had that which is often far more effective than beauty pure and simple—a strikingly pretty cast of countenance, and a charm of manner which, as I have already indicated, was as difficult to resist as it is to define. Though already twenty-one, and consequently by two years the senior of her Imperial mistress, she might easily have passed for younger than the Princess, more perhaps by reason of her great vivacity and frolicsome temperament than her actual looks.

Sir Edward, as he escorted his fair companion from one apartment to the other, moving, as he was directed, in the most erratic manner, apparently without plan or purpose, found himself very much in the same predicament as once before during that evening—that is to say, conversing with one who was too preoccupied to heed what he said. The Comtesse's eyes seemed to be everywhere at once, now sweeping the whole length of a crowded room which they had just entered, now glancing searchingly into some remote corner, and scanning the faces of those who occupied it, as if they afforded an absorbing subject of study.

"Are you looking for some one, Comtesse?" Sir Edward asked at last, finding that all his courtly eloquence awoke no response. "Perhaps I can aid you."

The Comtesse looked up at him archly.

"Am I tiring you, Sir Edward?" she said, quietly ignoring his question. "I fear you find it troublesome ploughing your way through these crowded rooms."

Sir Edward knew how to interpret an answer in whatever guise it came, and hastening to repudiate the notion that he could feel any fatigue under such enviable circumstances, he once more resumed his ungrateful task of entertaining a half-listening partner.

"Is it true, Comtesse Renee," he asked, presently, "that Princess Margaret has been taken ill to-night?"

The Comtesse gave a little start of alarm.

"The Princess?" she exclaimed, looking at him with an air of innocent surprise.

"I heard it rumoured that she had been seized with a sudden faintness, immediately after the Royal polonaise, and had been obliged to withdraw to her apartments."

"If that were so, I must have heard of it," the Comtesse said. "I am not in attendance upon her Highness to-night, but—why, to be sure," she exclaimed, "I have seen and spoken with the Princess within the last ten minutes, Sir Edward. People have been fabling."

They had now entered the apartment immediately adjoining the ballroom, whence at that moment, a rush of couples emerged, crowding the space before them and bringing their strange pilgrimage to an abrupt stop.

Suddenly the Comtesse made a quick side movement, as if to avoid being hustled in the crush. Then, with a little cry of annoyance, she detached her arm from that of her escort, and looked with a rueful countenance on the floor in front of her.

"What a plight!" she exclaimed, in a tone of dismay.

Following her look, Sir Edward saw to his surprise that a large length of the billowy lace flounce of her gown had been wrenched off, and lay trailing on the ground in front of her. How it could have happened puzzled him somewhat, for he had been careful to protect her from the crush, which proceeded entirely from his side of the room, and, moreover, he had heard no sound of a tear, such as might have been reasonably expected under the circumstances.

However, the thing had occurred, of that there could be no doubt. The Comtesse's little cry had at once attracted the notice of those in their immediate neighbourhood, and before Sir Edward could come to his partner's assistance, a dozen officers had rushed up precipitately, all eagerness to be of service to the pretty Comtesse. One of these, an Arminian lieutenant, wasp-waisted and profusely bear-greased, like most of his kind, instantly produced a handful of pins and a dainty pair of scissors from some hidden recess behind the flaps of his uniform, and picking up the precious length of lace, was proceeding to pin it deftly to the gown from which it had been torn, when the Comtesse, declining his offices with a petulant little air, declared that she would have no pins; the lace must be properly sewn on.

"Ah, you can help me, Doctor Hofer," she exclaimed, of a sudden, taking an impetuous little start forward towards that personage, who, as Sir Edward now noticed for the first time, had been standing a few steps off watching the incident with a smile of amusement. "Will you kindly give me your arm and take me away. But quick, quick, please! I must have this repaired at once by proper hands."

Doctor Hofer flushed perceptibly, and his large grave eyes lighted up with a sudden gleam of comprehension. He bowed, stepped forward, and before Sir Edward quite realised what was passing, the Comtesse, gathering up the trailing length of lace, had

94

placed her arm in his and was moving away through the throng that drew aside to let her pass.

As she did so, she caught the eye of her late cavalier, and stopped for an instant with a comic gesture of regretful apology.

"I am dismissed, then, Comtesse," Sir Edward said, in a half-whisper, glancing meaningly at her new partner.

"Not dismissed, Sir Edward; only relieved," she answered, with a bewitching little smile; and the next moment she was gone.

Sir Edward was still gazing after her with a perplexed air, when he felt a hand lightly laid upon his shoulder, and, turning round, saw Sir John Templeton standing beside him.

"I believe you have something to say to me, Sir Edward?" he said.

"I have, indeed," the Ambassador exclaimed, with animation, linking his arm in that of the old diplomatist.

"Then I am at your service," Sir John said. And, threading their way through the festive crowds, the two men went in quest of a convenient corner where they could converse without fear of being interrupted.

CHAPTER IX
The Mending of a Torn Flounce

Meanwhile the Comtesse Renee, on the arm of her newly-chosen cavalier, had passed out of the room into the grand corridor where Doctor Hofer had stood earlier in the evening to watch the royal procession on its way to the ballroom.

"Quick, through that door on the right!" the Comtesse whispered, accompanying her words with a slight pressure on the arm she was leaning upon.

The doctor obeyed silently, and steering for the spot indicated, passed swiftly through the door, which communicated with a short passage leading direct to the great entrance hall of the main building. Instead of traversing the hall, however, the

Comtesse, now leading her companion, turned abruptly to the left on entering it, and passing along at the side of the grand staircase, disappeared with him a minute later into a corridor at the back, which was curtained off from the hall, and guarded by an Imperial lacquey, stationed there apparently to prevent the intrusion of unprivileged visitors.

The man bowed profoundly as the Comtesse approached, and drew the curtain aside to let her and her escort pass.

As it closed again behind them, the Comtesse gave a little sigh of relief, and momentarily, slackened her pace. The stillness here was soothing and the coolness most refreshing after the rush and bustle in the heated rooms they had just left. The passage, which was carpeted with a thick pile of British manufacture, led, as Doctor Hofer knew, to what had once been the private apartments of the late Emperor Fritz. At its furthest end it opened out into a kind of vestibule, from which a flight of stairs mounted to a similar vestibule on the first floor, with the aspect of which the reader is already familiar.

As they approached these stairs, Doctor Hofer, who had not spoken a word since they started, turned his head and looked down inquiringly at his fair guide.

"Will you tell me what is our destination, Comtesse?" he said, in a voice which betrayed the speaker's excitement.

She looked up at him with a little moue.

"We are going to get my gown mended, sir," she said. "If you have anything to mend in the meanwhile, it would be well to lose no time about it. It will take my maid exactly fifteen minutes to readjust this strip of lace, and I can afford to wait no longer."

With these words she tripped lightly up the stairs, and Doctor Hofer followed with a quick-beating heart. When she had reached the top step she paused until he was at her side again. Then, pointing straight in front of her, she whispered:—

"The door opposite, which stands slightly ajar, leads to a room where you can wait for me, Doctor Hofer. I shall be here again in fifteen minutes, and shall expect you to escort me back. Do not fail me."

And without stopping for him to reply, she hurried on and vanished into one of the numerous apartments that gave on to the vestibule.

With a few quick strides Doctor Hofer had reached the door she had pointed out to him, and entering closed it noiselessly behind him. One glance around him, and a cry of pleasure escaped his lips.

In the middle of the room, in an attitude of anxious expectancy, with her body slightly bent forward and her lips parted as if in dread or suspense, stood her Imperial Highness Princess Margaret of Brandenburg. A deep flush suffused her cheeks for an instant, and was followed by a pallor which seemed by contrast almost deeper still. But she did not stir when he entered. Attired as she was in her full ball costume of cream white and silver brocade, daintily trimmed with costly lace and lilies of the valley, she looked, as she stood out motionless against the background of green palms immediately behind her, like some fair creation of an artist's imagination rather than a living being of flesh and blood.

Doctor Hofer gazed upon her in silent admiration.

"Margaret," he murmured, at last.

The word came from his lips in a whisper only, but it caught her ear, and she raised her hand with an impulsive sweep, as if to expunge its unwelcome record.

"Where is my brother, Doctor Georg Hofer?" she asked, in a low, stern voice.

"God knows it, Princess. I do not know it," he answered, earnestly.

"If you do not know it, who, then, shall know it?" she said, coldly.

He looked at her with a pained expression.

"You believe me guilty, Princess," he said, "of this hideous crime which the world imputes to me?"

"Are you not the faithful servant of the Duke of Cumbermere?" she answered, shortly.

"I have never denied it," he replied.

"The Duke," she went on, "is levying war—nay, not war, but black, treacherous rebellion—against the Emperor."

Doctor Hofer was silent.

"Are you still his faithful friend, Doctor Hofer?" the Princess continued.

"If I am," he answered, slowly, "that does not prove that I would not give all I possess, my life itself—all, Princess," he added, with sudden passionate ardour, "save one thing alone, to see his Majesty safely back in his capital."

"You know, then, that the Emperor is in Noveria?" she asked, with a little gasp of dismay.

"I fear it," he answered, sadly.

"A captive in the hands of his bitterest foe, of him whom you serve and uphold?" she exclaimed, with flashing eyes. "And you would have me believe that you are innocent of this shameful betrayal of one who had loaded you with favours, who has trusted you and honoured you, and made you his friend?"

"Let me prove it, Princess," Doctor Hofer replied. "Great God," he cried, "were it under any circumstances conceivable that I could have lent my hand to this dastardly thing, can you, dare you, believe I would have done so knowing it would cost me that which I prize above all earthly things—the one sweet hope which has become the breath of life itself to me? Margaret," he went on, seeing her tremble and half-avert her head to hide the effect his passionate speech produced upon her, "I had hoped and prayed for this interview—not to plead my cause before the only tribunal whose sentence I dread—but for a purpose which you alone can aid me to achieve."

"I?" the Princess exclaimed, turning to him with a start. "What is it? Speak."

He bent a look upon her full of proud yet tender reproach.

"If you really, truly, believe me culpable of what would render me for ever dishonoured in men's eyes, Princess," he said, "it would be useless for me to name it. For the favour I have to crave you can grant only to one in whose faith and honour you place firm trust."

He waited for her response. But none came. She stood struggling with herself, and watched the result, silently, expectantly.

"Why are you not free, Doctor Hofer?" she said at last, in a softened tone, "you are here to-night, but as a prisoner to whom a brief respite has been granted. Can I believe that my brother suspects your loyalty without some just cause?"

"Princess," he said, "for that which the Emperor has done he can account to himself alone. I know of no offence—save one—by which I may have forfeited his pleasure; and for that offence I will gladly answer before a whole world of Emperors, so long at your lips do not condemn it."

"You are bold, too bold," the Princess answered, with a tremor in her voice. "If I thought it possible that some mad desire of realising a hope that can never be realised had misled you thus to cast truth and honour to the four winds and become a traitor to the brother who is dearer to me than my own happiness."

"Margaret," he interrupted her once more, almost sternly. "Your lips utter what your heart does not believe."

"Disprove it, then," she cried passionately. "Have I not a right, a sister's right, to demand such proof? If you know the fate that has

98

befallen the Emperor, you must know by what means he has been treacherously lured to it; and if you possess that knowledge—"

"What if I do indeed possess it?" he broke in eagerly. "What if I possess it since last night, Princess, and am yet powerless to use it? Powerless for want of one day's freedom to act at will?"

"Ah," the Princess cried, stepping back, with a look of cold suspicion, "is it this you have come to ask of me? To assist you in regaining your liberty?"

"If I thought it were in your power to procure it for me, Princess," he replied, "I would not hesitate to ask it of you boldly. But I know it is not. All I desire is the means of communicating the knowledge I have gained to one who will use it as I cannot use it."

"And how can I aid you in effecting such a purpose?" the Princess asked.

"You can do so by consenting to despatch this letter under your Imperial seal, Princess," he answered, drawing a letter, as he spoke, from his breast pocket. "If I dared intrust it to the tender mercies of the Arminian post office," he went on, seeing her start back and change colour, "or if I had one solitary friend upon whose faith and integrity I could place reliance, I would not ask this favour of you. If you refuse it, nothing rests for me to do—"

He stopped short.

"But what?" the Princess asked.

"But to suffer in silence, Princess, a wrong far greater even than that which his Majesty the Arminian Emperor has done me. I can say no more," he continued. "My life, I know, and more than my life, is in peril, in grave hourly peril. But, by the love which governs my heart, and which I have sworn to live for—in spite of all obstacles, in spite even of your pride, Margaret, which is as sweet and precious to me as the love it would crush, yet contends with in vain—I swear that I would willingly yield up that life, if by sacrificing it I could undo what I believe has been done, basely, treacherously, indeed, but without my knowledge or connivance."

"But how can you hope to undo it?" the Princess said. "Can you bring life and liberty to another, you who are yourself deprived of liberty and in imminent peril—for you are in peril," she added, clasping her hands with sudden desperation. "I know it, I know it too well."

"I know not what may be in my power to do," he answered. "But rest assured, if anything can be done, this letter, and nothing else in the world, will accomplish it. Ah, the folly of it!" he broke out. "Could I only have dreamed of this! The Emperor, in depriving me

99

of my freedom, has unwittingly constituted me, not his prisoner, Princess, but his gaoler."

"His gaoler?" she murmured, looking at him with an expression full of bewilderment.

"You cannot understand me," he said.

"But you can believe me—you alone, Princess. Margaret," he continued, in a soft, appealing voice, "I ask you to trust me—nothing more. Can you see me look into your eyes—thus, and believe me capable of wronging you, my Princess? Is there no memory left of that one precious moment when those eyes made confession to me of that which your lips would fain have denied? I treasure that memory, and revere it as my costliest possession, Margaret; nor shall I cease to treasure it until I hold what will render it more than a memory: an abiding fulfilment of the hope it promised."

There was a ring of proud assurance in his voice which thrilled her. Yet it awoke no responding emotion in her own breast. She knew she had given her heart to this man, but she knew, also, that she had done so without that hope and faith which rendered the gift a gain to the giver. She had wrestled with her pride and her sense of duty, and had not conquered them. Alas, it had not needed the stern fiat of the Emperor to blast her hope of future happiness. That hope had not survived its birth; nay, it had been stillborn.

"Why remind me of that which is best forgotten," she said, in a low, almost plaintive voice, which tried to be calm, failed. "Have I not suffered enough for this one moment of weak folly?"

"Suffered, Princess?" he said. "Suffered since when? Since this cruel suspicion entered your heart, poisoning its faith in him who has won it—ay, won it, Margaret, for all you may say to the contrary, won it where the greatest of the earth, suing in all their power and glory and splendour, have failed to win it. That is my pride, Princess, and I would not part with it for the most coveted crown in Christendom. Would I then deceive you in that which I know to be nearest and dearest to you? You do not believe it, you have never believed it."

Something like a tear glistened in the girl's eyes, and she turned away, afraid of her own weakness. He spoke the truth, and she knew it. Had she, indeed, ever really doubted him? The proud, fearless tone she loved so well, the manly dignity, and the simple ease of his bearing towards her, which contrasted so favourably with the air of humble deference, the constrained respect she was accustomed to meet with from all who approached her, which had, as it were, bridged over the immeasurable distance that separated her, the Royal daughter of Brandenburg, from this obscure son of a

Noverian chaplain; could it be a mere outward veneer, hiding a soul as base and treacherous as mind can conceive?

There was a soft tapping at the door, which gave warning that the time was flying. Doctor Hofer heard the sound, and knew its meaning. Countess Renee was waiting, and there was danger in further delay.

"Princess," he said softly, "my time is spent. Have I pleaded in vain?"

She turned and looked full into his eyes.

"Go," she murmured. "Heaven forgive me if I do wrong to trust you."

He bent low, and, raising her hand to his lips kissed it with silent passion.

"And the letter?" he said.

"Oh, no, no," she cried, shrinking back with an air of sudden repugnance. "Not to me. The Comtesse will take it. You may trust her; it will be safest in her hands."

The door opened, and Comtesse Renee looked in.

"For heaven's sake," she whispered, "delay no longer. You will ruin everything."

Doctor Hofer hesitated an instant, as if there were something he had still left unspoken. But the Princess motioned him anxiously to leave her, and, resigning himself, he bowed and withdrew in silence.

As the door closed behind him and the Comtesse, the Princess dropped wearily on to an ottoman, and sat there long with clasped hands, gazing dreamily into the space before her.

Had she done right? She knew not. She only knew that she had followed her heart's instinct; and if that had lied to her, what would the rest matter?

CHAPTER X
A Fateful Letter

The reappearance of Doctor Georg Hofer among the company below had meanwhile been watched for by more than one person with considerable anxiety. The Empress's unexpected commands that he should attend the State ball had placed those intrusted with his safe custody, which recent events had rendered almost an affair of national importance, in a position of some embarrassment. There was nothing in the Emperor's order to prevent his secretary from partaking in whatsoever pleasures, social or otherwise, he might feel an inclination for, provided only that he was, under no circumstances, permitted to quit the capital. Indeed, his Majesty had expressly commanded that Doctor Hofer should receive all the consideration due to one holding his much-envied office.

It was this that made the responsibility resting upon those concerned with his charge peculiarly harassing, and the sense of relief they felt when his tall, manly figure once more became conspicuous among her Majesty's guests was proportionately great.

The Comtesse Renee was keenly alive to the discomfiture her absence had occasioned, and she enjoyed it with a mischievous relish. Yet, with all her love of romantic adventure, combined as it was with a spirit of mischief which would have done credit to the immortal Puck himself, the Comtesse had by no means light-heartedly undertaken the task she had just brought to a successful issue. She knew its perilous nature far too well.

While the excitement lasted it had afforded her a certain pleasure; when it was over, a reaction set in, and she felt the need of a few moments' quiet and seclusion, to recover herself—perhaps, too, to ponder at leisure over the sequel by which the interview she had been the means of bringing about had been followed.

Alas for the little Comtesse! She had hardly selected a suitable spot for her musings—a window niche in one of the rooms overlooking the terrace, and too far from the ballroom to be much frequented—when she was disturbed in a manner she had little dreamed of.

She was sitting half-concealed behind the curtain which hung before the window recess, dreamingly drinking in the cool air which came in breezily through the open casement, when she became aware of some one approaching her, and heard herself addressed by a familiar voice.

Looking up with a light start she saw Sir Edward Hammer standing beside her, and close behind him a personage whose countenance was unknown to her.

"Pardon the intrusion, Comtesse," Sir Edward said blandly. "Sir John Templeton is desirous of a few minutes' conversation with you. May I commend him to your kind notice? He has an important favour to ask of you."

And without awaiting her reply he bowed and retired, leaving her alone with the stranger.

There was something in the manner of the introduction, and in the grave tone with which it was accompanied, that sent a slight chill to the heart of the little Comtesse. She knew Sir John Templeton's name, if not his face, and a faint apprehension seized her as she thought of a possible connection between his appearance at this particular moment and the occurrences of the last half-hour.

"I shall be very pleased to be of service to a friend of Sir Edward Hammer's," she said, half rising in response to Sir John's profound bow. "What favour is it you have to ask of me, Sir John Templeton?"

"The same favour, Comtesse," he replied, in the most ordinary tones, "that you have just bestowed upon Doctor Georg Hofer; that of procuring me an interview with her Imperial Highness Princess Margaret."

The Comtesse sprang up as if electrified. The suddenness of it all took her speech away.

"Do not be alarmed, Comtesse," Sir John went on in his gentle, reassuring way. "I was perfectly well aware that this meeting was to take place. But it is imperative that I should see the Princess at once. Will you conduct me to her?"

The Comtesse stared at him with wide eyes. But she had now regained some of her usual self-possession, and replied, with a little laugh:

"What you ask is impossible, Sir John Templeton. I am not privileged to grant interviews with the Princess without first obtaining her Highness's consent."

"That is a pity," Sir John said; "for in that case I shall be obliged to obtain the required interview by applying direct to her Majesty the Empress; a step which, for the Princess's sake, I would have gladly avoided."

"The Empress?" Comtesse Renee exclaimed, turning pale. "Do you mean—"

She stopped short, and continued after a moment:

"For what purpose do you wish to see the Princess?"

"That, Comtesse," Sir John replied, looking at her steadily, "is perhaps hardly a fair question. But I will tell you. I merely desire to obtain possession of a letter which Doctor Hofer has just confided to her Imperial Highness's keeping."

The Comtesse sank back into her seat with a scared expression.

"The letter?"

A quick flash of intelligence lighted up Sir John's face.

"Ah, Comtesse," he said, "that, of course, alters the matter. Since this letter is in your hands, it will not be necessary for me to trouble her Imperial Highness. You will give me the letter."

"Sir," exclaimed the girl, "this is pure insolence! I have no letter. And if I had, by what right do you claim what is not yours?"

"By a right which it would take too long to explain to you, Comtesse," he answered. "But rest assured that it is a right which Princess Margaret would be the first to recognise and respect."

"Then claim the letter of her," the Comtesse said pertly, with a flash of defiance in her blue eyes.

"When I know that you hold it, Comtesse?" he rejoined, with a smile. "It will take less time and cause less trouble than to claim it from her Majesty the Empress, which I shall certainly do without a moment's delay, unless you comply with my request. Believe me, Comtesse," he added quietly, "I mean to have this letter. Will it ease your mind to know that my only purpose in obtaining it is to return it to the person who wrote it?"

"Why?"

"Because it will be safer in his hands than in yours."

"Then I can return it to him myself," the Comtesse said quickly.

"Doubtless. But I have my reasons for desiring to undertake the task myself."

"You intend to acquaint yourself with its contents," the Comtesse exclaimed.

"You are mistaken, Comtesse. I know its contents."

"You know them?"

"As well, I think, as if I had written the letter myself."

The Comtesse was puzzled. To yield up this letter which had been intrusted to her on behalf of her Imperial mistress, and for the safe despatch of which she had solemnly answered, seemed a base betrayal of a sacred charge and a crime against the Princess herself. Yet what could she do? The man who stood before her was obviously as stern of resolve as he was courtly in speech.

She tried all the wiles she could think of to escape from the cruel dilemma in which she was placed. But Sir John Templeton proved invulnerable. He remained polite but firm.

Tears of anger rose to the girl's eyes.

"My God!" she exclaimed. "What shall I do?"

"I grieve to distress you so deeply, Comtesse," Sir John said kindly. "But I cannot act otherwise. Let it console you to know that you can at this moment render no greater service to Princess Margaret than by doing as I bid you."

"But what can I say to her? How shall I explain—"

"Tell her Imperial Highness what I have said to you," he answered. "It will suffice."

"You are inflexible, then?" the Comtesse asked, with a sudden gleam of resolution in her eye.

"I have no other choice," he replied.

"Then I at least have another choice," she cried, stepping back, "and I will take it."

And with a swift movement she snatched the letter from her bosom, and grasping it for an instant with both her hands, stood defiantly before him.

"You can force me to deliver up this letter, Sir John Templeton," she said, in a dry, disdainful voice. "But you cannot prevent me from first tearing it into fragments."

"I shall certainly not prevent you, Comtesse," he rejoined without stirring, "because it will not be necessary for me to do so."

"You mean—"

"I mean that you will give me the letter intact. You forget that my intention is to restore it to its rightful owner, and I desire to place it in his hands unopened."

His simple tone of quiet assurance baffled her, and she stood irresolute.

"Will you now give me the letter, Comtesse?" he said.

He held out his hand, and slowly, almost mechanically, she placed the letter in it. Then, with an hysterical sob, she sank back into her seat, and covered her pretty little face with both her hands.

Old Sir John stood for an instant regarding her with an expression of kindly pity.

"Comtesse," he said, touching her arm softly, "in a quarter of an hour, if you so desire, you can learn from Dr. Hofer's own lips that I have spoken the truth, and that the man to whom you have delivered this letter is his friend."

When she looked up, he was gone.

Two minutes later Sir John Templeton was swiftly making his way towards the winter garden adjoining the Palace-terrace. A startling change had come over his countenance. The soft, kindly light that had shone in his eyes when he left the Comtesse Renee von Seckendorf had vanished, and a stern, angry look had taken its place.

"The fools," he murmured as he glanced ever and anon contemplatively at the cover of the letter he held in his hand. "To have concealed this from me! Was it crass stupidity or design?"

The address on the letter was harmless enough; or, at least, it was apparently not such as could have caused its present possessor much surprise. The envelope, in fact, was directed to her Imperial Highness Princess Margaret of Brandenburg, and it was not difficult to detect that it covered another sealed letter inside. Doctor Hofer, as will be readily conceived, had not been able to foresee that the opportunity would be afforded him of holding private converse with the Princess; all he had dared to hope had been that he would succeed in contriving some means during the evening of conveying his request to her in writing, either direct or through the medium of the Comtesse Renee.

Notwithstanding, harmless as it appeared, it was plainly evident that there was something about this letter which had deeply impressed Sir John Templeton, and it was not until he entered the winter-garden that his brow relaxed, and his face resumed its usual serene and tranquil expression.

The huge conservatory, owing to the close and somewhat vapoury atmosphere which prevailed there, was not a spot to attract loungers at this season, and save for one or two solitary couples, whose desire for solitude outweighed the discomforts of a heightened temperature, and the few passers who used this means of egress to the cool terrace beyond, the place was almost deserted.

Sir John Templeton had scarcely advanced more than half-a-dozen yards along the middle walk when a tall figure emerged swiftly from a side path and confronted him. It was Doctor Georg Hofer.

Sir John Templeton stopped.

"I trust I have not kept you waiting, Doctor Hofer," he said. "The delay has not been entirely of my making."

"I have come here at the request of his Excellency Sir Edward Hammer," Doctor Hofer said stiffly, ignoring the old gentleman's courteous apology. "I understand from him that you have a communication of importance to make to me. What is it?"

The tone was distant and haughty. But Sir John appeared not to notice it.

"It is merely to return to your hands a letter," he said, "which I believe at this present juncture is better there than in the custody of the Arminian Post Office officials, even though intrusted to them under the seal of her Imperial Highness Princess Margaret of Brandenburg."

Doctor Hofer stood for an instant speechless, astonishment and anger depicted on his face. Then something like an expression of despair swept across it, and he said in a hard, toneless voice:

106

"You have intercepted this letter, then. By what means?"

"By the simplest," Sir John Templeton replied. "I asked for it,"

"And you know to whom it is addressed?"

"I know to whom it is not addressed, Doctor Georg Hofer," Sir John answered, looking him steadily in the face.

"You have read it?"

In lieu of replying. Sir John handed him the letter in silence. He seized it eagerly, and a sigh of relief escaped his lips as he observed that the seal was intact.

"Why have you done this?" he asked abruptly.

"To prevent a catastrophe greater than that which this letter was designed to avert," Sir John replied.

Doctor Hofer glanced once more quickly at the letter, and back again to the speaker.

"You tell me this, and yet you pretend not to have gained knowledge of its contents?" he said in a tone of angry suspicion.

"Why should I pretend?" Sir John rejoined. "It is a knowledge I do not require. It is sufficient for me to know, what indeed the merest child would have divined, that this letter contains an enclosure of an important nature, which it was your purpose to convey to Noveria."

"Well?"

"The means you adopted for its transmission were singularly ill-chosen. You could scarcely have devised a surer method of placing the Arminian Government in possession of that knowledge which you have been so anxious to conceal from them than by transmitting it under the Royal seal of a daughter of the house of Bradenburg."

"They would dare to tamper with her Imperial Highness's correspondence?" Doctor Hofer exclaimed.

"They would assuredly dare what they have dared before, and that upon more slender grounds. We are not living in ordinary times. Extraordinary circumstances may justify extraordinary measures."

"Measures which it seems you have thought fit to thwart."

"In this instance, yes."

"You have chosen a curious method of serving the Government that trusts you," the Doctor said, with a curl of his lip.

"I have chosen this means of serving you, Doctor Georg Hofer," Sir John Templeton retorted. "Is it possible that you have not considered what would be the fate of the sender of that letter, if those into whose hands it would be certain to fall were to share the belief that prompted him in writing it?"

Doctor Hofer shot a quiet, searching glance at the speaker, who, however, went on without heeding it:

"That belief I know to be erroneous. The Emperor Willibald is not in the hands you think him in, Doctor Hofer."

"You speak with great assurance," the Doctor replied. "It is a pity your knowledge does not enable you to say what has become of his Majesty."

"I shall know even that," Sir John answered, "before the world is a few hours older."

The stern tone of his words startled his listener more than the assertion they conveyed. But before he could reply, Sir John Templeton resumed his usual manner:

"I repeat, we are not living in ordinary times. I warned you to take no step to-night without first consulting me. My first warning was intercepted, my second must have reached you. You have disregarded it. But, whether you acknowledge the service I have rendered you or not, of this you may rest assured: had this letter been posted it would never have reached the hands of the personage for whom it was intended."

"What do you know of this personage?" Doctor Hofer asked, darting another quick look of suspicion at the speaker.

Sir John Templeton paused deliberately before he answered.

"I know this, sir, that the personage to whom the enclosure in this letter is addressed is not his Royal Highness the Duke of Cumbermere."

There was a moment's silence, during which the two men stood regarding each other fixedly. But the name pronounced by Sir John Templeton seemed to have produced a strong effect upon the Doctor. He crunched the letter fiercely in his hand, and something of the desperate expression which had settled on his face when he first learned of its interception swept over it once more.

"Ah, this is insufferable," he murmured at last. "Come what may, I will make an end of this doubt and suspense. You have made it your object to thwart and foil me, Sir John Templeton—to what end I know not," he went on, in a firm tone. "But there is still one means left, which even you cannot prevent me from employing, to open the eyes of his Majesty's advisers to that which I alone can see. Since none other will avail, I will employ it. The Imperial Chancellor will not deny me a hearing."

He turned away abruptly, and the next moment he would have gone. But Sir John Templeton was at his side in an instant, and detained him.

"One word, Doctor Georg Hofer," he said, "before you do that which may be irreparable. Doubtless you will have no difficulty in obtaining a hearing of his Excellency the Imperial Chancellor. Grant heaven he may not believe what you tell him. If he does—"

"If he does?"

"If he does," Sir John went on, "the consequences be upon your head. It is not I, believe me, but you who are blind—blind to the friendship of the man who is serving you, and blind to the folly of an act which would have been more than venturesome three weeks ago, but will now of a certainty be fatal."

"Fatal? Pshaw," Doctor Hofer exclaimed, impatiently; "to whom? The Emperor?"

"Not to the Emperor, sir, but to one whose life is at this moment as precious to his Majesty as that of his own flesh and blood, and to save whom from the fate you would blindly invoke he would sacrifice—perhaps, even the Kingdom of Noveria itself."

Doctor Hofer gazed at him in astonishment.

"To whom do you refer?" he asked.

Sir John glanced cautiously around him. Then, bringing his lips close to his companion's ear, he whispered a few words into them.

The effect was extraordinary. Doctor Hofer staggered back as if he had been struck by a bullet. At the same moment a female figure entered the winter garden, and advanced quickly toward the spot where they were standing.

It was the Comtesse Renee von Seckendorf.

As she recognised the old diplomatist she stopped abruptly within a few feet of the two men, and looked from one to the other with an air of mingled alarm and confusion. Sir John Templeton greeted her with a courtly bow, and casting a significant look in the direction of his companion, drew back without a word, and passed out of the garden by the same door through which the Comtesse had just entered.

Once more traversing the crowded reception rooms, where the festivity—if the term is not misapplied—was still in full progress, he made his way swiftly to the grand entrance, and two minutes later had left the palace.

Meanwhile Comtesse Renee stood looking with a troubled expression at the pale and disturbed face of Doctor Georg Hofer. Sir John Templeton's parting words, when he left her with the ill-fated letter in his hands, had filled her with a vague hope that after all everything would be well. What she had just witnessed caused her heart to misgive her again.

"Is the letter safe?" she asked at length, in an anxious whisper. "Has he returned it to you?"

Doctor Hofer nodded affirmatively. He was still struggling to regain his self-possession.

"Who is this extraordinary man?" the Comtesse asked. "And how did he know—"

Doctor Hofer turned quickly, and laid his hand on her arm.

"It is useless to discuss this, Comtesse," he said. "What he knows, he knows. How or whence he obtained that knowledge who shall say? It is his, and better his, I think, than another's."

He added the last words in a subdued tone, reflectively.

"You trust him, then?" the Comtesse inquired, with some surprise.

"He is a friend," he answered, shortly.

Although her curiosity was sorely piqued, Comtesse Renee recognised that further questions would be useless. She had been driven hither by her anxiety to assure herself that Sir John Templeton had really not deceived her, and, having satisfied herself of the safety of the letter, she was just as anxious to escape again, with the least possible delay. To prolong the interview, after the incidents that had preceded it, was, she well knew, undesirable—not on her own account, for she herself cared little for the gossip of evil tongues, but for the sake of her Imperial mistress, whom her presence here might compromise by implication.

Doctor Hofer was so much wrapped up in himself that the Comtesse was gone before he noticed that she had turned away and left him, and he only bowed in a half-conscious, mechanical way as she swept along towards the door by which she had entered a few minutes before.

For some time he remained alone in the winter garden plunged apparently in deep and engrossing thought. When he once more mixed with the company in the palace, the expression in his face was again stern and haughty, and all trace of the unusual agitation which had recently possessed him was gone.

BOOK III
THE REVELATION

CHAPTER XI
Arnoldshausen

There are many estates in Brandenburg more magnificent than Arnoldshausen, but none more prettily situated. The village itself, which forms part of the domain, lies in a quiet valley opening out in the west on to a vast plain that stretches hence almost without break or undulation to the range of diminutive hills behind which the great city of Berolingen lies sheltered—a distance of over thirty miles. On the brow of the hill above the village stands the Mansion, a building of some antiquity, with its quaint turrets, verdigrised with age, gleaming out between the green tops of the trees that conceal the main structure from view. It had been in the possession of the Von Arnolds, who were originally a Brandenburg family, for the better part of two centuries. But it had rarely happened that one of its proprietors had honoured the estate by selecting it even temporarily as his residence; certainly not within the living memory of the present villagers.

Consequently, when the news reached them that the young Baron had decided to take up his abode in the old place, it caused a flutter of excitement in the little hamlet such as it had scarcely ever experienced. The villagers were simple, hard-toiling folk, who depended for their knowledge of the outer world and its doings upon such scraps of news as occasionally reached them from this or that absent member of the younger male community who happened to be serving his regulation three years' term in the Imperial Army. Newspapers were a rare curiosity to them, to be passively admired as a marvel of human ingenuity rather than actively studied as a source of profitable information. The nearest town was three miles off, and it was seldom visited except on grand market days, on the occasion of the annual fair, and once or twice during the year, perhaps, by some of the more enterprising spirits among them on a particularly fine Sunday afternoon; it contributed little to the enriching of their knowledge and general intelligence beyond temporarily widening the tiny circle of their ideas and interests.

The re-entry of the lord of the soil upon his long-vacated property had been followed by various changes round about them, not only in the direction I have particularised; nor were these changes altogether such as met with their unqualified approval. In fact, to say the truth, they had been somewhat disappointed in the young Baron. So long as the estate had been the property of the Crown of Brandenburg, to which it had fallen by forfeit, together with the Arnold estates, in the fateful year 1866, the villagers had been obliged to prefer whatever petitions or complaints they had to make to the Crown Steward, by written documents drawn up and executed in the officially prescribed form; a process wearisome in itself, and especially disheartening to men whose want and grievances rose readily enough to their lips, but became extremely puzzling when required to be put in due shape and form on a piece of official parchment.

The advent of an individual landlord, visible in the flesh and accessible in person, should, they thought, have relieved them of this grave and long standing difficulty. But, young though he was, and ever ready to listen to whatever his dependants had to bring before him, Baron Frederick von Arnold was by no means the man to grant off-hand what they chose to request of him, nor to rest content with the mere verbal assurance that matters were exactly as they pleased to represent them to him. He had proved, in short, as inexorable in regard to the formality of documentary procedure as the Crown Steward himself, and while his personal relations with his people were characterised on his side by great affability and solicitude for their well-being and prosperity, they really left the village very much in the same position as it had been in before, which, by-the-way, was a tolerably fair one.

This circumstance, then, met with their disapprobation. But there was another which perhaps troubled them even more. The Baron's presence at the Mansion had not been attended by any appreciable increase in the intercourse between the Arnoldshausen domain and the estates of the neighbouring gentry. Some few of the surrounding landed proprietors had called at the Mansion, but it had been invariably when Baron Frederick was absent inspecting his Noverian possessions, which had generally been the case before he brought his young wife home, and as none of these calls had been returned, these attempts at establishing visiting relations were soon discontinued.

On the other hand, however, the village appeared to have become a centre of attraction to gentry of quite another description, whose undisguised interest in the owner of the property and his doings was a source of much speculation on the part of the inhabitants.

Who these strangers were, and what prompted their inquisitive proceedings, no one was able to say; but they were looked upon with strong suspicion, which was increased by the fact that Herr von Arnold had issued strict orders to the village elders enjoining them to make daily reports at the Mansion, giving a description of every stranger who passed through the village, and stating the nature of every question and inquiry such passer made with reference to the inmates of the Mansion. These orders were duly obeyed. But they were felt to be unusual and irksome.

It is not to be supposed for an instant that the villagers of Arnoldshausen, who were loyal Brandenburgers and faithful subjects of their sovereign, would under any circumstances have countenanced in their very midst proceedings of a character inimical to the interests of the Empire of which they formed an infinitesimal part. But if anything could have induced them to wink at doubtful loyalty on the part of their more immediate lord, it would have been the circumstance that he was thus spied upon by officious nondescripts whose suspicions, if they were such, were in their opinion a direct insult to the Emperor who had restored him to his own. They resented this espionage, and regarded it as an imputation upon their own credit and honour. To their minds, the Von Arnolds, in spite of their long connection with Noveria, a connection of which the good village folk had but a very hazy and confused notion, were sterling Brandenburg stock, and hence above all debasing suspicion. They had never quite understood the reason for the expulsion of the family from a soil which had been theirs ever since the remote dark ages, which to the folk of Arnoldshausen meant any period that transcended the memory of the oldest member of the community. In short, the rights of the case had always seemed extremely doubtful to them, and they had regarded the sudden reinstatement of the young Baron much in the light of a tardy recognition of this fact on the part of the sovereign whose ancestor had arbitrarily expropriated him.

In view of this state of feeling, it is scarcely a matter for surprise that the information obtained in the village regarding Baron von Arnold, his mode of living, the visitors he received, and other such like details, by those whose curiosity tended that way, was of a very limited kind, and even, such as it was, very grudgingly bestowed. Latterly, although the number of strange faces to be seen in the vicinity of the estate had by no means decreased, the inquiries in the village had almost ceased; probably because the inquirer recognised the futility of pursuing their investigations in this direction.

It caused quite a little stir, therefore, among the villagers when early one morning a post chaise from Friedrichsdorf, the nearest station-town, drew up before the humble inn at the entrance to the village, and mine host was summoned forth to reply to a few queries addressed to him by its occupant.

Mine host was as surly a devil as may be met with on a fine summer's day either in this or any other part of the world, and he came forth prepared to polish off the newcomer in his usual curt and defiant fashion. But he reckoned this time, to transpose a homely phrase, without his guest.

The questions put to him by the stranger were few, short, and precise, and the manner of the man who put them was unmistakably one that commanded respect. Moreover, there was nothing about them to rouse feelings of resentment in the most sensitive of breasts, although they undoubtedly gave rise to a certain amount of bovine surprise on the part of the worthy innkeeper.

The first inquiry the latter was called upon to answer was as to whether the Mansion could be reached more quickly on foot than by the carriage drive which wound round the hill. Learning that, if one knew the way, the distance on foot through the wood was shorter by fifteen minutes than the drive round the hill, the stranger leaped from the chaise, and delivered a series of sharp, short questions as to this quicker route, which fairly bowled mine host over.

"Can you provide me with a trustworthy guide?" the stranger asked, cutting short the man's confused explanations.

Mine host scratched his head, and then, beckoning to a youth standing among the small group of gaping women and children who had gathered in the road near by, intimated that he was one whose knowledge of the locality might safely be trusted.

"But," he added, "if you have any message for the Baron, you may as well save yourself the trouble of climbing up the hill. He sees no one, unless he knows him."

This was said in a tone implying a query, to which, however, the stranger, who was already preparing to start off with his newly acquired guide, made no reply.

"May be," the host continued, tentatively, "a note or a message left with me would do as well, and be likely to reach the Baron all the sooner."

"Does Herr von Arnold usually visit the village in the morning?" the stranger asked, turning suddenly.

The man shook his head, and smiled as if to say, "If you can't understand me, it's not my duty to say any more." But he made no audible reply.

The stranger glanced at him for a moment keenly, then turned on his heel, and, accompanied by the youth, proceeded at a brisk pace along the road towards the hill beyond the village.

The chaise remained behind to await his return; and mine host, having seemingly no better occupation, fell into conversation with the driver, whom he treated to a bumper of small beer and sundry other delicacies, which, seeing that his fare had given no authority for the display of such magnificent hospitality, astonished the recipient most agreeably.

Mine host, it may be mentioned, was one of the village elders, and among the duties that had recently fallen to his lot was that of reporting at the Mansion as accurately as his intellectual means would permit whatever information he could elicit as to the objects and intentions of those who passed through the village or honoured it with their presence in a more permanent manner; from which it may be gathered that, if Baron Frederick von Arnold was subjected to a species of espionage, he apparently retaliated in kind.

Yet there was nothing in the aspect of the Mansion, or in that of its owner, as he sat that morning with his young bride on the beautiful garden terrace overlooking the green valley below, which could have led anyone to suppose that apprehensions of a serious kind were entertained regarding the security of the one or the safety of the other. A more frank and fearless countenance than that of the young Baron it would be impossible to find. There was at this moment, it is true, a shade of anxiety upon it, which seemed to grow deeper as his eyes rested ever and anon questioningly upon the somewhat pensive features of his beautiful companion. But it detracted in no way from the manly openness which characterised it; on the contrary, it rather set it off in more striking relief.

The Baroness Marie von Arnold, once Demoiselle Hofer, the sister of the man on whom so many grave suspicions now rested, bore a strong resemblance to her brother. Her beauty was of that rare kind which is beyond all question of individual taste and opinion. An artist would have pronounced it perfect, a type in itself of absolute feminine loveliness. But it required no sense of artistic perfection in the beholder to enable him to appreciate, at a glance almost, the full power of its exceptional charm. Indeed, all the art in the world could never have succeeded, either in fixing it upon canvas, or revealing it by any other method of artistic reproduction. Like a beautiful landscape over which the travelling summer clouds, alternating with the bright and brilliant sunlit sky, cast innumerable hues of light and shade, and reveal at every moment some fresh undreamed charm and beauty, its aspect was for ever changing, and remained for ever new. It was here that the likeness between the brother and sister ceased. The features were the same, indeed, but it was the sameness of form only, such as may be seen to exist between a shape hewn out of hard, cold granite, and its counterpart executed in the softest and warmest of marble. The commanding brow, the large, startlingly expressive eyes, and the proud, dignified poise of the head; none of these peculiarities were missing. But they were blended with such infinite feminine grace as to give them a stamp entirely their own.

One would have thought that upon a creature of such surpassing loveliness life could have bestowed nothing but smiles. And yet there was that in the expression on her fair face at this

116

moment which told of some hidden unrest, some haunting care agitating her spirit. There was a curiously apprehensive look in her eyes, as they wandered dreamily over the green expanse of the valley beneath her, and the nervous play of the slender white fingers that rested idly upon the terrace balustrade beside her betokened a mind harassed and at war with itself.

Presently she became conscious that her husband's gaze was upon her, and she turned her head with a start and a half-smile.

He rose, and stood beside her, placing his hand caressingly upon her fair hair.

"Why so sad and pensive. Marie?" he said, tenderly.

She sighed.

"I was thinking," she said.

"Thinking?" he echoed.

She suddenly rose, clasped her two arms about his neck, and looked long and searchingly up into his face.

"Tell me," she said, "why did you accept this gift from the Brandenburger? I should feel happier and easier had it never been bestowed."

"Do you regret it, Marie, that I accepted it?" the Baron asked.

"Regret it?"

"Would our paths have met, had I acted otherwise? Whatever sins Brandenburg may have to answer for in the past, it is at least to her King, the Emperor, that I owe—this."

"Ah, that it should be so," she exclaimed, with a little flash of petulance. "But is it really so?" she continued. "Had you not seen and loved me, though I never knew it, before all this happened? And why—"

"You forget," he said, "that it was when you had no eyes for such as me, Marie. What if I had sought this favour as the one and only means to realise what I could never hope to realise by other means?"

She averted her head with a troubled look.

"It is what I have long feared to believe," she murmured.

"Feared?"

"My brother always said it. He wrote it again and again. He thought you had forsaken the cause for—for this. It was the reason of his vehement anger, his distrust. Oh, why does he thus distrust you?" she exclaimed, with a little burst. "He is so good, so tender."

He took her hand in his, and kissed it lovingly.

"If you trust me, Marie, and my love and loyalty," he said, softly, "all will be well. Rest assured, I shall yet make my peace with him."

"Perhaps, had you gone to Berolingen and seen him, as he desired," she said, "he might have relented. It was unwise to refuse."

"He will still relent," the Baron answered.

"Not if you oppose him," she said, thoughtfully. "You have other plans than his, is it not so? And he knows it. What if those plans should fail? Is it safe to be so trustful? Think of the past, and the cruel wrong done to a Prince whose rights are rooted in the soil of ages. What trust can be placed to a Sovereign who claims possession to the fruit of that grevious wrong? Ah, you smile," she added, with an impetuous little toss of her head. "Perhaps men may find it easy to unlearn the creed with which they were born. I am only a woman."

"You mistake me, Marie," he said, gravely. "God forbid that I should wish you to forsake a creed which is part of your very being. But no creed, however sacred, can alter accomplished facts; and it is with these we have to reckon; to reconcile what we desire, ay, perhaps even what is right, with what is possible."

She shook her head slowly and resolutely.

"Ah," she said, with a sigh, "how it always pains me to hear you speak thus. There can be no question of compromise between the house of Noveria and that of Brandenburg. The idea is hateful to me. You place trust in this young Emperor. Yet how does he requite that trust? By watching you, and setting his police spies to dog your every footstep. They are here, about us now. They surround and pry upon us wherever we turn. I know it, and I fear them."

She spoke quickly and nervously, and her hand, which had stolen into his as she proceeded, trembled perceptibly.

He drew her tenderly towards him.

"Fear nothing," he said. "These men cannot harm us."

"But your actions may be misinterpreted," she went on, with increasing ardour; "nay, they have already been misinterpreted. Are there not those who believe that you have had private dealings with this man, that you have held secret, dangerous intercourse with him? But it is not so; you can assure me that it is not so."

She looked into his eyes, wistfully, almost fearsomely. He smiled, and gently stroked her forehead.

"Why let these fears harass you, Marie?" he said. "Such thoughts are for men only. Let them strive and struggle. It is man's province, not woman's."

"It would kill me if they should ever doubt you," she murmured. "Have I no part in you and your fair fame?"

"Such part, indeed." he said, with sudden intenseness, "that I will accept no other judge of my actions than you, my own. But it must be your heart that judges me, Marie. May I claim, whatever comes, to plead alone before that one supreme tribunal?"

She glanced at him in mild surprise at the earnestness of his tone.

"My heart?" she said softly. "Has not that judged you already? And could its judgment, once pronounced, ever be reversed?"

"Let me hear it," he exclaimed. "How does your heart judge me?"

She paused an instant, as if wavering between doubt and resolve. Then she raised her eyes once more, and fixed them with a sweet, earnest expression upon his face.

"I judge you," she said, in a low, vibrating voice, "as I shall ever judge you, as long as I hope to live: spotless in honour, unswerving in faith; as loyal to the Prince you serve as true to the woman you love."

The shadow of a cloud passed over his face. She observed it, and a look of wonder crept into her eyes. It was for a moment only; then she smiled upon him again, serenely, confidently.

"You are silent," she whispered.

Her voice seemed to thrill him. He clasped her to his breast with a sudden impulse, and held her there in a passionate embrace.

"Marie," he said, "what if I told you—"

But the sound of footsteps approaching quickly along the gravel path leading from the house checked him, and he stopped abruptly.

It was the servant, who came to announce a visitor. The Baron frowned, and waved the man off with an impatient gesture.

"I will see no one," he said angrily. "Why are my orders not obeyed? I do not receive strangers."

The man hesitated.

"The gentleman says he has a communication of the utmost importance to make to you, sir," he stammered, "and I thought—"

"I know of no communication important enough to interest me," his master replied. "Tell him so. If he has a message, let him leave it. Go."

The servant retreated quickly, and the Baron, ruffled by this inopportune interruption, paced the terrace with angry strides.

He had not recovered his composure, when the man reappeared, this time with every trace of surprise and alarm upon his countenance. Without a word, he placed a card in his master's hand, and retired a few steps to await his orders.

The effect of the card upon the Baron was a strange one. He took it, glanced at it, and gave a sudden start of surprise. Then a

119

perplexed look came into his face, followed by one of disquietude, and letting the card drop upon the table, he gazed for some moments thoughtfully into vacancy.

"I must see this man at once," he said at last, shaking off the mood, and speaking hurriedly to the Baroness. "I trust our interview will be short."

And followed by the servant he left the terrace, and passing quickly along the gravel walk disappeared a moment afterwards into the house.

The Baroness pursued him with her eyes until he had vanished. Then she took up the card he had left behind him from the table, and looked at it.

On its face it bore the usual inscription of the owner's name, which, however, conveyed nothing of especial significance to the mind of the Baroness. What riveted her attention were the words which had been hastily scrawled in pencil beneath it, and which apparently explained the servant's alarmed countenance and her husband's concerned manner.

"Sir John Templeton?" she murmured at last. "On the business of his Majesty, the Arminian Emperor?"

For fully a minute she stood staring at these words, without uttering a sound or making a gesture. But her face had grown paler, and her lip quivered tremulously. Slowly the card glided from her fingers and fell to the ground, where it lay unnoticed; and still she stood, now gazing out over the hill-side into the far, far distance with that same sad, earnest expression that had settled upon her face when, ten minutes before, her husband first broke in upon her silent musings.

CHAPTER XII
The Meeting of the Arminian Sovereigns

Berolingen in its time has been the scene of many strange and impressive events, but it may be safely asserted that no more strange and impressive spectacle has ever been witnessed within its walls than that which it presented on the memorable 26th of June in the year of the young Emperor Willibald's disappearance.

I may claim to speak on the subject in some degree with the authority of personal experience. I was in Berolingen, then the capital, not of the great Arminian Empire, but of Brandenburg only, when his Majesty King Willibald I., standing on the balcony of his palace between his great Minister and the wiry old strategist whose fame will last as long as that of his venerable Sovereign and his fellow-servant, addressed his people assembled below in their thousands on the eve of the great Fanco-Arminian war. By a piece of singular good fortune, due chiefly to my diplomatic position, I chanced within a year afterwards to be an eye-witness of the reception of his Majesty, now Arminian Emperor and King of Brandenburg, when he re-entered his capital at the head of his incomparable army fresh from the stupendous victories in far-off Franconia.

Both these events have remained indelibly impressed upon my memory, as they doubtless have upon the memory of every one who witnessed them. The scenes on both occasions have been described again and again by better and more able pens than mine, and if I mention them here, it is merely by way of comparison with the strangely different spectacle I am now about to bring before the reader. Strangely different indeed! and yet in many respects remarkably similar.

The morning of the 25th of June, the day following the State ball described in previous chapters, had broken in all the glory of a magnificent summer tide, and almost simultaneous with its dawn the entire city of Berolingen was astir. A kind of instinct seemed to have seized the people that the event they had so long apprehended with so much sullen suspicion and suppressed resentment was about to take place. The contemplated meeting of the Arminian Sovereigns in council had been kept a profound secret. Yet the intelligence had spread abroad, and there was scarcely one among Berolingen's million souls who was not accurately informed of the time and place of the meeting. The precise effect of the tidings upon the temper of the masses was as difficult to gauge as were the intentions with which they appeared suddenly to have become inspired. For, that this extraordinary spirit of watchfulness which caused them to leave their beds at earliest dawn on a summer's day and parade the streets was the outcome of some deliberate intention, could admit of no doubt it was in all save the actual fact a rising, methodical, premeditated, and silent, but none the less ominous and threatening; and the authorities knew and recognised it to be such.

Rumours as to the unruly spirit pervading the city had reached the Government the day before, and precaution had been taken to provide for a sufficiently early display of the forces of law and order to prevent the elements of subversion, which were believed to be at work among the citizens, from gaining anything like a point of vantage in the contest that was likely to ensue. But

121

when it came to the execution of the well-laid plans of the authorities, the latter were met at the outset by a difficulty upon which they had not counted.

It had been supposed that the centre of the trouble, if any, would be the heart of the metropolis; that is to say, that the people would congregate, as a matter of course, in the Grand Avenue of Limes, the Castle Square, and the adjacent quarters, where the chief events of the day were to pass, and it was in these parts of the city that the police had mustered at an early hour in strong bodies. But towards 8 o'clock communication reached headquarters from every part of the immense city, giving notice of the outbreak of more or less serious disturbances, and asking for immediate reinforcements. Even in the outlying suburbs disorderly crowds had massed, threatening violence, and necessitating the despatch of extra constabulary to maintain peace and quiet. The consequence was that before noon the ranks of the police in the streets and squares in the immediate vicinity of the Royal Castle had become alarmingly thinned, and although by this time all the principal routes leading to this great centre had been occupied by the mounted troops ordered out ostensibly to do honour to the Sovereigns who were to pass along them on their way to the council, considerable disquietude was felt as to the possible results, should unorganised attempt be made by the riotously disposed to attack or break through this military cordon.

The anxiety experienced on this score increased markedly towards 1 o'clock, the hour fixed for the assembling of the Sovereigns in the Royal Castle, when a strange thing happened, which entirely disconcerted the authorities. As if on a preconcerted signal, the inhabitants of every suburb of the capital, men and women alike, suddenly commenced to swarm in endless crowds towards the Avenue of Limes, the streams from all these distant quarters converging and meeting in this already crowded centre and hopelessly blocking every street and thoroughfare in a circumference of several miles. This manoeuvre, for it can scarcely be regarded otherwise, was accomplished so simply and with such rapidity, that long before the contingents of police which had been drafted into the various suburbs during the morning could communicate with the central authorities and receive orders to quit the evacuated quarters, they were practically cut oft from all access to the main body in the heart of the town.

Let the reader, in order to fully conceive the meaning of this occurrence, imagine for a moment that the entire inhabitants of greater London were to flock at a given signal from every corner of

122

the vast metropolis towards one particular centre, say, the vicinity of Buckingham Palace, for instance, on the occasion of a grand court pageant, thus swelling the crowds already assembled in that neighbourhood to an extent unprecedented even in the history of London mobs; and this after fully half the police force of the great city had been withdrawn to maintain order in the suburbs. The picture presented to his mind will convey something at least faintly resembling the spectacle I am endeavouring to describe.

Berolingen differs, however, from London in this respect, that it is not studded with large open parts, wherein congregated masses of this description may find breathing spaces even under such extraordinary conditions as here related. It was consequently in the streets that the crowds gathered, and from the Grand Avenue of Limes, whence some dozen of the principal thoroughfares of the inner town radiate towards all quarters of the city, every street was soon densely packed for a distance of miles in all directions.

In the Grand Avenue itself, and the two or three chief adjoining streets along which the route of the various royalties lay, the crush was naturally the greatest, and it extended hence like one unbroken sea of humanity as far as the Castle Square, where strong detachments of cavalry were drawn up, barring the way to all save those privileged to enter the Castle.

Here there were every now and then ugly rushes on the part of some among the countless multitudes that filled every inch of space outside the military cordon. But no organised assault was attempted. Indeed, the marvel was the comparative self-control exercised by these dense throngs, not only here, but everywhere, even in the surrounding streets, where, had anything in the nature of a serious disturbance arisen, the police would have been altogether powerless to grapple with it. In short, one spirit seemed to pervade everyone, and it was a spirit of calm resolution. Not that the elements of disorder and lawlessness were by any means wanting. Indeed, they made their presence felt in all parts of the city. But they found themselves, to their surprise, confronted and controlled by a power they had not reckoned with. Wherever they gave the slightest sign of activity, they were immediately suppressed, sternly and resolutely, not by the usual forces with which they were accustomed to wage interminable war, but by the people itself.

It was plainly evident that a tacit determination existed on the part of the populace to countenance no ruffianism. The Berolingers had a fixed purpose, and, strangely enough, in spite of all the many indications to the contrary, that purpose seemed to be to carefully

123

avoid any conflict with the representatives of the law—for the present.

Such, then, was the general aspect presented by the Arminian capital at the hour when the monarchs of the Empire were preparing to leave their various quarters and proceed in state to the Royal Castle to deliberate on the momentous question of electing one amongst their number to assume the functions of supreme head and leader in place of the vanished Emperor.

The authorities, military and executive, were utterly puzzled. There was no mistaking the attitude of the people. It meant defiance, and something more. But this self-possessed, almost dignified demeanour seemed so strangely out of keeping with the revolutionary sentiments that were supposed to underlie it, that it was difficult to grasp its meaning. In vain the Government waited throughout that morning for reports of hostile outbreaks in this or that quarter, which might afford some indication as to where the central seat of the threatening disturbances lay, or a clue as to the ultimate intentions of the mob. None of any importance came. The people were waiting, waiting steadily, patiently—for something; what, no one was able to say.

At the stroke of 1 o'clock the first Royal carriage, preceded at a distance of fifty yards by two mounted police officers, and accompanied by a small escort of the Imperial Guard, left one of the palaces in Willibald-street, and rolled rapidly through the double row of troops that lined the course towards the Avenue of Limes, along which it proceeded at the same rapid pace in the direction of the Castle.

Its occupants were the Kings of Suabia and Neckarstadt, and their countenances, as they glanced occasionally right and left over the sea of faces upturned to them on either side of the great Avenue, gave unequivocal evidence of the uneasiness prevailing in their minds. A low murmur, sounding like the rumble of distant thunder, greeted them along the entire route. Otherwise the reception they met with was in all respects similar to that which had been accorded them on the day of their arrival in the capital. There was no actively hostile manifestation, not even in Castle Square itself, where an incessant stir and movement among the crowds was now perceptible, like the seething and bubbling that may be observed on the surface of an immense cauldron just prior to the moment when its contents reach the boiling point.

In rapid succession the rest of the Sovereigns now followed one another from all directions. The King of Wettinia, the Grand Dukes of Zahringen and of Castel, the three Dukes of the Thuringian

States, the Sovereigns of Mecklenthal and Strelitzburg, and the host of smaller Sovereign Princes, each with his attendants and outriders, and accompanied according to his rank and consequence by a more or less imposing military escort, passed into the Avenue within a few minutes of each other at different points, the accompanying cavalcades in some cases meeting and mingling into one.

For the space of a quarter of an hour, as all these splendid corteges proceeded towards the Castle Square, the spectacle in the streets was one of imposing grandeur. Between the various points where the carriages issued into the Avenue mounted dragoons and orderlies could be seen galloping to and fro, conveying orders and directing the movements of the individual parties in such manner as to prevent them from clashing and obstructing each other. At the street corners along the route the extra contingents of police stationed there to prevent any sudden rush on the part of the crowds that blocked these thoroughfares as far as the eye could reach drew closer together as each cavalcade passed, backing their steeds the while into the compact wall of human beings behind them until the animals reared from sheer astonishment at the living obstruction they met with. But the precaution was unnecessary. In no single case was an endeavour made by these stolid spectators to oppose the restraint thus forced upon them, or otherwise to interfere with the customary order of things. They merely watched the pageant, recognising the occupant's of each carriage as it passed before them and rolled on its way to its ultimate destination—the Castle Square.

Here the scene was somewhat different. As one cortege after the other arrived and passed through the ranks of the cavalry drawn up in front of the Castle entrance in a strong phalanx curving crescent-like from one end of the Square to the other, the movement among the assembled populace increased perceptibly; though under ordinary conditions it might have been ascribed to nothing more serious than the natural excitement which always pervades large congregations of this description when the moment of supreme interest arrives. There was a certain tension noticeable, however, on the countenances of those whose position was to the front, nearest the troops, which could scarcely be accounted for by the eager interest they felt in the proceedings before them. Indeed, their intention seemed to be attracted elsewhere, and once or twice, when a momentary interval occurred in the precession of carriages entering the archway to the inner castle yard, their eyes could be seen to wander anxiously in the opposite direction towards some spot on the other side of the Square facing the Castle.

This curious attitude of expectancy on their part was a subject of considerable speculation to many who were viewing the scene below from various coigns of vantage in the Castle itself. The windows of the Grand Council Chamber on the first floor of the main building, where the monarchs were now assembling, overlooked the Square, and from here a vast bird's-eye view was afforded, not only of the multitude gathered there, but also of the streets beyond, where the people stood in seried masses, the sea of heads extending between the houses in all directions to an immense distance, like living streams all converging to one common centre.

The sight was indeed one to strike a thrill to the boldest heart. Such a congregation of the populace had never been known within the history of Berolingen, and its meaning could scarcely be misconstrued. In the few moments since the first members of the Sovereign Council had entered the chamber, where they stood in groups near the large windows gazing anxiously upon the extraordinary spectacle outside, some foreboding of the events that were preparing seemed to have seized their minds, and the air of suspense which pervaded the room deepened from minute to minute as the number of those present gradually increased until it was nearly complete.

In the embrasure of the middle window stood King Albert of Wettinia and Leopold, Prince Regent of Wittelsbach, engaged in earnest conversation. The former looked grave and concerned, the latter stern and somewhat contemptuous. The Prince, being quartered in the Castle itself, was the only one of the monarchs who had not taken part in the procession through the streets, and his view of the temper of the populace was therefore merely based upon what he now saw from the window. His arrival in Berolingen, too, it will be remembered, had passed almost unnoticed, and he had not had the opportunity, like his fellow sovereigns, of gauging the feelings which their presence evoked by the nature of the reception accorded to them on that occasion. In consequence he was inclined to treat the misgivings to which the Wettinian monarch was now giving expression very lightly, and to scout the notion of there being any intention on the part of the people to interfere with the Council or its illustrious members.

"What your Majesty regards with so much concern," he said, "is, I think, merely the result of ordinary popular curiosity. The mob has come out to gape and stare, not to threaten."

126

"Your Highness forgets," the King replied, "that no intelligence of to-day's proceedings has been officially vouchsafed to the public. Mobs of this size do not gather at a moment's notice. This one has unquestionably assembled premeditatedly, and in accordance with a long-determined plan. All Berolingen is astir."

"Are we to expect a revolution, then?" the Prince said. "Such movements do not generally commence in this fashion. Moreover, the troops are in any case a sufficient safeguard. Where would these sansculottes be in case of a conflict?"

"I think the result would be more than doubtful," the King rejoined. "Although the troops are mustered in considerable force, they are scattered over an immense area, and their positions are extremely disadvantageous. The streets were virtually already in possession of the populace before any of the troops had left their barracks. This unforeseen circumstance has materially interfered with the dispositions of the military commanders, and if it was deliberate design it has certainly effected its purpose. A glance from that window will convince your Highness that in case of need no reinforcements could reach the precincts of the Castle save by the one route which we have just traversed."

The Prince cast a quick look across the square and into the densely packed streets beyond, and was silent.

"But heaven forbid," the King went on, "that any conflict should ensue. The consequences would be too fearful to contemplate. It is this we should avoid at all costs."

"If it be forced upon us the responsibility will rest with the people, not with us," the Prince said. "But, frankly, I do not share your Majesty's apprehensions. Were there any deliberate design in this extraordinary conflux of idle crowds there would surely have been some evidence of it by this time. It seems, at least, that there has been no attempt to prevent our assembling. The Council, as your Majesty sees," he added, casting his eye over the sundry groups in the chamber, "has so far been permitted to reach the scene of its deliberations in safety. Our number is nearly full."

Indeed, just as he spoke, the last of the procession of the Arminian Princes entered the Castle Square, and a minute later, passing through the cordon of troops, disappeared into the archway entrance below.

At that moment, visible to the monarchs at the window, a small white flag suddenly shot out of the topmost story of one of the houses opposite. The occurrence, insignificant in itself, had a startling efface upon those who witnessed it from the Castle. But the effect upon the people below was more startling still.

The appearance of the flag was followed by a moment of complete stillness outside. The confused babel of tongues, the din and the uproar, to which the ear had gradually become almost insensible from the sheer persistency of the sound, ceased with a suddenness that was more surprising to those assembled in the Council Chamber, by contrast with what had gone before, than if a cannon-shot had been fired off in their midst, and one and all stood gazing at each other alert and attentive.

The interval of silence can scarcely have lasted longer than two or three seconds. Then followed a general roar, accompanied by a curious shuffling noise, like that which attends the quick movements of a body of soldiers at exercise when carrying out their drill officer's commands, only on a far larger scale.

What it meant no one knew. There was certainly something out of the common going on below, as was evidenced by the excited looks of the multitude, and the attitude of surprise assumed by the troops, who were still stationary in the same position they had been occupying for hours. But to all appearances it was nothing of a serious or alarming nature. Other sounds, of a far more ominous kind than those proceeding from the Square, had become audible to the occupants of the Council Chamber; and not only to them, but also to the surging throng outside. They came from the distance, and were heard in various directions far above the voices of those immediately below.

Could the white flag have been a signal, not to the crowd in the Square, but to the people in other parts of the town? The simultaneity of its appearance with the cries and shouts that could now be heard resounding in the distant portions of the city admitted of but one interpretation; the two incidents bore some relation to one another, what relation it seemed not difficult to guess.

There is a peculiar ring in the voice of vast multitudes, however far distant they may be, which conveys, even to the untrained ear, unmistakable evidence of the passions that uplift it. The distant sounds now wafted across to the Castle by the wind were undoubtedly the sounds of rushing, struggling masses; and of masses that were triumphing.

The Prince Regent of Wittelsbach himself, with all his contempt for mob organisation when opposed to military discipline, could hardly pretend to be deaf to this unmistakable note of triumph, though he affected to regard it with unconcern. The noise in the distance rose and fell with the breeze, and, though it continued without interruption, it appeared for the moment to be stationary. At least there was no sign that the disturbance, if it was

128

such, was extending in the direction of the Castle. After all, it seemed impossible to believe, if the populace had intended any hostile manifestation against the Council, that they would have chosen some remote portion of the town to make it in, after allowing the monarchs to pass through the streets unmolested.

The Council was now assembled in its full number, and whatever might be passing in the city outside, there was nothing to prevent it from proceeding to its deliberations. Its first business—which, according to the views of certain pessimistic minds, would probably prove to be its only business, and that, too, abortive—was the election of a president.

The King of Wettinia, it was known, had laid claim to this office by right of seniority, a right which the Wittelsbacher, as was equally well known, was resolved to contest. A flutter of excitement, therefore, passed over the august assembly, causing it momentarily to forget the incidents which had just engrossed its attention, when the Prince Regent, leaving the side of his royal rival, was seen to approach the Chief Secretary of the Council, Prince Hohenburg, and after a short conversation with him silently take his place at the table. It was the signal for the rest to follow suit, and in a few moments every member present had taken his seat at the huge horseshoe-shaped table which occupied the middle of the chamber.

After a short, impressive pause, the Secretary of the Council, who was seated with his three assistant secretaries at an oblong table drawn across the space between the two ends of the horseshoe, and who thus faced the five and twenty Sovereigns, rose to read the summons convening the conclave, issued, as the document formally put it, by two illustrious members of the Council, to wit, his Majesty King Albert of Wettinia and his Royal Highness the Prince Regent of Wittelsbach.

The reading of this momentous document, however, had scarcely commenced, when it was unceremoniously interrupted by the hasty entrance of an officer in the uniform of a colonel of the Imperial Guard.

The intrusion was so extraordinary, and the expression on this man's countenance was so grave and full of concern, that the assembled monarchs with one accord half started up from their seats, and the Secretary of the Council broke off in his reading with a snap that sounded almost as if his jawbone had suddenly sustained a fracture.

Outside in the Square the din of voices had risen to a pitch that no longer left any doubt as to the attitude of the mob collected there, and the uproar in the distance had now assumed dimensions which indicated that the disturbance was rapidly extending towards the Square.

One glance at the stern face of the officer sufficed to enlighten the King of Wettinia as to the nature of his errand. The Prince Regent was the first to recover his voice.

"What is the meaning of this intrusion, sir?" he asked, regarding the colonel with a frown.

"The meaning, your Royal Highness," the officer replied with military bluntness, "is that revolution has broken out in Berolingen, and I have thought it my duty to inform your Majesties and Highnesses of the fact."

"A revolution!" exclaimed the Prince. "But where are the troops? Are they incapable of coping with a 'mere mob?'"

The colonel coloured.

"Sir," he rejoined, "if you are pleased to issue any commands to me they shall be promptly obeyed, whatever the cost may be. My orders, however, are to guard the precincts of the Castle."

"Well?"

"It will become impossible to fulfil that duty unless I receive speedy reinforcements. I have five hundred men under my command. We are walled in by a multitude numbering a hundred thousand."

"Walled in? Do you mean that the Castle is practically at the mercy of the mob?"

"This is no ordinary mob, sir," the officer replied gravely, "but the entire populace of Berolingen. And they are in deadly earnest."

"But the troops, man, the troops," the Prince cried in astonishment. "Two-thirds of the whole garrison, thirty thousand men at least, are in the streets."

"And well occupied, if one can judge by sounds," the officer retorted dryly, glancing significantly towards the street.

"Then what is to be done?" the King of Wettinia exclaimed. "Do you anticipate an attack upon the Castle?"

"Within ten minutes, unless help arrives, or,"—he hesitated—"or your Majesties and Royal Highnesses will consent to agree to the terms of the people."

"Terms?" cried the Prince. "Are we beleaguered by an army? What are these terms?"

"They demand, firstly, that the Council of Sovereigns shall instantly break up, in which case your Majesties and Royal Highnesses, with two exceptions, who shall remain in Berolingen as hostages pending his Majesty the Emperor's safe return, will be permitted to leave the city unharmed. The second condition is that the Emperor's private secretary, who is a Noverian, and believed to be implicated in a plot against his Majesty, shall be at once delivered up to the representatives of the people."

For an instant the illustrious assembly to whom these words were addressed stood speechless with amazement. Then the Prince Regent sprang to his feet in an access of rage.

"Do you," he exclaimed, in a voice trembling with passion, "an officer holding his Majesty the Emperor's commission, dare to present yourself before us with such an insolent message?"

"I have done my duty, sir," the man replied, simply, "and I merely request your Royal Highness's commands as to the nature of the answer I am to take back."

"And if we refuse to comply with these insolent demands?" the King of Wettinia asked.

"The Castle will be stormed," the officer replied.

"And you, sir?" the Prince Regent said sternly.

"I shall defend it as long as I remain alive," the colonel answered, with quiet dignity. "I am responsible for the safety of its occupants."

"Then go, sir, and do your duty," the Prince said coldly. "We are men, not women; and if there is dying to be done—"

But the rest of the sentence was drowned in the terrific tumult that now arose outside. It came with a burst so sudden that the stoutest heart might well have quailed before it.

Rushing to one of the windows, the colonel gazed out, and fell back instantly, pale and aghast.

"They have broken faith, the scoundrels," he murmured wrathfully. "But, by heaven, we will sell our blood dearly."

And without another word he darted from the room and was gone.

Several of the monarchs had followed him to the window. But the sight that met their view caused them to retreat again hurriedly. The entire Square and the streets beyond presented one mass of struggling humanity, all pressing or being pressed relentlessly towards the Castle. The cries, shouts, and shrieks were deafening, and seemed to come from every imaginable quarter at once. The Square alone, roughly computed, must have held at least 30,000 persons, on whom the pressure of perhaps fivefold that number was now being exerted from the mob in the adjacent streets.

And between this overwhelming multitude, and with excitement and apparently unreasoning fury, and the five and-twenty Sovereigns assembled in the Council Chamber there was a paltry body of 500 mounted troops—a mere handful when compared with the fearful numbers opposing them.

The events of the last fifteen minutes had followed one another, in such quick succession that they had left those whom they most nearly concerned no time to realise the significance of each successive stage. But here was a situation which it required not a moment's reflection to grasp. The storming of the Castle could, under the circumstances, be a matter of a few minutes only, and what it meant to these five and-twenty crowned heads was perfectly plain.

No one spoke; every ear was strained to listen to the sounds outside. The large folding-doors of the Chamber opened on to the grand staircase, at the foot of which stood two officers on guard. At the door itself another two officers were stationed, whilst in the gallery running round the staircase and in the lobby immediately adjoining the Chamber the adjutants and officers in attendance upon the individual Sovereigns were scattered in several groups. Gradually this space became more and more crowded, as the servants and officials from all parts of the Castle came, pale and terror-stricken, to seek refuge and safety where, alas! had they only reflected, they must have known that it was least likely to be found, in the proximity of the illustrious Sovereigns.

Below all was commotion and confusion. Officers, lacqueys, grooms, gentlemen of the Imperial household, were hurrying to and fro asking questions or shouting commands. Doors were being opened or slammed in all directions; the muffled shrieks of terrified women sounded from the remoter regions of the Castle; and mingling with all these sounds of alarm and dismay in the building, the roar and the turmoil outside rose higher and higher, approached nearer and nearer. It was a scene of indescribable excitement.

In the Castle courtyard the ordinary guard was drawn up, and the glittering helmets of the men could be seen opposite the great archway entrance leading to the Square almost immediately beneath the windows of the Council Chamber itself. Here, too every one, save the soldiers themselves, who stood stolidly awaking events, seemed beside himself with panic and amazement. Bewildered officials were flying aimlessly across the courtyard stumbling, colliding, impeding each other's movements. Cries were raised to close the archway gates. But even had these huge, ponderous masses of iron been so easily movable at a moment's notice, the thing was already impossible. The archway itself was blocked by a heterogenous crowd of civilians and soldiers, all struggling to resist the tremendous pressure of the on-rushing multitude outside.

All this time not a shot had been fired, not a stone flung at the Castle windows; a circumstance that emboldened the King of Wettinia and two or three of his fellow-sovereigns once more to survey the scene in the Square. But they had hardly shown themselves at the window when they were recognised by those below, and a perfect storm of triumphant yells rent the air, causing them for a second time to fall back precipitately.

At the same moment several of the officers-in-waiting outside burst into the Chamber, the foremost exclaiming that the Castle was taken. And, indeed, across the lobby and beyond the grand staircase, over the heads of the groups of servants, officials, adjutants, and others, now thickly clustered there, the people could be seen in the distance pouring into the courtyard in one tumultuous, unbroken stream. On came the rush, the fiercely jubilant shouts now resounding both within and without the Castle walls, filling the spacious yard and the entrance hall below.

"They are making for the Chamber," cried several voices. "Stand by the Princes."

But on came the torrent, rising, rising. The staircase was one overwhelming mass of shouting, cheering, struggling human beings. On they came, carrying everything before them. What could that puny body of men before the entrance to the Council Chamber hope to accomplish against the tremendous impetus of such numbers? Before they could take measures, either for defence or attack, they found themselves jostling one another, compressed into a narrow space, a seried, compact group—a mere temporary impediment, a paltry barrier, that might perhaps stem the surging tide for an instant, but no longer.

In the Council Chamber stood the five and twenty Sovereigns grouped in threes and fours, pale, erect, and silent, waiting for that which they told themselves must come. They were soldiers every one of them, trained in the severe discipline which has made the Arminian army the great, almost invincible body it is. Whatever might occur, they would comport themselves as became their military honour and their ancient lineage. Their hands were on their sword-hilts, and slowly, resolutely, as the onrush grew more terrific, they drew the weapons from their scabbards ready for action.

The spectacle was impressive in its dignity, and almost grandly simple in its contrast with the mad scene of excitement outside. The resolute knot of men in the doorway, standing firm and determined, shoulder to shoulder, every face set sternly, and every muscle exerted to resist the onflow from without, was all that could

133

be seen from the interior of the room. But the clamour beyond told the ear what the eye could not perceive.

For the space of a few seconds it seemed as if the incoming rush was checked, and a voice from among the group at the door raised a faint cheer of encouragement, which, however, was instantly drowned by counter cheers from countless throats in the distance. Then some one cried:

"Stand fast. The guards have cleared the courtyard. They hold the archway."

But the reassuring news came too late, so far as those to whom it was addressed were concerned. The pressure upon them had become irresistible. They now yielded, and came tumbling, stumbling, pell-mell into the Chamber, followed by the rush.

A strange and startling sight was now witnessed by those in the Chamber. Once the barrier removed, the van of the storming party came to a temporary halt. Whether momentarily daunted by the presence of these five and twenty pale and determined men who stood, sword in hand, in an attitude of military firmness waiting to receive their assailants, or whether, in obedience to some prearranged plan, they advanced only a few steps into the room, arraying themselves on either side of the door, and thus forming a wide lane through which those who followed behind them came pouring in, but again only to deploy, as it were, in the same manner as the others, with necks straining backwards, and eager, expectant faces, as if watching for some sign or coming event outside.

Suddenly the influx ceased. The hubbub of voices was hushed to a low murmur, and through the now open lane, which reached as far as the eye could carry, the solitary figure of a man was seen advancing from the staircase with a quick, dignified step.

One moment of breathless silence and intense suspense, then a great gasp of amazement, audible even above the ceaseless roaring of the multitude without, burst from the august assembly in the Chamber. The next instant, with that sudden revulsion of the feelings which causes men to pass from the extreme of one emotion to the extreme of another, these five and twenty Sovereign Princes raised their swords high aloft and sent forth a cheer that would have done credit to the throats of any picked thousand men among their subjects.

And indeed well might they cheer.

The figure that now stood upon the threshold of the Council Chamber, surveying the scene before him with a calm, critical smile, was his Majesty Willibald II., Arminian Emperor and King of Brandenburg.

CHAPTER XIII
How the Revolution of Berolingen Was Averted

Until this day it has never been exactly ascertained how the famous Berolingen rising of 25th June, which ended in so strangely dramatic a manner, came about, nor whose was the master mind that planned it. For that it had been planned in its every detail, with a care and a foresight worthy of the finest tactician history has shown, admits of no doubt.

The most astonishing thing about it to the circumstance that the plan itself can have been known to comparatively only a few people, and that those who executed it when the critical moment came, blindly, unquestioningly, were admittedly taken as completely by surprise as the authorities against whom it was directed. It is true, of course, that in the excited state of the public feeling it required but the tiniest spark to ignite the flame of revolution. But to control and direct it to the manner in which it was controlled and directed, towards one stern, distinct purpose, was a work of a very different kind, the accomplishment of which is by no means so easily explained.

That the riots in the suburbs and the outlying districts of the capital, which broke out in the course of the morning, were the outcome of a deliberate manoeuvre to divert the attention of the authorities and necessitate the withdrawal of a large portion of the police forces from the centre of the town, is beyond question. The accumulation of vast masses of the populace in all the streets adjoining the Castle Square, whereby the troops stationed there were cut off from all communication with the rest of the town, was also no less certainly the result of deliberate design. No such movement could have been foreseen, and the police in these thoroughfares, which lay quite out of the route of the day's proceedings, proved utterly powerless to cope with the overwhelming crowds that began to stream into them from the most unexpected quarters of the city within an hour only of the procession of Sovereigns through the chief streets of the capital.

Both these incidents, it is needless to say, had occasioned great disquietude at headquarters, and were the cause of much perplexity on the part of the authorities, whose arrangements they hampered in so unforeseen a manner. Still, in themselves they had given no cause for serious apprehension. The Government had been perfectly alive to the possibility of some hostile demonstration on the part of the populace; they had even anticipated an active attempt at mob violence in certain quarters. But the point of attack, if any, would, they had imagined, be the Castle Square, or perhaps some particular portion of the route along which the Princes passed on their way to the Council, the object of the party of discontent being avowedly to prevent the meeting of the Sovereigns at all cost.

While, therefore, the procession of the Princes was on its way, the anxiety of those responsible for their safety was strained to the highest pitch, but once it had passed over without untoward incident of any kind happening, all apprehension for the moment ceased. No one dreamed of danger now. The Square itself had been closely packed with a comparatively quiet and orderly mob since the earliest hours of the morning, and even the concourse of people that stretched from here over the wide bridge which spans the river between the palaces, the Grand Opera House, and the Museums, and for quite a mile and a-half along the entire length of the Avenue of Limes to the Arch of Victory at its farther end, huge and vast though it was had given no actual signs of threatening trouble, or at least certainly none that could have led to the assumption on the part of the military and police authorities that these crowds of sightseers were animated by the one joint purpose of attacking and overpowering the guardians of the law at a given signal, after the procession had passed.

Yet such was, indeed, the plan; and it would have succeeded to perfection—with what ultimate consequences to those against whom it was more particularly directed, who can say?—but for one event, which altered with one stroke the whole aspect of affairs, and surprised attackers and attacked alike.

To attempt to describe with any approach to accuracy the precise sequence of the incidents which culminated in the closing scenes of the last chapter is, I fear, an impossible task. Among the thousands and thousands who were eye witnesses of them there is probably not one whose testimony would be found to tally exactly with that of his neighbour. Under the circumstances, therefore, I perhaps cannot do better than select from the conflicting mass of evidence at my disposal, the experience of one single individual, and, while supplementing it where feasible by the independent accounts of others, make it the basis of this part of my narrative.

I trust that it will not detract from the reliability of this testimony when I say that the single individual in question is the humble author of these pages himself. My duties had, of course, necessitated my mixing with the crowds in the streets on that eventful day, and for a very good reason I had taken up my position in the Castle Square. The reason was this. Late the previous night I had received the following somewhat mysterious note, written, however, in a hand with which I was not unacquainted:—

"If you desire to witness the most interesting part of to-morrow's proceedings, station yourself at an early hour well in view of the Royal Castle. You will not regret it."

The note was signed "A journalistic friend," and guessing the identity of my informant I did not hesitate to follow his advice. I have since often regretted having done so; for, stirring though the scenes were which I had the good fortune to witness from my coign of vantage in the Castle Square, my kind and well-meaning friend was after all destined to prove a false prophet, inasmuch as the particular interesting event he was doubtless alluding to did not come off, as the reader now knows, whilst the real centre of interest was unexpectedly transferred to other parts of the city.

Indeed, the people in the Square, and first and foremost the ringleaders of the movement which took place there, were as utterly mistaken as to what was actually occurring elsewhere as the inmates of the Castle itself. Had they been less excited, it is possible that the simultaneity of the appearance of the white flag in one of the windows opposite the Castle and the outburst of triumphant shouts and cries in the more distant portions of the town would have struck them as capable of a different construction from that which they placed upon it. The hoisting of the flag was undoubtedly intended to serve two distinct purposes. The one was to announce to the mob in the Square that the last member at the Sovereign Council had passed into the Castle. It was the pre-arranged signal for the crowd, prompted by the few initiated ones distributed amongst it, to swerve suddenly, as it did, in such wise as to close up the route through which the procession had come, and consequently deprive the troop of cavalry drawn up before the Castle entrance of this only means of communication with their comrades in the streets beyond. The other purpose was to convey tidings of the successful accomplishment of this manoeuvre to those assembled along the route itself, with the view to their commencing the sudden attack upon the troops lining it which was to form part—and, indeed, no unimportant part—in the day's revolutionary programme.

Thus, while the great bulk of the military forces in the city were engaged in repulsing the fierce onslaughts made upon them simultaneously in all possible quarters, the mob in the Square, separated from the actual scene of strife, and backed by the almost limitless crowds filling and blocking the thoroughfares north of the Castle, would practically hold the Castle and its gallant little band of defenders at their mercy, and be able to deal with both at their leisure.

The plan, it must be acknowledged, was an excellent one, and, so far as its first part was concerned, it proved an unqualified success. Hearing the sudden hubbub in the distance, and judging from the jubilant tone of the shouts that burst upon them that all was progressing satisfactorily in that direction, the ringleaders in the Square, who had formed themselves into a compact body to the front of the huge crowd facing the troops, proceeded to carry out their programme in the most deliberate and methodical fashion. No violence was attempted, nor had any been intended in this quarter, unless the small troop guarding the Castle entrance should resort to desperate measures of defence, in which case it is to be feared that a quick and terrible fate would have overtaken them. The officer in command was merely approached by the spokesman of the group, a citizen of considerable standing in the capital, who, after tersely informing him of the true position of affairs, demanded firmly but respectfully to be conducted with three of his companions to the presence of the Arminian Princes.

A short parley ensued, during which the officer at first sturdily refused to budge. But recognising the utter helplessness of his position, and concluding from the rapidly increasing sounds of the disturbance in the distance that he could look for no immediate help from other quarters, he finally consented with great reluctance to convey the demands of the people to the Sovereigns in Council, provided an undertaking were given that the mob would be held in check pending his return. With the stipulation that the limit of his absence should not exceed fifteen minutes, these terms were agreed to, and he went.

The conduct of this officer has been impugned by some who affect to be particularly well versed in the code of military honour. But, inasmuch as the subject of their structures was subsequently tried, and not only honourably acquitted, but actually commended for his behaviour, by a court-martial presided over by one of the fiercest disciplinarians in the Arminian army, it is scarcely necessary for me, a mere civilian, to take up the cudgels in his defence. In an emergency of the extraordinary kind I have described, with such tremendous interests at stake, time was obviously the only thing to be gained, and it was to gain it that the officer in question acted as he did. Had he acted otherwise, it its almost certain that Sir John Templeton's sombre prediction recorded in a former chapter would have been fulfilled to the letter; that is to say, that the Arminian Emperor would have re-entered his capital to find himself the only Sovereign left in the Empire.

During the worthy colonel's absence the pact entered into by the party in the Square was kept religiously. The sudden transformation of the comparatively quiet and orderly multitude assembled there into a surging, plunging sea of wildly excited beings, as witnessed by the astonished officer from one of the windows of the Council Chamber, was not due, as he supposed, to a breach of faith on the part of those whom he had trusted, but to a very different cause. The news that the Emperor was in Berolingen, and on his way to the Castle, had spread like wildfire through the city. The occupants of the Square were the last whom it reached, and preoccupied as they were with the events that were passing under their eyes they had at first treated it as a myth, with incredulity and derision. When, however, the whole truth flashed upon them, and they saw that what they had mistaken for the triumphant cheers of an insurgent mob had been in reality the people's wild manifestation of joy at the long-despaired—of return of their Emperor, incredulity made way for amazement, and amazement for such transports of jubilant delight that the very castle walls shook as from a sudden concussion.

It was this yell of exultation, sent forth simultaneously from tens of thousands of throats, which had suddenly interrupted the determined speech of the Regent of Wittelsbach, and startled the gallant colonel into fancying himself and his men basely betrayed.

How it had all happened—where the Emperor was first seen and recognised, and by whom—it is impossible for me on anyone else to say with any certainty. There are hundreds of Berolingers, each of whom to this day proudly claims to have been the first to recognise and hail him, as he entered the Avenue of Limes by the Arch of Victory in an ordinary open carriage drawn by two horses. One thing only is certain, that some time before any portion of the populace as a body became aware of his presence in their midst, he was already surrounded by a strong guard of soldiers, under whose escort he was proceeding as rapidly as circumstances would allow along the same route which had just been traversed by his fellow-Sovereigns.

But far faster than horses could gallop travelled the news of his arrival. The magic words, "The Emperor is coming," flew from mouth to mouth. Necks were craned, hands upraised, handkerchiefs waved, caps and hats thrown up into the air—in short, every

139

imaginable demonstration of frantic joy was indulged in. Roar followed upon roar, until the clatter of the horses' feet could no longer be distinguished. The people jostled and hustled and trampled upon each other in their frenzied anxiety to get near the carriage and catch a glimpse of the man for whom they had been mourning, plotting, scheming, and vowing vengeance for more than three sad weeks. No troops in the world could have safeguarded their charge from the headlong onrush of these shouting, screaming, cheering crowds, mad with the maddest of all excitements, senseless, exuberant joy.

But the troops were by this time long supplanted and replaced. A body of some hundred resolute citizens, the very men who had been selected for a task of quite another description, which the reader will have no difficulty in divining for himself, had now surrounded the carriage on all sides, and by offering a determined front to the howling mob which rushed in upon it from every quarter, prevented the carriage and its illustrious occupant from being overwhelmed and torn to pieces from the very excess of loyal affection. This band of self-appointed guards was swelled as it proceeded at each street corner by others of a like stamp, who, seizing the situation at a glance, rallied to the side of their sorely pressed comrades, and kept back the struggling, fighting crowds, which had they not been so restrained, would have swept them away instantaneously, as a torrent sweeps away a dam when once the bursting point has been reached.

Such, then, was the escort which accompanied his Majesty the Emperor Willibald through the streets of Berolingen to his castle on the day of his long-looked-for return; and a safer escort no monarch has ever been able to boast of. His progress was of necessity slow and much impeded. But he reached the Square at last, and—but the rest the reader knows.

Indeed, what more could I add? What passed in the Council Chamber of the Royal Castle after the Emperor's entry would doubtless be supremely interesting to record, were it only possible to obtain one single authentic account of that memorable scene which is not flatly contradicted by some other account of equal authenticity. The versions vary again here in a hopeless fashion, and probably no single one is quite correct.

Those who know the character of the young Emperor—and he is pretty well known to the world at large at the present day—may be safely left to conclude for themselves what kind of welcome he gave his illustrious guests, who had assembled under his roof much after the fashion of Penelope's suitors—at least, we the public of

140

Berolingen thought. That he understood the position, and rightly appreciated the attitude of his own subjects, may be inferred from the fact that when, in response to the thundering acclamations of the crowd out-side, he appeared on the balcony of the Castle a minute or two after his entrance into the Council Chamber, he was alone, and stood there for fully two minutes, with his hand raised in salute, gazing proudly and, as I thought—for I saw him— approvingly at the vast multitude shouting and gesticulating below. Suddenly a voice started the first bars of the Arminian national anthem, with the music of which no loyal Englishman is unacquainted. It was one solitary voice. But in a few seconds the whole immense gathering had taken up the song. All discordant shouts ceased as of one accord, and the grand, wonderful melody rang out to the skies in a strain that must have thrilled every heart present.

Truly, it was the most stirring scene I have ever witnessed, and one that I shall never forget.

I refrain from drawing a picture of the spectacle presented by the streets of the capital during the rest of that extraordinary day. The people for a time were beside themselves, and lost to all sense of dignity and decorum. Excesses were committed upon which I prefer to remain silent, and many a sad sight, too, was witnessed in those portions of the city where the crush had been greatest and the inevitable results consequent upon the dashing of excited and unbridled masses had been most numerous.

Gradually something like order was established. But the general excitement and jubilation lasted until the evening, when the entire city burst into a flood of light, almost every house being illuminated by such hasty means as could be provided on the spur of the moment. The thoroughfares were now paraded by endless crowds of sightseers, and giant processions and deputations, hurriedly improvised, wended their way through the jubilant throng towards the Castle, all bent upon giving some fresh and signal vent to their satisfaction at the termination of a suspense that had become well-nigh intolerable. Numerous versions of what the Emperor had said and done on confronting the Council of Sovereigns, some of a most preposterous nature, were floated and eagerly discussed among the people. Otherwise the sense of animosity against the Sovereigns themselves, which the events of the last few weeks had awakened in the population, seemed to have vanished completely, and some of the more favoured ones were even greeted with lusty cheers when they once more made their appearance in the streets.

Strangely enough, one thought appeared for the moment to have entirely passed from the mind of the people. No one inquired now what had been the cause of the Emperor's absence, or whence he had so suddenly and unexpectedly reappeared. He was there, visible and in tangible shape, in their midst again, and this sufficed.

During the evening it occurred to some of the enthusiastic souls to finish up the day's excitements by proceeding in mass to the Victoria Hotel under the Limes, and bringing Prince Ottomarck a grand ovation. In their view the great ex-Chancellor, and no other, could have brought about the happy event they were now celebrating, and it was meet that he should be paid the honour which was his just due.

The idea was seized with avidity, and once more the mad torrent took its headlong course, and the multitude collected in front of the Prince's hotel. But this time disappointment was in store for the people, and they clamoured in vain for their idol to appear.

Prince Ottomarck was no longer in Berolingen. He had left the hotel as soon after the news of the Emperor's safe return as the condition of things permitted, and driving in a closed carriage to the northern railway terminus, had chartered a special train to convey him back to Fritzensruh.

CHAPTER XIV
The Arminian Emperor and His Chancellor

In less than two hours after the reappearance of the Arminian Emperor in his capital the news of his safe return had been flashed all over Europe. In the tremendous international complications that had arisen throughout the world since the day on which he strangely vanished from sight, people had almost forgotten to speculate upon his fate. Having given him up for lost, they had no longer reckoned with the possibility of his return, and it took some time before the full bearing of the event upon the political situation was realised.

Yet realised it was, perhaps soonest by those who had taken advantage of the Emperor's absence to plan the downfall of the mighty Empire that acknowledged his sovereignty. The position of these schemers had now become one of considerable difficulty.

Franconia, in particular, found herself awkwardly situated. She had gone so far in her imperious demands that she could hardly retreat with dignity, yet to embark upon a war with a united Arminia was a contingency which she had never contemplated, and which she now felt it necessary to avoid by every means diplomacy could provide. Russia, too, whose attitude during the last three weeks had been such as to cause alarm to every pacifically disposed statesman in Europe, had her peace to make with the neighbour she had used so ill. Whether and how it would be accomplished was a question which was to exercise the minds of European statesmen in general, and Russian, Franconian, and Arminian statesmen in particular, for many days to come.

For the moment, however, the gravest question of all, and the one upon which all these others hinged, seemed to be whether the return of the Emperor would put an end to the troubles Arminia was beset with at home. The situation in Noveria, so far as the immediate future was concerned, remained unaltered. It is true there was nothing now to stay the Government from proceeding with the utmost rigour to quell the rebellion and annihilate the insurgent forces. But to do so effectually would not be possible without the employment of a considerable portion of the army required for the defence of the Empire itself—a fact to which its enemies must of necessity be alive.

Such, then, was in brief the position the Emperor found himself called upon to face upon his return to Berolingen, and he did so with characteristic promptitude and energy. While the people were exulting at the happy event which, according to their views, had with one stroke settled all difficulties, his Majesty was closeted with his Chancellor listening to the reports of the heads of the various Governmental departments, who had been hastily summoned to the Castle for the purpose of enlightening the Sovereign on the state of affairs generally.

In the Castle itself the aspect of things had meanwhile undergone a marked change since the stirring scenes which had signalised its Imperial matter's re-entry. By far the greater number of the Princes were still within its walls, it being deemed unsafe for them to pass through the streets until public feeling should have calmed down again. There was consequently still much stir and bustle in all parts of the building, but it was of a very different kind from that which preceded it. In the corridors, at the grand entrance, and on the central staircase a host of Imperial servants were busy removing the traces left by the memorable events of the afternoon, whilst the constant to-and-fro of officials between the various

143

offices of the household, and the frequent arrivals and departures of messengers and orderlies passing between the Imperial Cabinet and the Ministerial Departments in the town, lent the place a busy appearance which it had not known for many a week.

In the palace, as well as in the cottage, there are certain not easily definable signs which denote unmistakably the presence of the master, and they were now visible here. Voices were hushed and footsteps softened, whilst every one, and particularly those who moved about in the proximity of the Imperial apartments, seemed to be on the alert, as if they expected every moment might bring them under the keen scrutiny of their Sovereign's eye. There was a good deal of curiosity, and perhaps still more of anxiety, mixed with this general air of expectancy. The people of Berolingen were content with the mere fact that the Emperor had returned again, and did not trouble their minds—at least, for the present—to inquire what had so long kept him away. But here, in the immediate entourage of the monarch, the conditions were different, and every mind was engrossed with the one thought: What had happened? What was going to happen? The Emperor had reappeared as mysteriously, if not as quietly, as he had vanished. But what had been the cause of his absence, and what would follow upon it?

These questions formed the burden of every one's talk, wherever there was talk going on in the Castle—that is to say, among the illustrious guests who were still assembled under its protecting roof, as well as among the lacqueys and serving-men in the kitchens and house-hold offices; in the officers' quarters, as well as in the guardroom. They were questions none could answer. His Majesty had as yet vouchsafed to open his lips to no one on the subject, and there was no one who dared question him. His first order, after bidding his Royal visitors welcome and expressing—so one version has it—his profound regret that circumstances should have prevented him from appearing sooner to do the honours of his house in person, had been to despatch a messenger to the Dowager Empress announcing his arrival, and informing her Majesty that he would wait upon her as soon as the state of the streets permitted of his leaving the Castle without fear of molestation. He had then thanked and graciously dismissed those who had constituted themselves his escort through the streets of the capital, and having turned to the assembled Sovereigns and begged them, with a fine touch of irony, which must have caused them some uncomfortable reflections, to excuse his further presence at their deliberations, on the plea that they had been good enough to provide him with business of a more urgent and pressing nature to attend to, he had almost immediately withdrawn to his apartments, leaving the members of the august assembly to recover from their surprise and confusion as best they could.

In the Imperial Cabinet, meanwhile, Count Capricius was undergoing an ordeal of an unenviable kind. His reception by the Emperor when, after much difficulty, he reached the Castle in obedience to the Imperial summons, had been ominously cold and contemptuous. His Majesty had brusquely interrupted the warm speech in which he had endeavoured to express his pleasure and relief at seeing his beloved master safe and sound in his capital again, and had told him with his characteristic bluntness to eschew idle sentiment, for which the present moment was ill suited, and proceed at once to business. Report had then followed upon report, to all of which the Emperor had listened attentively, but in silence.

Occasionally an ominous frown gathered on his brow, and he darted an angry look at the Chancellor, who stood by anxiously awaiting the result of this trying audience. But one after the other of the Ministers and Privy Councillors entered the Imperial Cabinet, fulfilled his duty, and was dismissed with a wave of the hand, and still no word escaped the monarch's lips that enabled the Chancellor to guess from what direction the wind was likely to blow.

At heart Count Capricius had come prepared to witness a violent outburst of wrath on the part of his Imperial master, whose displeasure when things went awry was wont to vent itself in no measured terms. But this calm was worse than the storm he had expected, and increased the sense of misgiving which filled him.

It was strange to see this gray-headed Chancellor, with his fine martial bearing and commanding figure, standing with a crestfallen air, humble and faltering, before the youthful monarch, who, as far as years go, might have been his grandson. Yet there was that about the latter which made you forget his lack of years and only remember his exalted station. The personality of the Arminian Emperor is perhaps as well known to the world in general as that of any other prominent European ruler. He has been described and dissected so often in the public prints of this and other countries that there is scarcely anything now left to say about him. Yet, curiously enough, one feature—and to my mind the most striking of all—has rarely, if ever, been dwelt upon in these multifarious descriptions. I mean the extraordinary resemblance he bears to his late grandfather, the great Emperor Willibald I.

In stature he is, indeed, smaller than the illustrious founder of the Armininan Empire. But in face his likeness to him is remarkable. The keen, gray-blue eye, with its quick, penetrating glance, is the same, though it perhaps expresses more of the indomitable energy and stern will-power, and somewhat less of the exceeding kindliness of heart which endeared the old Emperor, especially in his latter years, to everyone who knew him. The proud lines of the mouth, with its characteristically pursed underlip, and the graceful sweep of the fair moustache, the ends of which, boldly upturned, lend the whole countenance a certain air of manly resoluteness—all these traits recall the venerable monarch, whose face is still indelibly engraven in the hearts of the nation which he raised to a first power on earth.

Much has been said of the brusque manner of the young Emperor Willibald, his contempt for what may be termed general conventionalities, and his disregard of the feelings of those who serve him. Maybe it is all just and true. But what of it? A character must be judged as a whole, whether it be the character of a common toiler of the earth or that of a ruler over forty odd millions of men. And taken as a whole, a finer specimen of this kind than Willibald II., Arminian Emperor and King of Brandenburg, may be sought for in vain. That he is intensely proud no one can deny. But even if there be a spice of arrogance in his pride, it is, on the other hand, leavened with a stern sense of duty, which raises it immeasurably high above the mere vapid silliness of ordinary conceit and vanity. Relentless of purpose, he spares himself as little as he does others in his pursuit of that which he was once determined to attain. Military to the core, like all his predecessors, with few exceptions, he carries the strict principles of discipline and subordination into every business that happens to engage his attention—and to what kind of business, be it governmental, administrative, military, or purely social, has he not at some time or other given his personal attention? The world may sneer and snigger at the spectacle of a modern Harun al Raschid appearing at this latter end of our humdrum nineteenth century, or may affect virtuous indignation at seeing a monarch, young, self-confident, able, and, untiringly active, repudiate the notions of his time and, regardless of custom and the claims and opinions of those who surround him, elect to stand forth alone, without props, a sufficient support in himself.

After all, in this age of sovereign nonentities it is by no means an unimpressive sight to see a king who is not merely content to possess his crown, but is also determined to wear it, who not only performs the formal functions of his exalted office, but also accepts all its burdens and responsibilities. Such is the Emperor Willibald, and whatever theoretical views his critics may entertain as to the most ideal form of government and similarly abstruse questions, they must give him credit for a personality as eminent and striking as any known in the world's history.

No one was more keenly alive to the originality of the young Emperor's character than the man who now stood before him in the Imperial Cabinet, anxiously awaiting his judgment upon the conduct of affairs during his Majesty's absence. That judgment came at last, and it was pronounced with a pithiness that savoured almost of contempt.

"Well, my dear Capricius," the Emperor said, breaking silence at length, after the last of the Ministerial reporters had accomplished his task and had been dismissed, "considering the short time you have been at work, you have certainly managed to make a pretty mess of affairs."

He stood, as he spoke, with his arms crossed, confronting the burly Chancellor, with an expression on his face that was rather humorously pitiful than angry or resentful.

"Your Majesty will be pleased to consider," the Chancellor stammered, "that the extraordinary difficulties with which we were faced—"

"Nay," interposed the Emperor, "I see no extraordinary difficulties, save those of your own creating. You have blundered, my dear Capricius, blundered deplorably; and your first and foremost blunder was to suppose your Emperor was a fool."

"Your Majesty—"

"What, sir, did you not lead the world to think I had gone blindly on some fool's errand, to treat in my own person, forsooth, with a mere handful of rebellious rogues, whom a company or two of my troops would have easily swept from the face of the earth? You have accomplished the feat of making your Sovereign the laughing-stock of Europe for the space of three whole weeks, and I owe you little thanks for it."

There was an angry flash in his eye, and his lip curled disdainfully. The Chancellor stood silent. These signs of storm rather relieved him than otherwise. At least, he knew where he was. But he could scarcely conceal his surprise at the Emperor's apparently accurate knowledge of what had occurred during his absence.

"If your Majesty had only deigned to enlighten us," he murmured, after a moment, respectfully.

But he got no further. The Emperor turned upon him like lightning.

"Deigned to enlighten you!" he cried, surveying him sternly from head to foot. "Am I to render an account of my doings to my

147

servants? When I think fit to enlighten you, Count Capricius, you may be assured that you will receive enlightenment as full and complete as you can desire. For the present let it suffice you to know that I have been busy during these three weeks in mending what you and your precious Ministers have been at pains to spoil. Unfortunately," he added, "no mending will undo the disgrace my Empire has sustained in the meanwhile. By heaven, to think that a ragged and undisciplined Noverian rabble should have succeeded for three whole weeks in bidding defiance to the entire forces of Royal Brandenburg! I could forgive and forget everything but that."

The thought seemed to agitate him deeply, far more than the insolence of Franconia, which he treated with contempt, or the animosity of Russia, in whose friendship he had never believed. The Chancellor, an Arminian soldier with all an Arminian soldier's instincts of blind submission and self-repression, watched his Sovereign silently, as he strode angrily up and down the room, venting his displeasure every now and again in occasional exclamations and expletives, which were far from complimentary to those to whom they were applied.

"I presume," Count Capricius at last ventured to remark, "that your Majesty will order the troops concentrated in Noveria to proceed to immediate action?"

"Will I do so?" the Emperor said, stopping short in his impatient promenade. "I have done so, sir."

The Chancellor looked up with an air of surprise.

"But you remind me," his Majesty continued, "that it would be well to ascertain whether my messenger has reached the Ministry of War in safety. I made out the order en route for the Castle, and handed it for instant despatch to the young lieutenant off the Third Uhlans who rode next to my carriage. Let an orderly proceed at once to the Ministry. And mark, I will have no treating or parleying with these insolent rebels. I demand instant unconditional surrender and submission to such sentence as the military courts may pronounce. Otherwise no quarter. You understand me. Let this be seen to."

While the Chancellor hurried into the ante-chamber to carry out the Imperial commands, the Emperor resumed his walking exercise with renewed vigour. He evidently felt the necessity of working off the angry feelings that had been accumulating within him. When the Chancellor returned he wore a thoughtful took.

"Your Majesty is aware, of course," he said, "that the Duke of Cumbermere himself has assumed the command of the insurgent forces?"

148

"Well?"

"It might give rise to awkward questions were his Royal Highness to fall into our hands. Would it not be expedient, therefore, in view of possible contingencies, to facilitate—"

"The Duke's escape?" the Emperor exclaimed. "On the contrary, I desire that every means shall be adopted to prevent such a calamity."

"But if we secure his Royal Highness's person—"

"He shall be dealt with as traitors deserve," the Emperor said, sternly. "Were my own brother guilty of the perfidy of which this precious Duke has been guilty, I would make an example of him."

"But the courts of Great Britain and Austria," the Chancellor said, dismayed at this inflexible determination, in which he saw fresh and incalculable dangers; "has your Majesty reflected upon the inevitable complications that must ensue in such an event?"

"Let us leave the courts of Great Britain and Austria to act for themselves when the occasion arises," the Emperor replied, grimly. "I fancy they will not be inclined to baulk me here. It surprises me somewhat," he added, "to find that the Duke of Cumbermere possesses so anxious a champion in the Imperial Chancellor. It used to be otherwise."

"Your Majesty can scarcely charge me with being the Duke's champion," Count Capricius answered, nettled by the ironical tone of the Emperor. "Your Majesty must concede that I have never placed any trust in his Royal Highness's sincerity in desiring an amicable settlement of the questions pending between him and the Crown of Brandenburg. If your Majesty has been deceived—"

"The fault is mine? Is that it?" the Emperor said. "On my faith. I almost despair of ever convincing you that my head is better than yours. Let me tell your Excellency, however, that if you do me but scant justice, you certainly overrate both yourself and his Royal Highness the Duke of Cumbermere. I am not so easily led by the nose as your Excellency appears inclined to suppose. While his Highness has been plotting and scheming, I have acted—with what success the result will show."

There was a shade almost of doubt in the tone of these last words, which struck the Chancellor, and emboldened him, perhaps, more than the resentment he felt at the Emperor's scathing reference to his estimate of his own efficiency, to hazard a piece of sarcasm, for which he might have paid dearly.

"Your Majesty, then," he said, "has practically settled the Noverian question single-handed?"

149

The Emperor regarded him for a moment with a severe glance.

"Your shrewdness does you credit, Count Capricius," he said; "but honour to whom honour is due. If the Noverian question should indeed be settled—and God grant it may prove so—it will not be my doing alone."

"I can only join heartily in your Majesty's prayer," the Chancellor said, "that all may prove as your Majesty anticipates."

"But meanwhile you reserve your own opinion as to the likelihood of this happy consummation?" the Emperor observed, with a good-humouredness that surprised his Minister.

"I cannot deny," the Chancellor rejoined, "that the fact that the Duke of Cumbermere is at this moment bearing arms against your Majesty seems scarcely to augur well for the fulfilment of your Majesty's wishes."

"But if we capture and hang this venturesome Duke as a rebel?" the Emperor asked, with a coolness that caused the Chancellor to start back aghast.

"God forbid!" he cried. "Your Majesty cannot seriously contemplate such an act. It would alienate every loyal heart Brandenburg has gained in the annexed kingdom during all these years. Nay, it might-even be said—"

He stopped short, hesitating to give expression to his thought.

"Pray proceed," the Emperor said.

"It might be said, sire," the Chancellor continued, "that this rebellion in Noveria had been deliberately planned by the Crown of Brandenburg itself in order to ensnare the Duke of Cumbermere and cause him to forfeit his liberty and his life to the power which has despoiled him of his possessions."

The Emperor fixed his eye searchingly upon the speaker's face.

"Which means?" he said, curtly.

"I pray your Majesty not to misunderstand me," Count Capricius said, conscious of the delicate ground on which he was venturing. "Of course, no one who knows your Majesty will credit so monstrous a story. But unfortunately the world at large judges by appearances only, and I fear that your Majesty's well-known relations with the Baron von Arnold, who is believed to have had a weighty voice in the councils of the Duke, may, unless satisfactorily explained, be liable to a most unhappy misconstruction."

"Ha, what about this Baron von Arnold?" the Emperor exclaimed abruptly, apparently quite ignoring the insinuation conveyed in the Chancellor's last words. "My Government, I am informed, have been mighty eager to court-martial the friends of the Duke of Cumbermere. I trust, at least, that they have bestowed some attention in this quarter, too."

"Your Majesty may be quite easy on that score," the Chancellor replied. "Baron von Arnold has been kept under the strictest surveillance. I can answer for it that no communication whatever has passed between Arnoldshausen and the Duke of Cumbermere or his agents."

"A fig for your surveillance," cried the Emperor in great dudgeon. "What if I tell you that, to my certain knowledge, this Baron von Arnold has until three weeks ago been in daily intimate communication with his Royal Highness the Duke of Cumbermere—nay, more, that he has just successfully eluded the vigilance of your watchers and escaped from Arnoldhausen to join the Duke?"

Count Capricius stood dumbfounded.

"Your Majesty astonishes me," he stammered. "It was only yesterday that I received the most reassuring reports from the agents charged to watch the movements of the Baron. Unless your Majesty has been strangely misinformed—"

"Pshaw, it is your information that is deficient, not mine," the Emperor said.

"Then," exclaimed the Chancellor, "if your Majesty will be guided by my counsel, you will issue instant orders for the definite arrest of the man whose sister has recently become the wife of Baron von Arnold. I will stake my head that no other than Doctor Georg Hofer, your Majesty's private secretary, is at the bottom of this foul conspiracy."

"There I am inclined to agree with you," the Emperor remarked, drily. "But not so fast, my dear Chancellor. There is a person who is just now of even greater consequence to us than Doctor Georg Hofer. I mean the Baroness von Arnold herself. I have reason to believe that the Duke of Cumbermere possesses no stancher friend in the world than the wife of Baron Frederick von Arnold."

"I rejoice to see that your Majesty has at last recognised this important fact," the Chancellor said.

"At last?" the Emperor retorted. "Had I ever doubted it, Count Capricius, believe me, much of that which has now become history would never have come to pass. But enough of this subject," he broke off. "We are losing valuable time. I have no more need of your Excellency's services for the present. There is work here,"—pointing to the mass of documents and reports piled up in a huge heap upon

151

the Imperial writing-table—"sufficient to occupy me until we meet again."

"But the Franconian demands?" the Chancellor inquired, somewhat aghast at this abrupt termination of an audience which so far left him no wiser than he had been before. "I beg to remind your Majesty that the term stipulated for the definite answer to this insolent ultimatum expires at 10 o'clock to-morrow morning. Has your Majesty considered—"

"Considered?" said the Emperor with flashing eyes. "What is there to consider? If my presence at the head of my army is not answer superabundant to impertinences of this character, let his Excellency the Franconian Ambassador fetch his answer from me in person. By heaven, he shall not lack it!"

He waved his hand imperiously, in token of dismissal, and the Chancellor, bowing deferentially, retired. At the door, however, he turned back once more.

"And with reference to the Baroness von Arnold," he said, "I may assume that I have your Majesty's authority to order the immediate arrest of this lady."

"Nay, my dear Chancellor," said the Emperor, "it is not my custom to adopt such drastic measures against ladies. Moreover, your suggestion, as usual, comes somewhat late. I have already issued my instructions with regard to the Baroness von Arnold to one upon whose skill and discretion I have reason to place implicit confidence. He is empowered to convey my commands to the Baroness in such form as will render them more palatable than your Excellency might be inclined to make them."

"Then the Baroness—"

"Will be in Berolingen to-morrow," the Emperor answered briefly, turning his back upon the Minister.

Still the latter tarried.

"May I venture to ask," he said, "who it is that your Majesty has thus honoured with your confidence?"

The Emperor raised his eyebrows as if in surprise at the audacity of the inquiry. Then he strode deliberately across the space that separated him from his bold questioner, and stood facing him for several seconds with an expression which made him regret his temerity.

The Chancellor prepared himself for an explosion of wrath. But he proved mistaken.

"I will tell you, sir," the Emperor said at last, in sharp, cutting tones. "It is the man to whom I perhaps owe it that I still possess the crown I wear—no thanks to your Excellency and the rest of my Ministers."

With these words he turned abruptly on his heel, and left the Chancellor standing at the threshold confused and abashed. Whether the latter understood to whom the Emperor was referring is a matter for conjecture. But he bit his lip furiously, and withdrew in silence.

CHAPTER XV
In the Imperial Ante-chamber

Berolingen had slept at last upon the exciting events of the 25th of June, and the capital had once more resumed its ordinary appearance. Gossip of every description was still rife among all classes of the inhabitants as to the possible consequences of the momentous crisis through which the country had just passed. Rumours, springing no one knew whence, that the Government had fallen, that the Imperial Chancellor had been dismissed in disgrace, and that some vast, far-reaching conspiracy had been unmasked, in which personages of the most exalted station were involved, and which had aimed at nothing less than the complete overthrow of the Imperial supremacy, were being busily weighed and discussed in the cafes and in the streets, in the places of public business and in private circles. But inasmuch as they were practically no more than the echoes of the same sombre convictions which had laid hold of the public mind and exercised it during the past three weeks, their effect was harmless enough.

A sense of absolute security had now come over the people, and the only place where there was still real excitement bubbling among them was the Bourse—a fact that will scarcely occasion surprise when it is remembered that, according to the careful computations of a well-known contemporary statistician; the unprecedented fluctuations in the public stocks and securities of Europe on that one single day represented a sum of no less than two hundred millions sterling. The cost to financial Europe of these three eventful weeks of the world's history has been estimated by the same eminent authority at a total figure of such magnitude that it would take the ordinary reader's breath away were I to mention it.

The busiest man in the whole Arminian Empire that day was the Emperor himself. Yet he of all others should have been sorely in need of rest. He had not snatched even a quarter of an hour's sleep during the night, but had worked uninterruptedly at the task he had set himself with his usual dogged persistency and disregard of everything but the stern call of duty until the day dawned and the Castle was again astir. At six o'clock the Chief of his Military Cabinet had arrived, and remained in conference with his Majesty until eight, leaving him, as he admiringly confessed, as fresh and vigorous as if he had just risen from an eight hours' undisturbed slumber. Then Minister after Minister had followed to receive the Imperial comments upon the voluminous documents submitted the previous afternoon, every one of which the Emperor had carefully perused, mastering its contents, however intricate, down to the very smallest detail, with that extraordinary facility that never ceased to astonish those who knew him.

Until noon he had been thus occupied, with but few intervals, devoted to the reception of the various Princes and Princesses of the Imperial family, and one or two favoured members of the diplomatic corps, among the latter in particular Sir Edward Hammer, with whom he had conversed for some time very graciously.

Towards 10 o'clock his Excellency the Franconian Ambassador had arrived at the Castle, causing an extra flutter of excitement among the groups waiting in the Imperial ante-rooms and in the corridors and lobbies outside. The object of his visit was well known, and every one remained on the tip-toe of anxious expectation during the few minutes that he was closeted with the Emperor.

It was a remarkably brief interview, and its result could only be guessed at. The Ambassador had entered the Imperial presence with an air of uneasiness which he endeavoured in vain to carry off by an extra display of pomposity. When he issued forth again, scarcely five minutes afterwards, his face was pale, his lips were compressed, and his whole demeanour was expressive of intense agitation. He hurried through the ante-room, taking no heed of the chamberlain who escorted him with all due ceremony to the door of his carriage.

What had passed between him and the Emperor during those few minutes no one knew, nor ever learned. The next person who was ushered into his Majesty's presence, immediately after the Ambassador had left, found him quietly engaged in sticking tiny flags of various colours into an immense military chart of

Franconia, which lay spread out upon a low table in the middle of the Imperial study. To all appearances he had been thus occupied for the last half-hour or so, and beyond a certain grim smile of satisfaction that hovered about his lips there was nothing to indicate that he had recently passed through any unusual emotion.

It may not be uninteresting, however, in this connection, to recall two significant paragraphs which appeared on the evening of that day in the Government organs of Arminia and Franconia respectively.

The latest edition of the Berolingen 'Official Gazette' of that day contained the following notice:—

"His Majesty the Emperor worked for several hours during the morning with the Chief of his Military Cabinet, and issued orders of an important character respecting the concentration of the Imperial forces. All leaves of absence granted to officers of the Imperial army have been peremptorily cancelled, and the annual levy of recruits has been ordered to take place immediately. His Majesty subsequently received his Excellency the Franconian Ambassador in a short audience."

The journal of the Government issued the same evening at Patropolis brought the following reassuring piece of news:—

"Satisfactory explanations have now been forthcoming from the Arminian Government with regard to the frontier questions and the undue amassing of troops in the border garrisons. His Majesty the Arminian Emperor has given our Ambassador at the Court of Berolingen personally the most explicit assurances of his friendly and pacific intentions, and has expressed his regret at the unfortunate misunderstanding that has arisen. The incident is now closed."

But the audience of the Franconian Ambassador, with its abrupt termination, was only one among the many excitements that set all brains in the Castle a-thinking and all lips a-whispering that morning. Nor was it by any means the incident that gave rise to most speculation. Rumours of the Emperor's decision to adopt stringent measures against all those who were suspected of having aided and abetted the Duke of Cumbermere in his treasonable proceedings had reached the Castle, and were discussed on all hands with the utmost interest. The quasi-arrest of the Baroness von Arnold, whose alleged secret machinations were currently reported to have deeply incensed the Emperor, was understood to be but a preliminary to a host of other arrests shortly to be expected, and persons of every degree and kind were named as being on the list of these suspects.

155

The probable fate of Doctor Georg Hofer, the Imperial private secretary, was in particular a subject of eager conjecture. It was known that soon after the Emperor's return Doctor Hofer had solicited an audience of his Majesty, which had been peremptorily refused. Failing in his attempt to gain speech of his Imperial master, the Doctor had then resorted to the expedient of addressing a letter to his Majesty, which, however, had been returned in like manner, unopened, with the curt notification that the Emperor would hold no communication with his secretary until such time as he should himself appoint.

As the morning wore on, fresh topics of interest arose, which diverted the general attention from the Imperial Secretary. Telegrams from headquarters in Noveria began to arrive in quick succession, bringing details of the movements of the Imperial troops. The Emperor's orders to proceed to attack the insurgent forces had been promptly obeyed, and already during the night news had come in of skirmishes between portions of the rebel forces and the advance detachments of the Imperial Army.

The result of the contest was of course a foregone conclusion. In spite of their numbers, which had increased enormously during these three weeks of inactivity on the part of the Arminian Government, and in spite, too, of the fact that the country folk in the Noverian province sided more or less openly with the partisans of the old dynasty, especially since the report had spread that the young Duke of Cumbermere himself was at their head, these untrained and undisciplined rebels could stand no chance whatever against the regular forces opposed to them. But the Emperor, so it was rumoured, was determined to effect the capture of the Duke of Cumbermere at all costs, and had issued commands to direct the attack in such wise as to prevent the possibility of the Duke's escape. Hence, for all that was known, it might be evening before any definite news of the destruction of the insurgent forces arrived.

Meanwhile everyone was discussing what would happen to the Duke when he was captured. Would he be treated as an ordinary rebel? Would he forfeit his liberty, perhaps his life? And, if so, what would be the consequences? The Emperor, all the world knew, would brook no interference with his own affairs, nor allow any considerations of sentiment or even policy to weigh against that which he deemed to be just and right. Yet the Duke, although he belonged to a deposed dynasty, and had, like his father before him, throughout all these years steadily refused to hold any intercourse with the European courts, because he considered that they had shamefully acquiesced in the act of despoliation which had deprived him of his hereditary rights, still possessed powerful friends and relatives among the reigning families, who would be sure to intercede in his favour. Hence complications might arise, leading heaven knows where to. In short, in this, as in every other direction, the same question confronted these anxious speculators: How was it all going to end?

Had they but known it, the end was even then preparing.

Towards 1 o'clock the Minister of War arrived at the Castle, followed almost immediately by the Imperial Chancellor. They met in the grand vestibule, and after conversing privately for a few moments, proceeded together to the Imperial antechamber.

As they passed through the somewhat crowded room, those who respectfully made way for them scanned their faces with eager curiosity. It was evident that matters of paramount interest had brought them here at this hour, and from the pleased expression on the countenance of the War Minister it was not difficult to guess that news of some decisive action in Noveria had arrived.

The Chancellor's face was grave, and there was a touch of anxiety in his eyes. But he, too, could scarcely conceal the pleasurable excitement that was working within him, and when, in response to a whispered query addressed to him in passing by a gray-headed old warrior in a field-marshal's uniform, he was seen to hold up a telegraphic despatch with a significant smile, all doubt as to the nature of the business that had brought him and his colleague to the Castle was over. The old field marshal was immediately surrounded by a dozen eager questioners, and before the two Ministers had reached the Imperial aide-decamp, whose duty it was to announce them to his Majesty, the news that the rebel forces, with their leader, had made unconditional surrender, was in everyone's possession.

That the Noverian rebellion, like the revolution in Berolingen, should have ended without bloodshed was news so gladdening that for the moment the graver question of the capture of the Duke of Cumbermere was entirely lost sight of. In an instant everyone was excitedly commenting upon the welcome tidings, and exchanging congratulatory observations with his neighbour.

The incident of the entry of the two Ministers had engrossed the general attention to such a degree that the arrival of another personage, who had followed almost at their heels, had passed quite unobserved—a fact the more remarkable in that the personage in question was totally unknown to every one present, and would, therefore, under other circumstances, have been the subject of the keenest scrutiny to the occupants of the Imperial ante-chamber.

157

This new-comer, in fact, was Sir John Templeton. Taking advantage of the momentary delay in the progress of the two Ministers through the ante-room, he had managed to reach the aide-de-camp on duty at the door to the Emperor's apartments before they did, and he had just made himself known to that officer when the Chancellor and his colleague came up and demanded to be announced to his Majesty.

Sir John stepped back with a bow, to which the Imperial Chancellor responded with a frown of displeasure. The aide-decamp disappeared into the Emperor's cabinet, and returned almost immediately, leaving the door to the Imperial sanctum open. The Chancellor and the Minister of War stepped forward as a matter of course to enter, when to their astonishment the aide-de-camp barred their passage with a deprecatory gesture.

"I beg your Excellencies' pardon," he said. "His Majesty awaits Sir John Templeton."

And beckoning to that personage, he ushered him into the Emperor's cabinet, leaving the two dignitaries standing upon the threshold speechless with surprise and chagrin. The Chancellor in particular was white with disappointment and rage, and, when a moment later the officer reappeared and once more took up his position at the door, he so far forgot himself as to take him to task for having neglected his duty.

"His Majesty," he said, in a voice loud enough to be heard throughout the chamber, "cannot have understood that two of his Ministers are waiting to speak with him on State affairs of the utmost urgency. You will be good enough to ascertain if it is the Emperor's pleasure to delay receiving despatches of the most vital moment to the Empire which we have to lay before his Majesty."

The officer acquiesced silently, and once more entered the Imperial cabinet. He was back again in a twinkling, closing the door carefully behind him. The group in the ante-room had meanwhile drawn as close to the two Ministers as respect would allow in order to hear the result of this somewhat venturesome proceeding on the part of the audience-seekers.

"Well?" queried the Chancellor, as the aide-de-camp hesitated, with evident embarrassment. "What are his Majesty's commands?"

"The same that I have already communicated to your Excellency. His Majesty is engaged on important business with Sir John Templeton," the officer said, with manifest evasion, which exasperated the Chancellor.

"What were his Majesty's words, sir?" he asked, sternly.

"His Majesty's commands to me were that I was to go to the devil," the aide-decamp, answered, now with perfect imperturbability.

"Is that all?" the Chancellor asked, biting his lip.

"His Majesty desires your Excellencies to await his pleasure," the officer replied.

"Are these his Majesty's own words, sir, or yours?" the Chancellor asked, haughtily.

"They are mine," the officer rejoined, quietly. "His Majesty's own words were: 'Tell their Excellencies that they shall wait until they are blue in the face, if it so pleases me.'"

There was not a trace of humour in the expression with which the officer conveyed this unceremonious piece of intelligence. But it caused a slight titter among the listeners grouped around, which, however, was instantly suppressed. It is a dangerous proceeding in Arminia to laugh at the discomfiture of an Imperial Chancellor—at least, it is unwise to do so before his resignation had been handed in and accepted—and these wary courtiers and officials knew and well appreciated this important fact.

Disdaining to notice the involuntary manifestation of mirth called forth by the dry delivery of a message which had probably never been intended for literal transmission, the Chancellor and his colleague retired to a window recess, where they remained conversing until it should please his Arminian Majesty to grant them the desired interview.

They had not to wait long. After about ten minutes, the Emperor's bell rang. The aide-de-camp on duty darted once more into the Cabinet, and issuing forth again at once summoned the two Ministers to his Majesty's presence.

They glanced at one another in surprise, for the man on whose account they had been kept waiting had apparently not quitted the Emperor. Was he to be present while important affairs of State were being discussed? Such a thing would be without precedent in the history of Arminian governments.

But there was no time to demur now, even had their Excellencies been so inclined. The eccentricities of their Imperial master were incalculable, and they had no alternative but to submit to them in patience.

CHAPTER XVI

159

The Revelation

Part One

While these little scenes, trifling perhaps in the view of the ordinary reader, but of exceeding interest to these whom they concerned, were being enacted in the Imperial ante-chamber, two of the persons about whose fate, unknown to themselves, so many minds were busy speculating, sat closeted in the library, which, as the reader may remember from a former description, separated the abode of the Imperial secretary from the apartments of the Emperor.

Those two persons were Doctor Georg Hofer and his beautiful sister, the Baroness von Arnold.

The arrival of the young Baroness at the Castle, under the courteous escort of Sir John Templeton, had passed almost without notice in the bustle and confusion that prevailed everywhere save in the immediate entourage of the Emperor himself.

It was nearly five months since brother and sister had met, and during that period momentous changes had taken place in both their lives—how momentous, indeed, neither of them at that moment realised. The thoughts of the one were full of the bitterness which had accumulated within him in the course of these last few weeks; those of the other were divided between her teaming desire to conciliate the affection of the brother whom she had so deeply offended, and her agonizing anxiety as to the fate of the husband who had superseded him in her heart.

As she gazed upon the stern, implacable face opposite her, something akin to a feeling of resentment arose within the Baroness at the thought that in this her moment of dire trouble the brother upon whom she might have hoped to lean for support should have nothing but reproaches to address to her. For he had reproached her, almost before a word of welcome had passed his lips; had reproached her with her marriage, and with its consequences, not the least among which he declared was the destruction of his dearest and most cherished hope.

What hope? Certain recollections came back to her—of differences between them, which she had always regarded lightly, of certain schemes, from which she had shrunk instinctively, though but half-conscious of their real import. Indeed, what had she really known of the plans of this brother of hers? She had never learned enough of their nature either to approve or disapprove of them. How, then, could she have been the means of thwarting them?

But she had no mind at present to dwell upon these thoughts. What she had learned within the last few minutes had bewildered her senses, and she could fix her mind upon nothing save the one question: What had taken her husband from her side? He had left her suddenly, almost without warning, that previous morning after their short conversation on the terrace of Arnoldshausen, on a mission, as he had said, of paramount importance to the Duke of Cumbermere himself. It was all he would tell her, excepting to bid her be tranquil, and assure her that he was venturing into no danger; that he would not be separated from her for longer than a day at the worst, and that then she should judge him.

It was these last words that kept ringing in her ears; now more than ever, since this peremptory summons to Berolingen, which had startled her indescribably, in spite of the perfect courtesy and profound respect of the messenger who had brought it, and who had escorted her to the capital. She had not dared question him as to the whereabouts of her husband, nor had he opened his lips to her on any other subject but that of her brother, of whose safety he had been at pains to assure her; why, she had not known until this moment. The stupendous events that had taken place during these three weeks of supreme happiness to herself—a happiness that would have been perfect but for the growing fear that she had for ever forfeited her brother's love—the disappearance of the Arminian Emperor and its innumerable far-reaching consequences, the rising in Noveria—unfortunate Noveria—her brother's precarious position in Berolingen, and the treachery and deception to which he had fallen a victim—she had learned all this within the last few minutes from his own lips, and it had burst upon her with such overwhelming force that she could as yet scarcely realise it.

"Georg," she murmured at last, "it was cruel of you to leave me all this while without news. If I have made my own choice of happiness, can it justify you in casting me off, in severing the bond that has so long united us?"

He looked at her in surprise, and rising from his seat went over to her.

"I don't understand," he said. "It is you, not I, that have kept silence these three weeks, Marie. All my letters have remained unanswered—" He stopped short, struck by the puzzled expression on her face. "Marie," he exclaimed, "is it possible that these letters have never been permitted to reach you, that you have been left in

161

ignorance of all these inexplicable events? Ah, whose was the hand that intercepted them?"

"No word has reached me from you," she answered, with a troubled look, "since that terrible letter in which you threatened me with your curse, if I persisted in giving my hand to the man I loved. It was cruel, Georg; and it was not wise," she added, with a flash of pride. "We are of the same blood, and more easily led than driven."

The words seemed to incense him. He stepped towards her and seized her hand almost roughly.

"Do you know what you have done, child?" he said, gazing at her with a look of stern anger. "You have ruined the last hope of the house of Noveria. Its fortunes were in your hands, and you have destroyed them for the sake of this beggarly fortune-hunter, who has forsaken the cause of his country and basely betrayed the Prince he had sworn to serve."

The Baroness fell back with blanched lips. The reproach against herself was so startling that it made her momentarily forget the insult to her husband by which it was followed.

"I?" she exclaimed. "Surely this is madness. How can my heart's choice have affected the fortunes of Noveria?"

"How?" he said, still retaining his grasp on her wrist in the passionate anger that seemed to possess him. "Are you still blind? Do you know what first caused the Emperor to cool in his friendship towards his private secretary?"

He pronounced his title in a tone of lofty contempt, which left little doubt as to the value it possessed in his estimation. But the Baroness scarcely noticed it. She hung upon his lips with a shrinking dread of that which might fall from them.

"It was you," he continued. "Your refusal to follow me to Berolingen, which he attributed to my influence, first kindled his wrath, and it was from that moment that his coldness and distrust commenced—to end in this."

A strange, pained look crept into the eyes of the Baroness.

"Then it was at the Emperor's instance," she said in a low voice, "that you suggested my settling in the capital six months ago?"

"He had seen you," he answered.

"Seen me?"

"Twice."

"When?"

"Once in the Wettinian capital, and again a month later at Castel, where you came to meet me. Do you remember my companion on those occasions, Count Ravensburg, whose apparently sly and retiring habits excited your curiosity? It was the Emperor. The country was clamouring for his marriage, and he had set his heart on visiting the courts of Arminia in disguise, in order to judge for himself of the charms of those among whom it was proposed that he should select an Imperial consort. After Castel his interest in these secret expeditions suddenly waned, until your refusal to join me in the Arminian capital, when it revived once more. Then he again resumed these journeys, but thenceforward he went alone."

The Baroness stood silent, seemingly unable to grasp the full meaning of his words.

"And what would have occurred, had I consented to live in this place, which I have learned to hate as the hearth of all my country's misfortunes?" she asked, at last, without removing her earnest eyes from his.

"What would have occurred?" he ejaculated passionately. "You would have had the Arminian Emperor at your feet."

"For how long?" she asked,

"For how long?" he echoed.

"Yes; for how long?" she repeated. "Do you believe I would have concealed from him the abhorrence with which his very name inspires me?"

His lip curled disdainfully.

"Just because you would not have concealed it," he said, "I knew that he would have been captivated by a charm of double strength. Do you imagine I have studied him and his nature all these weary months in vain?"

"His nature?" she said, with a touch of angry scorn. "You speak only of him. But what of me? Have not you yourself taught me to hate this man and all that pertains to him? And do you suppose his love, even had it touched my heart, would have been powerful enough to remove the cause for that hatred?"

"What if it had removed it, Marie?" he said. "What if the Emperor's heart had yielded what the endeavours of years have failed to obtain from him and his predecessors—the restoration of Noveria to its rightful Sovereign? By heaven," he cried, bitterly, "had you but known it, this was indeed in your power to achieve; and with my aid you would have achieved it."

"At what price?" she asked, coldly.

"At the price of your hand and heart," he answered.

She had known what he would answer before he spoke; yet the words struck her like a blow.

"Georg, Georg," she exclaimed. "And you would have had me barter myself for this?"

"Have you not flung away what is far more precious for a name that will be uttered with loathing wherever true hearts beat for Noveria and her Prince?" he cried. "For this renegade and traitor you have sacrificed—faugh," he broke off, "the thought maddens me, even now."

He would have turned away from her with a gesture of impotent rage. But she had risen at his last words, and now stood before him with heaving bosom and flashing eyes, the beautiful counterpart of himself. For a moment neither of them spoke, but remained facing each other in total silence. Indeed, so deeply engrossed were they in themselves that, in spite of the stillness which reigned, they did not notice that the door communicating with the Imperial apartments had been quietly opened, and that a third person had entered.

Seeing the strange attitude of the two, the new-comer remained, half-surprised, half-expectant, standing upon the threshold, while through the door, which he left open, the curious faces of others could be seen peering into the room from the closet beyond.

At last the Baroness spoke in clear, ringing tones.

"You have uttered words which are unworthy of you," she said. "Now listen to me, my brother. I will uphold the honour and loyalty of him whose name I bear with my dying breath, against you and all the world, even if it cost me that which was my dearest possession until he won my heart—your brotherly affection. Nay, hear me out, for it is best we should understand one another once for all. Were he proved to be your bitterest enemy, Georg—which heaven forbid!—yet he would still remain the husband to whom I have given my love, my all, irrevocably; whose honour is my honour, and whose fate, come what may, shall be my fate."

An impressive pause followed these words. It was broken by the voice of him at the door—a voice which betrayed a strange emotion.

"Spoken like a true woman, Doctor Georg Hofer," it said. "Indeed, Baron Frederick von Arnold recognises but one judge between himself and the Duke of Cumbermere; and that Judge is his own wife."

The effect of this speech upon the two to whom it was addressed was very different. Doctor Georg Hofer started at the sound of the voice he knew so well, and drew himself up with a gesture of proud defiance. His sister, on the other hand, gave a great

164

gasp, and, turning quickly, faced the speaker with a look of half-incredulous surprise. As her eyes fell upon him, however, she uttered a cry of delight, and the next instant, before the last word had yet left his lips, she darted across the room and flung herself sobbing on his breast.

He had stepped forward quickly to receive her in his arms, and bending over her as she nestled in his embrace, he touched her hair reverently with his lips.

The scene that now followed would have offered wonderful possibilities to an artist gifted with a quick eye for contrasts. The group of onlookers in the closet beyond had meanwhile pushed forward into the room, and now stood in a cluster upon the threshold and in the doorway. The expression on the faces of all, save one only, was one of such consummate consternation and horror that one might have imagined they were assisting at the supreme crisis of some terrible tragedy rather than witnessing a touching meeting between a husband and a wife.

Dr. Hofer's face had suddenly undergone a complete change. His attitude was no longer one of defiance, but of speechless amazement. Twice he made an effort to say something, but his lips refused to articulate, and he stood merely gazing, as if in a dream, upon the scene before him.

The only person who seemed oblivious of everything around her was the Baroness herself.

At last, with a mighty effort, Doctor Georg Hofer shook off the numbness that had apparently seized him. He took a quick step forward, and then halted abruptly.

"Marie," he said, in a tone in which so many different emotions seemed to be struggling for utterance that it was impossible to fix and distinguish any single one, "if this man is your husband, he is not what you believe him to be."

She winced slightly, then, looking up, turned her head to him with an expression of silent reproach, but made no reply. Perhaps, however, the strange look on his face startled her, for she moved her eyes quickly from his to those of her husband, as if to appeal to him for an explanation. But he gave none. He merely returned her gaze with a steady, earnest look, which, if it contained a trace of anxious anticipation, was yet the same frank, fearless look she had always known and loved.

"Marie," her brother continued, now in cold, measured tones, "this man whom you claim as your husband is not Baron Frederick von Arnold. It is his Majesty Willibald II., Arminian Emperor and King of Brandenburg."

The words fell upon her like so many crushing weights. But for a moment she appeared unable to grasp their meaning. Then of a sudden the colour forsook her cheeks, and her eyes wandered with a helpless look of appeal to the countenance of him whom she had thus heard apostrophised, and whose gaze was still bent upon her with the same earnest, expectant expression as before. From him they glanced furtively to the group of stern and silent figures in the background, of whose presence she seemed only now to have become conscious, and back again once more to her brother. Slowly the comprehension of it all appeared to dawn upon her, her breath came and went painfully, and she trembled so violently that she was obliged to clutch for support at the arm from which she had just half released herself.

But the weakness lasted only an instant. With a sudden passionate gesture she flung herself entirely free and stood alone and unsupported with flaming eyes before the man in whom she saw represented at one and the same time all she had learned to hate and all she had learned to love.

All the while the young Emperor had never removed his eyes from hers; nor did the steady, earnest look on his face change even now for one instant. But his lips pronounced a word, in a tone so low and so tender that none but she could have heard it.

"Remember!"

As it struck upon her ear her features softened, and the warm blood returned to her cheeks with a sudden rush, suffusing them with a rosy tinge.

Remember! Had it needed his reminder? What memories, indeed, did not come crowding into her mind at this moment? And perhaps the loudest and most pressing of them all was the memory of what her brother had told her before this last astounding revelation came upon her. She glanced wistfully across at him, where he stood, pale and proud, apparently waiting for some utterance from her. Yet what could he expect? What dared he expect? She took a faltering step towards him, then wavered, and stood still again. It was a moment of intense inner conflict, each suggestive stage of which was depicted in her face with painful distinctness—a dumb, pathetic little history complete in itself. Suddenly, with a swift, impetuous movement, she raised her hand to her eyes, as if to banish the stern, unbending countenance from her sight; then she tossed back her fair head resolutely.

"Georg, Georg," she cried. "What is the Arminian Emperor to me? This man is my husband."

166

A quick flash of intense joy lighted up the young Emperor's face. The next instant he had clasped her once more passionately in his arms.

"Come," he whispered, simply. And, waving aside the silent group of men who blocked the doorway, he led her gently away.

CHAPTER XVII
The Revelation

Part Two

For the space of fully a minute complete silence reigned in the library; no one spoke or stirred. But, from the varied expressions on the faces of those who had witnessed this extraordinary scene, it was not difficult to gauge the emotions that were passing in their minds.

The group at the door, as the reader will no doubt have partly guessed, consisted of the Imperial Chancellor, Count Capricius, his colleague the Minister of War, the two chief officers of the Imperial household, and last, not least, Sir John Templeton.

The latter was the first to move, and as he stepped forward with the evident intention of approaching the Imperial secretary, who still stood motionless, gazing almost vacantly in the direction of the doorway through which the Emperor and his bride had just passed out, the spell that had bound his companions seemed suddenly to break. With an exclamation, which sounded ominously like an oath, Count Capricius strode forward, and intercepted Sir John Templeton's passage.

Doctor Hofer glanced at the two men with a look of haughty inquiry. Sir John stopped instantly, and drew back to await events.

While the incidents described at the close of the foregoing chapter were passing. Count Capricius, like his companions, had stood literally rooted to the spot, scarcely realising the true import of all he heard and saw. Now it gradually crushed in upon him, and, relieved from the restraining influence of the Emperor's presence, his blunt and somewhat impetuous nature, which, with all its foibles and shortcomings, was at bottom honesty and loyalty itself, asserted its sway, and his feelings took their natural course.

"Sir," he exclaimed, addressing Doctor Hofer in a tone of mingled desperation and rage, "this, then, has been the intrigue which has nearly cost Arminia her existence? Great heaven, what a fatality! The Emperor, upon whose marriage the future of the Empire depends, inveigled into a morganatic union with a chaplain's daughter."

The haughty stare on Doctor Hofer's countenance did not relax, and the Chancellor, almost wringing his hands as all the consequences of the event that had astonished him so completely broke more and more forcibly upon his understanding, turned away, incapable for the moment of giving further utterance to his feelings.

To him this astounding step taken by his Imperial master meant the collapse of all and everything. What would the world say of a sovereign who had callously sacrificed all his country's interests for the sake of gratifying a foolish passion for an obscure beauty—the low-born sister of a desperate adventurer? For, that Doctor Hofer was an adventurer, and an adventurer of the most dangerous type, had long become a rooted conviction in the mind of Count Capricius. It must be he, and he alone, who had made this monstrous thing possible. The Emperor's strong aversion to contract a marriage with one of the many European Princesses who had in turn been proposed to him had grown perceptibly since his relations with this interloping secretary commenced; so much so, indeed, that for the last six months no one had courage to moot the question to him again. His Majesty had forbidden all mention of the matter, declaring peremptorily that he would make his choice at his own time and pleasure, and required no counsel and advice on the subject.

Here, then, was the result. One hope only remained—that the Emperor would yet be persuaded of the folly of his own act and agree to an annulment of his marriage before the knowledge of it reached the public. Such things had occurred before now. Why should they not occur again? There was a notable case on record within quite recent times—a case where no less a personage than the uncle of his present Majesty, and a reigning sovereign like himself, had committed a similar act of folly, and been induced under pressure to revoke it. In what scathing terms had the Emperor, then Prince Willibald, referred to this well known scandal! Yet that sovereign's act was a far less reprehensible one in the Count's eyes, for at least it had involved no question of succession.

The precedent was valuable, and the memory of it, and of his Majesty's attitude on that occasion, momentarily reassured the Chancellor. He turned once more brusquely to Doctor Hofer.

"This unhappy union must be dissolved, without delay," he said. "His Majesty, I feel confident, is too much imbued with the sense of the duty he owes to his country to persist, on calm reflection, in maintaining a position that would be disastrous to its most vital interests. He will yield to true counsel, unless the pernicious influence to which he has succumbed should prove stronger than I believe it to be. It is to you, therefore, that we look—"

But Doctor Hofer interrupted him with a gesture of cold disdain.

"Your Excellency," he said calmly, "is singularly ill-advised in addressing these remarks to me. This marriage, which meets with so much displeasure on your Excellency's part, has had neither my consent nor approval, and I am the last person in the world likely to succeed in bringing about its annulment. The question that is exercising your Excellency's mind is manifestly one which no one can decide but those whom it most nearly concerns—the Emperor and his consort the Empress."

He laid a slight stress upon the last word, then turned on his heel before the Chancellor could recover himself sufficiently to reply, and striding haughtily to the door leading to his apartments, passed out of the room without another word.

The Chancellor gazed after him in dumb astonishment, until his stalwart figure had vanished. Then he cut a look of almost comically helpless appeal at his colleagues, who had drawn near during the foregoing conversation, and from them to Sir John Templeton.

"The Empress, indeed! Is he mad?" he ejaculated at last. "This marriage not had his consent? Is he insolent enough to suppose—by heaven, he shall learn at least that there are men in Arminia who will not submit tamely to his upstart pride."

And glowing with newly-kindled wrath, he advanced ponderously to the door, intending to follow the object of his resentment and renew the attack upon his own ground.

This time it was Sir John Templeton who intercepted his passage. Stepping quickly forward, he barred the way.

"Pardon me, your Excellency," he said. "But you are about to do what you will assuredly regret."

"What?" exclaimed the irate Chancellor. "Do you dare to meddle with me and my doings? Stand aside, sir."

"I will stand aside when you have listened to me," Sir John replied, unmoved. "Nay, no violence, sir," he added, sternly, as the Chancellor, beside himself with anger, made a gesture towards his sword hilt, as if he contemplated running his adversary through the body. "I am here at his Majesty's commands, and it will be well for you to respect them. When you have heard me, you will act as you please. But I doubt if your Excellency will then still think fit to carry out your present intention of renewing an argument in which you must infallibly be worsted."

At the mention of the Emperor's name the Chancellor's choler had received a slight check. But it now burst forth again afresh.

"Worsted? By this scoundrelly adventurer?" he cried, flourishing his arms fiercely. "Who in the devil's name is this Doctor Hofer that I should shrink from speaking my mind to him as I list?"

"That," said Sir John, "is a question very much to the point, and one which your Excellency would have done better to inform yourself upon sooner. I will answer it. The personage to whom your Excellency is pleased to refer to as Doctor Georg Hofer is better known as his Royal Highness the Duke of Cumbermere."

The effect of these quietly spoken words was astonishing. The Chancellor fell back with a look of blank incredulity, almost treading upon the toes of his companions behind him, while these latter stood open-mouthed, scarcely knowing whether they were to take the matter seriously or to treat it as a huge joke. Count Capricius himself was at first inclined to regard it as an insolent jest, and to resent it accordingly. But a glance at the old diplomatist's calm and serious face convinced him that, incomprehensible as it might seem to him, he had heard the truth.

"The Duke of Cumbermere?" he stammered at last, after a moment's silence. "This must be a fable."

"If your Excellency is of that opinion," Sir John rejoined, quietly, "I have nothing more to say. It is, however, within your Excellency's power to ascertain whether I have spoken the truth by appealing direct to his Majesty the Emperor for a corroboration of my statement. Whether it will be wise to do so under the circumstances, I leave your Excellency to judge for yourself."

"But if this is true," the Chancellor murmured, "the Emperor has in fact married—"

"The Emperor has married her Royal Highness the Princess Marie Victoria Augusta of Noveria," Sir John said, "sometime known as Demoiselle Hofer."

170

The four men stared at one another blankly. The news seemed too good to be credited.

"But all this is impossible," the Minister of War burst out at last, stepping forward with an air of complete bewilderment. "We have definite intelligence that the Duke of Cumbermere was captured at the head of the insurgent forces in Noveria this morning; nay, I hold in my hand a despatch written a few hours ago by his Majesty himself to the Commander-in-Chief of the Imperial Army in Noveria, ordering the extreme penalty of the law to be enforced against this unfortunate Prince, should he fall into our hands."

Sir John Templeton looked at the speaker in surprise.

"Do I gather from this," he asked, "that your Excellency has ventured to delay the transmission of this despatch?"

"And what if I have, sir?" the Minister answered, haughtily. "If my having done so should save his Majesty from a life long bitter regret by giving him time to reflect upon the inevitable consequences of an act which all Europe will condemn, I will cheerfully bear the responsibility, whatever it may cost me."

Sir John Templeton shrugged his shoulders.

"It is no concern of mine," he replied. "But this action, if I am not much mistaken, will cost your Excellency your portfolio, if not something more precious still. I know his Majesty to be very much in earnest in his intentions towards this particular captive."

"But, in the name of all reason," the Chancellor interposed, "if the real Duke of Cumbermere is in Berolingen at this moment, who is this man who has been acting as his double in Noveria?"

"It is the man, sir," Sir John answered, "who has played the part of the Duke of Cumbermere in America, while the Duke of Cumbermere assumed the character of Doctor Georg Hofer in Europe; in other words, Doctor Georg Hofer himself. As your Excellency will perceive," he went on, "he has somewhat over-acted his role, and seized the opportunity afforded him by his Prince's unfortunate position at the court of his Majesty the Emperor to attempt to step entirely into his shoes, and make a bold bid for the crown of Noveria on his own account. The fact that the person of the Duke of Cumbermere is practically unknown to his adherents in Noveria rendered the success of this fraudulent imposture only too easy. For obvious reasons, however, his Majesty the Emperor is naturally anxious that the identity of this arch traitor to his Prince and benefactor should be established beyond a doubt, to the satisfaction of Europe in general and Noveria in particular. Hence this stern order to proceed against the alleged Duke of Cumbermere with swift and merciless rigour. His Majesty is a keen judge of human character, and knows that the man who will sacrifice every instinct of honour and loyalty for the sake of living as a king is not the man to covet the doubtful distinction of dying as a duke."

It was evident from the looks of those who listened to this lucid exposition that it carried absolute conviction to their minds. Indeed, its correctness could scarcely admit of a doubt.

Some moments passed, however, before the four Excellencies recovered from their intense surprise. The first to speak was the Minister of War, who had grown strangely pale, and whose face was now twitching like that of a man suffering bodily pain.

"Great heaven!" he stammered, "then this despatch to the Commander-in-Chief in Noveria—"

"Is an instance of his Majesty's admirable foresight, sir," Sir John Templeton said. "The Emperor is at this moment impatiently awaiting the news that Doctor Georg Hofer has saved his life by confessing that he is not the Duke of Cumbermere. I need hardly impress upon your Excellency the urgent necessity of repairing this unhappy omission to obey his Majesty's commands without delay, while there is yet time."

There was, indeed, no necessity for this piece of counsel. Before Sir John Templeton had finished speaking, the Minister of War had turned and fled from the room like one pursued by a thousand evil spirits.

An interval of silence followed his abrupt departure, during which Sir John glanced with a twinkle of amused interest in his eyes at the faces of those who had remained behind. Two of them had sunk in a state of half-collapse into chairs, being too much overcome by all they had heard and witnessed to support themselves any longer upon their legs. The Chancellor alone was still standing. But somehow his big, burly figure seemed less big and burly than usual, and he was wiping his brow nervously, as if his wits had been scattered and he were busily engaged in sweeping them together again.

"It is all incomprehensible—astounding," he murmured again and again, pacing the room in great perturbation. "The Princess Marie of Noveria Arminian Empress—her brother the Duke of Cumbermere himself at the court of Berolingen—while the man whose every movement has been carefully watched and reported to us all these years from America, in the belief that he was his Royal Highness, proves to be—"

"Doctor Georg Hofer, the son of the late King of Noveria's private chaplain and the too much trusted friend of his namesake the Noverian Pretender," Sir John said. "The fact, I fear, is undeniable."

"But what object can his Royal Highness have had in placing himself in this extraordinary position?"

"The object," Sir John said, "is surely not far to seek. His Royal Highness is not unlike the Emperor in so far that he possesses a strong inclination to manage his own affairs; and, indeed, it is more than likely that he would have succeeded to perfection in this very instance, had his Majesty not proved to be an even greater adept in this rare art than the Duke himself. No doubt the chance circumstance that his Highness attracted his Majesty's attention and won his friendship when studying under the name of Georg Hofer at the University of Bonn five years ago first suggested to him the possibility of bringing the weight of his personal influence permanently to bear upon the mind of the sovereign from whom he had so much to claim, and thus to insure the successful issue of the negotiations which have been pending for so many years between the Government of Brandenburg and the unfortunate house of Noveria whose heritage it has swallowed up. The Emperor's pressing offers of service to the man who had gained his youthful confidence probably ripened this idea, which would otherwise have died at its birth, into a firm resolve; and so the extraordinary event we are now contemplating came to pass."

"But the Princess," said the Chancellor, who had followed these remarks with increasing interest. "When and where did his Majesty see her? And by what means did he discover the true identity of his private secretary?"

"If your Excellency will recall to mind the correspondence that passed between his Royal Highness and his substitute in America," Sir John replied, "It may perhaps save the necessity for any further explanation. When Baron von Ellermann, the Minister of Police, grew suspicious of this correspondence of his Majesty's secretary with the supposed Noverian Pretender, and employed the means at his disposal to ascertain the nature of it, he little dreamed that his Majesty's eyes would thereby be opened to a fact far more important than the comparatively harmless reports on the progress of Noverian affairs at the court of Berolingen, of which the contents of these letters were composed. I mean the fact—which had escaped his Excellency, and everyone else who examined these letters—that the writer, and not the recipient, was the real Duke of Cumbermere. Carefully worded though they were to dupe the inquisitive reader— and, indeed, his Highness appears to have been so much alive to the likelihood of his correspondence being thus tampered with that he strictly preserved his assumed character even in the letters that passed between him and the Princess his sister—the double imposture was not kept up cleverly enough to deceive so keen a mind as that of his Majesty."

"Yet his Majesty concealed this important discovery, not only from his own advisers, but from the Duke himself?"

"No doubt for very good reasons."

"This, then," exclaimed Count Capricius, "explains the sudden rupture that took place between the Emperor and his private secretary six months ago."

"Not quite, I think," Sir John observed. "Judging from my own experience, I am convinced that his Majesty divined the true identity of the supposed Doctor Georg Hofer on reading the very first letter his Minister placed before him. But some time elapsed, as your Excellency may remember, after that before the coldness sprang up between them which ultimately resulted in his Royal Highness becoming virtually a prisoner at the court of Berolingen."

"You mean that his Majesty had other reasons than the mere fact of the deception that had been practised upon him for acting as he did?"

"Obviously," Sir John answered.

"And what were these reasons?"

Sir John cast a side glance at the questioner.

"That, sir," he replied, "is for the present a secret which no one knows but the Emperor himself."

"And, of course, the Duke of Cumbermere?" the Chancellor said, quickly.

"Possibly," Sir John rejoined, curtly.

"But about the Princess," the Chancellor went on, returning again to the chief subject of his curiosity. "Where did his Majesty see her; and why all this secrecy and disguise in making her his wife?"

"Where his Majesty first set eyes on her Royal Highness it is impossible for me to say," Sir John answered. "That he must have seen her on one of the various expeditions which he was in the habit of making in company with his private secretary, as your Excellency presumably knows, is certain. As for the reasons which prompted his Majesty to approach the Princess in the character of a man who is known to be one of the most loyal and enthusiastic adherents of the Noverian cause, they are not difficult to guess. Love is as potent with emperors and kings as it is with us humbler mortals. His Majesty desired to gain not only the Princess's hand, but her heart; and I may leave your Excellency, whose acquaintance with the sentiments of her Highness is as complete as my own, to judge for yourself whether he would have been likely to secure the latter had he wooed her as Emperor of Arminia."

"True," the Chancellor said, reflectively, "there might have been some awkward conditions in such a case. On my faith," he added, admiringly, "his Majesty seeks his equal as a diplomatist and as a tactician."

The conviction that the Emperor, besides securing a suitable consort to share his crown, had done an exceptionally good political stroke, was fast dawning in his Excellency's mind, and caused him unmingled satisfaction. It had always been his great fear that the Emperor would let himself be persuaded to make some unwise concession to the Noverian Pretender, whose recent succession to the sovereign Duchy of Brunsbuttel upon the death of the late Duke had made the question of his formal renunciation of all claims to the crown of Noveria a matter of increased importance to Brandenburg. Failing such a solemn renunciation on the part of the Duke of Cumbermere, the Emperor, upon the demise of the late Duke of Brunsbuttel, had laid an immediate embargo upon that State, which with its rich revenues had become for the time, like Noveria, incorporated in the kingdom of Brandenburg. To obtain the removal of this embargo, and an unconditional recognition of his right to enter upon the succession to the Duchy of Brunsbuttel without prejudice to his claim to the Noverian crown, was known to be the primary object of the Duke of Cumbermere, and there had been good reason to believe that his Majesty personally was not disinclined to yield the point. What had caused him to change his mind, as he undoubtedly had, if it were not his displeasure at having been played upon by the Duke, was a matter which puzzled the Imperial Chancellor considerably.

But there were other points that puzzled him still more, chief among which was the circumstance that the Emperor, having once won the bride he had courted under so strange a guise, should have so long delayed making himself known to her in his true character. That he would have risked the consequences involved in his protracted absence from the helm of affairs for the mere sake of prolonging the calm enjoyment of an undisturbed honeymoon seemed indeed quite out of the question.

"It is all a complete mystery," the Chancellor said. "Surely, what his Majesty did to-day he might just as well have done three or four weeks ago, and all this terrible trouble and anxiety would have been spared us."

175

"Your Excellency always forgets," Sir John remarked, with a slight shrug of the shoulders, "that his Majesty could have no knowledge of the events that were passing in his own country, seeing that his Government took every precaution to prevent them from gaining publicity. Moreover," he added, with a twinkle of humour in his eyes, "the course of his Majesty's honeymoon may not have run quite so smooth as he expected. It is not always as easy to undeceive as it is to deceive, especially where the most precious possession a man can covet is at stake—the heart of the woman he loves. Indeed, the fear may not unnaturally have assailed his Majesty that the Princess's hatred of the Arminian Emperor would after all prove stronger than her love for the husband she had wedded. In short, your Excellency will readily perceive that the Emperor's task was not exactly an enviable one, and that, on finding himself at last face to face with it, his Majesty's courage may possibly have been slightly at fault."

The Chancellor was silent awhile. Then be turned abruptly to the speaker.

"Tell me," he said, eyeing him with a sudden look of suspicion; "you appear strangely well informed on all these matters. From what source did you learn that this famous Doctor Hofer was the Duke of Cumbermere?"

"Your Excellency, I fear, has but a poor opinion of my intelligence," Sir John said drily. "I learned that fact when I reached the Arminian frontier on my journey from Vienna a week ago."

The Chancellor regarded him with a frown.

"You are jesting," he said.

"By no means," Sir John answered.

"Your Excellency may remember that you were good enough to supply me with all the necessary materials for this conjecture."

"Ha, you mean this correspondence?"

"Precisely. The correspondence revealed to me what it had revealed to his Majesty the Emperor, and it required but a short interview with the supposed Dr. Hofer himself to render the conjecture a conviction."

"And you thought fit to conceal this important fact from his Majesty's Ministers?" the Chancellor cried, aghast.

"Has your Excellency reason to regret that I did so?" Sir John replied. "I had undertaken to aid the Government in finding the vanished Emperor, but not to betray the Duke of Cumbermere, whose life would assuredly not have been worth a minute's purchase had his true identity been disclosed under the unfortunate circumstances in which he was placed."

"The Duke knew, then, that you were in possession of his secret?"

"He learned it on the night of her Majesty's the Empress's state ball; an hour before I started for Arnoldshausen."

The Chancellor gave a jump.

"What?" he exclaimed in amazement.

"It was you who brought the Emperor back to Berolingen?"

"Has your Excellency ever doubted it?" Sir John rejoined.

"From whence did you derive the knowledge that his Majesty was at Arnoldshausen?"

"From the handwriting of the Duke of Cumbermere," Sir John answered.

"From the Duke's handwriting?" the Chancellor ejaculated, with a bewildered air. "You speak in riddles."

"The riddle is simple enough," Sir John rejoined. "Indeed, but for the unpardonable negligence of those upon whose information I needs had to rely, I should have known that Baron Frederick von Arnold and his Majesty the Arminian Emperor were one and the same person within an hour of my arrival in Berolingen."

The Chancellor's face assumed an expression of incredulity.

"Your Excellency, I see, is pleased to doubt my word," Sir John pursued, quietly. "Yet the conclusion I refer to was of the simplest imaginable, and was actually within your Excellency's own reach."

"How so?" the Chancellor asked, somewhat startled. "That this Baron von Arnold—"

"That this Baron von Arnold," Sir John said, "upon whom his Majesty's Government has been keeping so diligent a watch during all these anxious weeks, was no other than the missing Emperor himself. It was plainly evident from the correspondence between the supposed Dr. Georg Hofer and his sister that his Majesty had on more than one occasion seen the Princess Marie, and from the same correspondence it was not difficult to gather that the Duke, for reasons which I think are now sufficiently obvious, had used every endeavour to prevail upon his sister to take up her abode in the capital. She refuses, and within a few months enters into a supposed mesalliance with Baron Frederick von Arnold, whom the Emperor, for no apparent object, had suddenly called from his banishment and reinstated in his possessions. What more natural than the inference that the Emperor, failing other means of winning his beautiful bride, had paid his addresses to the Princess and married her as Baron von Arnold?"

"Natural enough, indeed," said the Chancellor, ironically. "And yet you missed it."

"I missed it, sir," Sir John Templeton answered sternly, "because there was one fact which apparently rendered the conclusion absurd; the fact that his Royal Highness had written several letters to the Princess subsequent to the Emperor's disappearance from Berolingen, and that therefore Baron Frederick von Arnold—in other words the Emperor himself—must have been all along fully aware of the disastrous state of affairs caused by his Majesty's unaccountable absence. I missed it, sir," he repeated with increased emphasis, "for lack of the important knowledge that, since the Emperor's disappearance, his Majesty's advisors had not been content with breaking open and copying the supposed Doctor Georg Hofer's letters, but had actually retained possession of the originals, thus unwittingly depriving his Majesty himself of the only source of information regarding the course of affairs during his absence—namely, his wife's correspondence with her brother."

A look of uneasiness came into the face of the Chancellor.

"Well, and what of it?" he said, stolidly. "Under the circumstances it was manifestly the duty of the Government to adopt every precaution to insure his Majesty's safety during his absence, and suspecting, not without reason, that this mysterious Baron von Arnold and his wife were implicated in some conspiracy against his Majesty, whose disappearance, as you will remember, was believed to be connected with the rising in Noveria, they deemed it prudent to prevent any knowledge of his movements from reaching them."

"I am deeply obliged to your Excellency for this interesting explanation," Sir John said, drily. "But unfortunately it does not explain why this all-important circumstance was withheld from me, and why I was left to discover by a chance glimpse of the Duke of Cumbermere's handwriting that these fatal letters, which had been represented to me as copies, were in reality originals, the transmission of which had been arbitrarily stopped by the Imperial Government."

"The point appeared trifling; and, moreover," the Chancellor said, with increasing uneasiness, "there were delicate considerations involved—in short, his Majesty, though he had ordered a strict surveillance to be kept upon his secretary's correspondence, had never authorised the detention of his letters. Of course, in the light of the present astounding disclosures—"

"The blunder stands completely revealed," Sir John said, with the utmost blindness. "Indeed, but for the circumstance that his

Royal Highness rejoices in so remarkably neat and clerkly a handwriting that it was probably considered necessary to make copies of these letters, I might never have had the opportunity of discovering the fact of their being originals; in which case his Majesty the Arminian Emperor would still be sojourning at Arnoldshausen in blissful ignorance that a universal conflict was raging in Europe, that his capital had fallen into the hands of a lawless mob; that the Duke of Cumbermere, his own brother-in-law, had been sacrificed to the fury of a fanatically-excited populace; that his fellow-sovereigns were likely to share the same fate, and that his chosen Ministers—but I may safely leave your Excellencies to complete the picture at your leisure," he broke off, with a sweeping bow, in which he included the two grand officers of the Imperial household, who had meanwhile risen to their feet with a scared expression. "I have duties to fulfil which are more urgent."

Saying which he turned away, and, traversing the library, vanished into the adjoining apartment, hitherto known as the official abode of his Majesty's private' secretary, before either the Chancellor or his two companions could give utterance to the feelings his words had called forth in them.

The three Excellencies remained standing in a group, gazing at each other with open mouths and somewhat rueful countenances, amazed, perplexed, and silent.

And so, with the reader's permission we will leave them.

CHAPTER XVIII
How the Noverian Question was Settled

The Arminian Emperor had won the day. No one realised this more fully and felt it more deeply than Georg, Duke of Cumbermere. He had played for a high stake, and had lost—had lost even more than he staked.

Proud man as he was, and conscious of his own personal power—else had he ventured to attempt single-handed what the combined wit and wisdom of his many counsellers had failed to accomplish?—the wound to his pride was almost the hardest part of what he had to bear. Almost. For his defeat touched him in a spot even more sensitive still—his heart; and the wound here was the greater that he knew, or at least believed, that, he would not have failed in his purpose as he had.

That purpose had been purely political. To use the influence he believed himself to possess over the mind of the young monarch who had been so curiously attracted towards him in his student days, in order to bring about a favourable settlement of the question of his succession to the Duchy of Brunsbuttel, and perhaps even an understanding in regard to his claim to the crown of Noveria, had been the sole object of the strange and daring enterprise in which he now saw himself so ignominiously foiled. To that object, however, another had been added in the course of time, and had, so he thought, thwarted it.

In coming to Berolingen, and placing himself under the Arminian Emperor, he had not calculated that he might find there something which would become more precious to him than that which he had come to seek. Although by several years the Emperor's senior, he had as yet no experience of the softer passions. His life had been that of a man who is born with a grievous wrong, and whose duty is to get it redressed; who inherits a solemn, immutable purpose, and knows no other thought or pursuit on earth than that of fulfilling it. All the softer elements of his character had been wrapped in his sister in whom he recognised the feminine counterpart of himself, and into whose soul he had from her earliest infancy instilled all those stern principles of undeviating loyalty to the righteous cause of the house they both sprang from which made up the sum total of his nature. He had loved her passionately, nay, even jealously. Until he separated from her a year ago, for the first time since she had outgrown her childhood, in order to carry out his bold venture at the court of Berolingen, the very notion of her marrying had been painful and repugnant to him in the extreme. That the question of her marriage might one day become a factor, and an important factor, in his own political schemes had never occurred to him.

And yet it had so proved. The experience of his own heart, which had felt for the first time irresistible power of love, had opened his eyes to a possibility he might otherwise have never dreamed of. Judging from its influence upon himself and his own actions, he had confidently reckoned upon a like result in the case of the young Emperor. The first meeting between the latter and the Princess Marie, of which her Royal Highness had been totally unconscious, had been brought about without any ulterior design on his part. The second meeting, which had passed in like manner so far as the Princess was concerned, had been deliberately planned,

180

and its effect upon the young monarch had been such as to raise hope in the Duke which he felt sure the presence of the Princess in the capital would make a reality. He knew her, and placed absolute reliance upon her strength of mind and the steadfastness of her principles. He knew the Emperor, too, and his resolute, wilful nature, his love of the uncommon, and his tenacity of purpose, which only grew in proportion to the greatness of the obstacles he found opposed to him. The result seemed almost a foregone conclusion.

How he had inwardly exulted at the prospect of seeing the man at whose hands he was suing for that which in justice should have been his unasked, himself a suitor for a possession against which, as he now knew, every other earthly possession was as nought! How he had chafed at the unexpected check his plans had sustained by the refusal of his sister to obey his summons to join him in Berolingen! He had considered this check merely a temporary one, and had trusted to time to overcome what he looked upon as the mere extravagance of girlish sentimentality. The sudden change in the attitude of the Emperor, the recall of Baron von Arnold, so inexplicable to him, and then this thrice accursed marriage, which he had in vain striven to prevent, had crushed his hopes irretrievably. But at least he had still derived some comfort from the reflection that fate alone, the cruel force of adverse circumstances, had destroyed his well-laid plans. What he now felt was the humiliation, so terribly galling to a proud, self-reliant nature like his, of having been outwitted by another, and that other the very man whom he had confidently expected to lead at will.

The hot blood rushed to his cheeks at the thought that he had been known to the Emperor all these months, that his most secret plans had been to him as an open book; for, could he doubt that his Majesty had fathomed that which none but he alone could have known? By what means it had been accomplished he was at a loss to conceive. But the fact was there. The tables had been turned upon him with a master-hand, and he now found himself in the very position it had been his design to place the Emperor in, that of a claimant, a humble supplicant for the costliest treasure a man's heart can covet.

It was characteristic that at this moment, when he saw the labour of these long years wasted, the entire fabric of his life's hope collapsed, the one thought predominant in his mind should have been, not the less of that for which he had striven with so much tenacity and self-sacrifice, but the threatened destruction of that

181

newer and sweeter hope which had been born in him within the last few months and had superseded all other in his breast.

The Duke of Cumbermere loved, and his love governed his thoughts, and would, he felt, govern his actions, as he hoped love would govern the thoughts and the actions of the Arminian Emperor. He scarcely evinced more than a passing interest in the important news conveyed to him by Sir John Templeton that the pseudo-duke—the friend who had betrayed him—had surrendered to the Imperial forces, and that the rebellion which once seemed so formidable, and which had added so terribly to his own grave difficulties, had ended in mere vapour.

"I am in his Majesty's hands," he said, coldly, in reply to the communication made to him by Sir John that the Emperor would deal with this abandoned traitor in accordance with the Duke's own wishes. "Let him act as he pleases."

Therewith he turned away.

But Sir John Templeton's task was not completed, and he stayed. To him the spectacle of this proud, determined nature, struggling with the humiliating sense of a position from which it seemed impossible for him to extricate himself without loss of dignity, was deeply pathetic. He thought of that first interview between them in this same room, not a week ago, when, bit by bit, he had drawn from him all those facts which he required for the elucidation of the strange mystery that was exercising every one's mind; all, that is to say, save one, the true object of his presence at the court of the Arminian Emperor. Yet even that one had been known to him, only the knowledge had been rendered useless by the foolish deception of others, which had diverted him from the conclusion it would otherwise have led him to.

Upon what trifles do not the greatest of events turn! It was an experience Sir John Templeton made every day of his life almost, and still the experience seemed ever fresh and new.

"Well?" said the Duke, seeing that he still tarried. "Have you any further communication to make to me? It seems there can be nothing more to apprise me of. His Majesty, who has his own notion of the laws of hospitality, has in turn violated the sanctity of my correspondence, held me a prisoner at his court, and finally taken the hand of the Princess, my sister, by force, or at least without the consent of him who alone had the right to bestow it. I know not what further indignity he may intend to impose upon me."

"I think none," Sir John Templeton replied. "Nor, if your Royal Highness will permit me to say so, do I think his Majesty's actions, which your Highness refers to in such scathing terms, will, on mature consideration, appear in so reprehensible light to the man by whom they were after all called forth. Pardon my frankness, sir, but justice is justice, and if his Majesty the Emperor has married her Royal Highness the Princess Marie without her brother's formal consent, he has not done so without having documentary proof of her brother's desire that he should pay his addresses to her; which, under the circumstances, he may well have been justified in regarding as tantamount to a consent."

"I do not understand," the Duke said, glancing at him with an uneasy look.

"Your Royal Highness," Sir John went on, "forgets that the Emperor has possessed knowledge of the whole correspondence which has passed between his private secretary and the supposed Duke of Cumbermere in America."

"Well?" the Duke said, impatiently.

"Copies of all these letters, sir, as you know, passed into the hands of his Majesty's Government, with the exception, however, of one, which was retained by his Majesty in the original, and consequently never reached its destination. That letter, which was written six months ago by the Emperor's private secretary to his American correspondent, contains a reference to the fact that a certain personage, whose identity it is not so difficult to guess, had become deeply enamoured of the beautiful Demoiselle Hofer, and dilates at some length upon the purpose to which this unexpected circumstance was to be turned. Can it surprise your Highness that his Majesty, thus timely forewarned of a scheme which threatened, not only the interests of his Empire, but those of his own heart, should have promptly turned the schemer's weapon against himself and made him the victim of his own plot."

The Duke's countenance had grown pale during this speech, and his brow had contracted as if with absolute pain. What a miserable unworthy farce it now seemed to him, now that it had failed, and he regarded it, so to speak, with another's eyes, this exchanging of roles with one who was his own servant, and who had ended by basely betraying him. The thought humbled him inexpressibly. The bitterness of failure lies less in the regrets it engenders than in the fact that it leaves a stigma behind it which nothing can wipe out. Who does not know that what is universally applauded as clever when it succeeds is laughed at as excessively foolish when it fails; that the same actions which success stamps with the stamp of greatness and genius become vile and contemptible in men's eyes when the curse of failure attends them? The Duke of Cumbermere, in spite of his pride, perhaps because of his pride, was not above the fear of ridicule, nor impervious to the opinions of his fellow men.

"His Majesty has retained this letter, you say?" he asked, after a moment's silence, in a low, constrained voice.

Sir John Templeton bowed an assent.

"And you have seen it?"

"I have seen it."

The Duke paced the room in considerable perturbation. Presently he stood still in front of his visitor.

"What is your object in telling me this?" he asked.

"I have done so at his Majesty's desire," Sir John answered.

"As a preliminary, I presume," the Duke said, "to informing me of the price his Majesty places upon this document?"

"As a preliminary to returning the document to your Royal Highness to deal with as you please," Sir John rejoined gravely, drawing forth the letter, and handing it to the Prince. "It is my good fortune, it seems," he added, with a twinkle of humour, as the Duke grasped the document with a sigh of relief, "to be the medium of restoring your Highness's letters, and this one, I may safely assume, will not have less value in your eyes than the last I had the honour to place in your Highness's hands, in which you had unwisely attempted to convey the intelligence to your friends in Noveria that the real Duke of Cumbermere was a captive in the Imperial Court of Berolingen, and not, as was supposed, braving the army of the Emperor at the head of a band of foolish, hot-headed rebels."

The Duke gazed at him in wonder.

"You knew this?" he said.

"Since I knew that the supposed Doctor Georg Hofer was the Duke of Cumbermere, as I confided to your Royal Highness on that occasion, the inference was inevitable," Sir John replied.

"And what are his Majesty's present intentions?" the Duke asked abruptly.

"They depend entirely upon your Royal Highness's intentions," Sir John said.

"Ha," the Duke exclaimed, "he thinks to make his own terms with me?"

"On the contrary, sir," the old diplomatist said. "His Majesty makes no terms whatever. He knows your Royal Highness too well to believe that you could under any circumstances depart from the firm principle which has governed your whole life, and which he both admires and respects, that of adhering unalterably to the policy of your late father, the King of Noveria. He is aware that it is impossible for your Royal Highness, consistently with that inherited

184

principle, to relinquish your claim to the throne of Noveria, and that consequently Brandenburg can never recognise your Royal Highness's succession to the ducal crown of Brunsbuttel."

The Duke fell back with an expression of dismay.

"In other words," he said, "his Majesty, knowing that he is in a position to withhold from me that which is mine by divine right, does me the honour to refuse its free acceptance at my hands? Truly, his generosity amazes me."

"Your Royal Highness misinterprets his Majesty's intentions, which are indeed conceived in a true spirit of generosity towards your Highness," Sir John said. "Does it not occur to you, sir, that his Majesty, having reason to believe that your Highness has a very precious favour to crave at his hands, may be desirous of assuring you that, should it be granted, it will be done without loss of dignity to yourself?"

"I do not follow your meaning," the Duke said, though the heightened colour now visible in his cheeks plainly belied his words.

"What I mean, sir, is this," Sir John went on. "His Majesty conceives that what honour forbids the Duke of Cumbermere to do for himself it may possibly not forbid the Duke of Cumbermere to do for his son. Should your Royal Highness, therefore, contract a marriage which meets with the approval of the crown of Brandenburg, his Majesty on his part promises to secure the succession to the Duchy of Brunsbuttel to the male issue of such marriage, provided the claim to the Noverian throne be formally renounced on behalf of that issue."

"Which means?" the Duke asked, fixing his companion with a penetrating glance.

"Which means, sir," Sir John answered, returning the look unflinchingly, "if I may venture to interpret his Majesty's sentiments, that the Emperor's love for his sister, the Princess Margaret, is second only to that which he bears to the Imperial lady who now shares his throne."

The Duke made no reply, but the light that glistened in his dark eyes, as he strode thoughtfully up and down the apartment, showed that the gentle thrust had gone straight home.

Sir John Templeton waited in silence for him to speak.

"Is this all you have to communicate to me?" he asked presently, interrupting his promenade.

"It is all," Sir John answered.

"Then I beg of you to leave me," the Duke rejoined, curtly. "You have supplied me with material for much earnest thought, and I require leisure to digest it."

185

Sir John Templeton bowed, and turned to go.

Before he had reached the door the Duke, obeying a sudden impulse, strode after him and placed his hand upon his shoulder.

"Do not misunderstand me," he said, in a tone of unusual warmth. "I am not ungrateful. You have rendered me a service I am not likely to forget, and I recognise it. Would heaven it had proved of more avail."

He left him as abruptly as he had approached him, and Sir John Templeton bowed once more and withdrew.

* * * *

Two hours later the Duke of Cumbermere sought an audience of his Majesty the Arminian Emperor, and remained closeted with him for some time. What passed at this interview it is impossible for me to say. The result, however, is a matter of current history, and within the knowledge of every well-informed reader.

The betrothal of the Duke of Cumbermere, the Noverian Pretender, to the Princess Margaret of Brandenburg, the favourite sister of the Emperor of Arminia, was an event in European history which caused too great a sensation at the time of its occurrence to require recalling to men's minds at the present day. The sensation was only surpassed by that attending the news that his Majesty had at last selected a bride in the person of her Royal Highness the Princess Marie of Noveria. As no rumour of such a possibility had reached the ears of the world, the most extravagantly romantic stories regarding the circumstances of the Emperor's courtship were soon in circulation. But, needless to say, none even remotely approached the truth. The world marvelled a little at the unprecedented rapidity with which the preparations for the Imperial nuptials were instantly pushed forward. But among the host of those who attended that imposing ceremony—and I was of the number—there were only half-a-dozen men who knew that the illustrious couple that day standing before the cathedral altar were, as a matter of fact, then receiving the priestly benediction for the second time.

Gossip at the Arminian Court was meanwhile, of course, busily engaged in connecting the various events of the past month, and constructing a fabric of its own, of which certain details may still interest the reader.

The disappearance of Baron Frederick von Arnold on the eve of the surrender of the Noverian rebels with their leader, the pseudo Duke of Cumbermere, admitted but of one explanation—namely, that the Baron had been implicated in the daring attempt of the now

186

notorious Doctor Georg Hofer to pose as the Duke, and having received private intimation of the impending failure of that attempt, had fled the country, together with his wife, the scheming sister of that luckless conspirator.

There were those, however, who maintained that the marriage of the Baron had been a complete fiction; that it had never taken place, and that such a personage as Demoiselle Hofer had never existed, or, if she had, that she had been a secret agent of the Duke's, who had passed for the sister of the Imperial secretary in order the better to facilitate the communications that passed between them. Others, again, professed to knew that Baron von Arnold had plotted to gain the hand of Princess Marie herself, but had failed owing to the timely intervention of the Emperor.

When some months afterwards, the real Baron von Arnold, with many other banished adherents of the Noverian Pretender, received the Emperor's permission—granted, it was said, at the instance of the Duke of Cumbermere himself—to return to his estates, these various stories were revived again, and since he returned without a wife the version which assumed his marriage to have been a fiction naturally carried the day. The Baron himself, who now again enjoyed the highest favour of his former patron, the Duke of Cumbermere—a fact which became a subject of much puzzled comment on the part of the curious who could not reconcile it with past events—vouchsafed no satisfactory explanation to those who had the hardihood to question him on the subject of his alleged participation in the famous Noverian conspiracy. Indeed, he is said to have silenced one particularly pertinaceous inquirer by assuring him blandly that, on reference to his diary, he had reason to believe that at the time of the occurrences in Noveria he was engaged on a scientific expedition to North Siberia, and must therefore disclaim all knowledge of West European affairs during that period; a statement which of course was accepted with a smile of intelligent comprehension by its recipient.

The Baron never set foot in Arnoldshausen, and shortly after his return sold that estate to the Duke of Cumbermere, who presented it as a peace-offering to his sister, the Empress, much to the dissatisfaction of the worthy villagers, who found themselves once more dependent upon the tender mercies of the Crown Steward for the recognition of those rights and privileges which they were incessantly labouring to maintain.

The commutation of the sentence of death passed upon the rebel leader, Doctor Georg Hofer, into a sentence of life-long incarceration in the fortress of Spandberg, met with little approval in the Arminian Press, which gave bold expression to the opinion that his Majesty, in dealing thus lightly with a most dangerous criminal, had erred lamentably on the side of leniency. But the Emperor, as everybody knows, cares not twopence for the opinion of the Press, and he went his own way. The sudden dismissal of the Minister of War, which took place at the same time, caused some surprise to those who knew how high he had stood in the Imperial favour. But the incident faded into comparative insignificance when, almost immediately afterwards, the Imperial Chancellor himself tendered his resignation, and the same was promptly accepted by his Majesty.

These, then, were the chief events that occupied the court gossips during the days immediately following the Emperor's return. To the world at large, of course, they were of too little moment to call for more than a passing notice. Moreover, general public attention was just then engrossed by something far more important. The sudden subsiding of the stupendous political hurricane which had swept over Europe for more than three weeks was a subject of no less amazement than had been produced by its equally sudden outburst a month before. Now that all was over, and people had leisure and the peace of mind to reflect calmly on the tremendous danger they had passed through, everyone's thoughts turned once more to the mysterious cause of it.

Volumes upon volumes have since been written upon the subject, and every possible theory under the sun has been propounded in explanation of the young Emperor's purpose in vanishing completely from men's view for so long a period.

I venture to think that, with the exception of the three personages who figure most prominently in the foregoing pages, no man living has fathomed the whole truth of that mysterious event; and even the three personages I refer to may perhaps find much that is new to them in the history I have just brought to a conclusion.

Before taking final leave of the reader, I would only add one more fact, which, if I may judge his sentiments by my own, he will not regard as the least interesting of these here related.

Among the countless trophies and mementoes of a career full of strange incident and restless activity, which adorn Sir John Templeton's residence in Vienna, there may be seen at this day a marble bust of her Majesty the Queen, executed by her Imperial Majesty the Dowager Empress of Arminia. It stands upon a handsome pillar to the right of the old diplomatist's writing table, and in a tiny gold frame beside it lies a card, on which the following words are written in a well-known hand:—

"To Sir John Templeton,

"As a mark of my esteem, and in grateful recognition of the services rendered by him to one who is very dear to me."

The signature affixed to these gracious words I may safely leave the reader to guess.

THE END

www.ingramcontent.com/pod-product-compliance
Lightning Source LLC
Chambersburg PA
CBHW050937120626
46552CB00001B/258